Whispers on the Color Line

Whispers on the Color Line

Rumor and Race in America

Gary Alan Fine
and Patricia A. Turner

UNIVERSITY OF CALIFORNIA PRESS

Berkeley   Los Angeles   London

University of California Press

Berkeley and Los Angeles, California

University of California Press, Ltd.
London, England

Cartoon from *The Psychology of Rumor* by Gordon W.
Allport and Leo Postman, copyright 1947 and renewed
1975 by Holt, Rinehart and Winston, reproduced by
permission of the publisher.

First paperback printing 2004

Library of Congress Cataloging-in-Publication Data

Fine, Gary Alan.
  Whispers on the color line : rumor and race in America /
Gary Alan Fine and Patricia A. Turner.
      p.   cm.
  Includes bibliographical references (p.) and index.
  ISBN 0-520-22855-3 (pbk : alk. paper)
    1. African Americans—Folklore.   2. Whites—United
States—Folklore.   3. Urban folklore—United States.
I. Turner, Patricia A., 1955–   II. Title

GR111.A47 F56 2001
398′089′96073—dc21   2001027089

Manufactured in the United States of America

13   12   11   10   09   08   07   06   05   04
10   9   8   7   6   5   4   3   2   1

The paper used in this publication is both acid-free and
totally chlorine-free (TCF). It meets the minimum
requirements of ANSI/NISO Z39.48-1992 (R 1997)
(*Permanence of Paper*). ∞

To our mentor, Alan Dundes

CONTENTS

ACKNOWLEDGMENTS

Every book, this one no less than others, is a joint venture. A world of support exists beyond the coauthors. At the University of California Press, we wish to thank, profusely and heartily, Naomi Schneider, who believed in the importance of the project throughout the years it took to reach fruition. We also thank our agent, Carol Mann, who in the early stages was instrumental in giving our ideas shape. Carol Beck gave us significant and cheerful editorial assistance. Among our colleagues, we particularly appreciate the advice, criticism, and comfort of Veronique Campion-Vincent, Bill Ellis, Patricia Johnson, Frederick Koenig, Janet Langlois, Jay Mechling, E. Ethelbert Miller, Susan Olzak, Michael Preston, Peter Tokofsky, Jeffrey Victor, and Richard Yarborough. We also thank our many Internet correspondents for the materials they provided over the years. Our staffs at Northwestern University and the University of California at Davis were also supportive of our efforts. Part of this manuscript was composed when the first author was a fellow at the Center for Advanced Study in the Behavioral Sciences in Palo Alto. He is grateful for the financial support provided by National Science Foundation grant SBR-9022192.

It should never go without saying, even when it goes without saying, that we thank our families: Kevin and Dan, and Susan, Todd, and Peter.

Last, but not least, we hope that this book will make a difference, even a small, nuanced difference, in the lives of our friends, black and white, who may come to understand each other just a little bit better because of what we have learned from them.

Introduction

Until the 1990s, the routine work of academic folklorists rarely inspired fiction writers or filmmakers. Whereas our colleagues in archaeology—the Indiana Joneses of the academy—have seen their lives celebrated and glamorized on-screen, those of us who toil diligently in dusty folklore archives and occasionally cart around cumbersome electronic interviewing equipment were accustomed to benign invisibility. But in recent years we have been discovered. It all began in 1992, during a peak slasher film period. Hollywood converted a short story by the prolific master of suspense Clive Barker into a stylish movie that attempted to capture the exhilaration and danger faced by a pair of intrepid folklorists. *Candyman* depicts the sometimes-sordid personal lives and persistently frustrating professional existences of one white and one African-American contemporary legend scholar who have embarked on a joint research project. When an unexpected racial angle seeps into the enthusiastic graduate students' seemingly innocuous fieldwork, their lives are threatened, and they pay an exorbitant price in their pursuit of scholarship. A success at the box office, *Candyman* inspired other filmmakers and television producers to make other movies and programs in the same genre. Throughout the 1990s more and more entertainment moguls have mined folkloric discourse for their plots. The popular Fox television series *The X-Files* relies heavily on contemporary legends, and films such as *Urban Legend, Dead Man on Campus,* and *I Saw What You Did Last Summer* also play on the genre.

Just as our colleagues in the field of archaeology alternate between laughing and crying at the multiple inaccuracies contained in, for example, the Indiana Jones films, we, too, find that the makers of *Candyman* took extensive liberties. But despite the many differences between the dangerous lives of researchers Helen Lyle and Bernadette Walsh and our more mundane existences, this particular film's plot deserves scrutiny.[1]

"Candyman" is the name assigned to the bogeyman in a legend based on the popular "Bloody Mary" cycle. As many a teenage girl would attest, Bloody Mary is an interactive ghost story in which one must chant "Bloody Mary" five times into a mirror. If you "believe," the fifth iteration will produce a bloody, disfigured white female who will strangle her misguided summoner. In many recitations of this legend, the teen-ager's hunky, horny date witnesses the gruesome encounter and is so severely traumatized that his hair turns white in the aftermath of the ghastly deed. The producers of *Candyman* transform the dreaded de-moness into an audaciously evil black male who assaults after the name Candyman is uttered five times, although he sometimes also murders innocent individuals who have not summoned him. Like menacing males in other legend cycles, Candyman has a sharp metal hook in place of a hand.[2]

At the beginning of the film, Helen and Bernadette classify "Can-dyman" as a contemporary legend (or "formula rumor") known pri-marily to young, sexually insecure white girls from privileged middle-class backgrounds. Within the safe boundaries of academic offices, they collect the Candyman story from students. One day an African-American cleaning woman overhears one of Helen's field tapes and in a matter-of-fact tone assures the skeptical folklorist that the Candyman routinely terrorizes Cabrini Green, a notorious Chicago housing proj-ect, where the impoverished occupants believe him to be responsible for a rash of vicious and unexplained murders. When the researchers start to investigate the woman's account, they find disturbing evidence that suggests that the creature they assumed to be fictional might indeed be real. Much to the dismay of their jaded mentors, they take their research outside of the university's safe environs, and disaster ensues.

When we reach beyond the movie's amusing and deeply flawed depiction of the day-to-day life of academic folklorists, *Candyman* offers a useful starting point. It testifies to the powerful presence of contemporary legends. These are stories that are known and believed by college students, cleaning women, and many others. They have an uncanny way of matching the concerns of average citizens. For teenage girls, the threat comes in their homes on evenings when their parents have left them alone. For residents of housing projects, the threat emerges when thugs outnumber law enforcement officials. Matters relevant to race invade the film slowly and surreptitiously. In spite of the racial identity of the bogeyman, the young folklorists seem unaware that this narrative's vigor is largely the result of its reflection of the racial disharmony that has long marked Chicago and its environs. As their understanding of the racial politics of their world increases, so, too, does the graduate students' comprehension of the power of folklore. Once they recognize that the stories were not just amusing anecdotes and charming fodder for conversations, but indicators of the despair of the narrators, they modify their mission.

But the slasher film's folklorists commit a crucial error. As they focus their efforts on collecting and debunking the legend, they overlook the truths that underpin the story. Consequently, the very real history of race and class hostility that permeates this section of inner-city Chicago ensnares them in the form of the violent Candyman figure.

JUST FOLKLORE? MERE RUMOR?

Within academic circles, folklore has enjoyed a long and respectable history. In the United States, the American Folklore Society was formed in Cambridge, Massachusetts, in the late 1880s. These scholars, like their European counterparts, were fascinated by the forms of expression found in everyday life. They believed that much could be learned from proverbs, riddles, folktales, ballads, and other vernacular idioms trivialized by many other researchers. Further, they maintained that members of ethnic groups and nationalities outside the western European and American mainstream deserved academic respect. Folklorists heeded the instructions issued in the *Journal of American Folklore* to "collect the fast vanishing remains of folklore in America: the relics of English folklore, the lore of the Negroes, and the lore of Indian tribes."[3] A century before the calls for multiculturalism, folklorists examined and published African-American spirituals, Native American myths, and Appalachian ballads. Although many of today's students of black literature are familiar only with the early twentieth-century folklore research conducted by Zora Neale Hurston and perhaps Sterling Brown, the collections of Thomas W. Talley, Newbell Niles Puckett, Elsie Clews Parsons, and several other pioneering folklorists offer valuable perspectives on the emergence of racial attitudes within the genres of folklore.

The goals of early American folklorists centered on the preservation of verbal and material forms of expression that they believed were destined for extinction, but they quickly realized that while certain types of folklore did diminish in popularity, others emerged. They also recognized that all human groups, be they Pennsylvania Dutch farmers or members of Congress, create folklore. Early twentieth-century scholars assumed incorrectly that increasing urbanization, more sophisticated channels of communication, and mass-mediated entertainment would inhibit and eventually annihilate folk expression. More recently, some individuals have predicted that the information superhighway's efficiencies would eliminate folklore. But as anyone on the Internet knows, folkloric expression is transmitted with robust frequency in cyberspace.

We disabuse our students of the notion that folklore belongs to the past or to less sophisticated communities by querying them about their own folk expressions. This is rather simple to do when we remind them of the many schoolyard games they played as children, the cootie catchers they constructed, and the rhyming taunts with which they tormented peers. As a result, they are usually willing to admit that folklore played a role in their lives when they were younger. But surely now that they are mature members of a university community, "mere folklore" must play only a minimal role in their lives. Here we ask them about the built environment of the campus, the rules of academic life, and the misfortunes that befall other students. Invariably students point to a strangely constructed building and claim that its seemingly incomprehensible layout is the result of a pitched battle between two architects. Students assure us that fruits and vegetables available on the dining hall salad bars are deliberately saturated with added carbohydrates so that weight-conscious female students will not develop harmful eating disorders. When we ask them how the university would respond to the suicide of a student's roommate, we are assured that a rule exists that will prevent the surviving roommate's mourning from compromising his or her grade point average. The student will be awarded a 4.0 (straight A's) for the semester. Many students claim to know of a male student who began to suffer extreme discomfort in his anal cavity. During a visit to the student health service, a doctor warns him that this malady is the consequence of homosexual intercourse. If he is going to continue to indulge in such conduct, he will have to get accustomed to this kind of discomfort. A heterosexual young man, the student fervently denies ever having had anal sex. Back in his room, however, he discovers ether, medical equipment, and other suspicious paraphernalia under his roommate's bed. The story alleges that his roommate has been drugging and sodomizing him.

Not surprisingly, female students are more likely to be familiar with the stories of the carbohydrates on the salad bar, whereas male students are more likely to describe the unfortunate ether victim. With some tales, the race of the teller is key to the story. For example, many white students are familiar with a story about Snapple brand beverages in which it is alleged that the corporation uses its profits to support radical antiabortion groups. In contrast, African-American students maintain that Snapple uses its profits to support white supremacist organizations. To verify their stories, students cite numerous sources. Some claim that they heard the story from someone directly involved in the events. Others claim that they heard it from a campus authority figure, such as a residence hall adviser or an employee of the campus health center. Stories like these flourish on most college campuses, but their popularity is not limited to academic settings.

As academics teaching folklore at the university level, we encounter numerous examples of contemporary legends. Aware that scholarship based on a sample of college students is of limited use, we have collected far beyond the gates of our campuses. What others dismiss as "mere rumor" or "just a legend" appeals to us because no other discourse better reflects the range of contemporary issues and attitudes, often in ways that cannot otherwise be expressed. Consider how boys and girls make sense of the novel and diverse candy products manufacturers present to them, the ways in which young men and women cope with the unfamiliar urges of their swiftly maturing bodies, the ways in which young people deal with the advantages and disadvantages of their newfound freedom, the ways African Americans explain corporate America's evolving attitudes toward them, and the ways white Americans validate their uncertainty about the scope of integration. In each of these examples—and numerous others—people tell stories. These repeated stories serve many purposes: they assuage anxieties, they entertain friends, they increase our sense of control, and they do so without directly proclaiming our own attitudes.

CONTEMPORARY LEGEND AND RUMOR RESEARCH

Although Jan Harold Brunvand was not the first folklorist to write about contemporary (or "urban") legends, his series of popular books has done more to inform the general public of the existence of these texts than those of any other writer. With the publication of his first book, *The*

Vanishing Hitchhiker, in 1981, a growing segment of the American public became familiar with the genre. In particular, journalists suddenly discovered that many of the stories they had tried in vain to authenticate were traditional. No wonder they could not find the actual woman who sold her husband's Porsche for fifty dollars! Here was an explanation for the lack of a paper trail in the story of the consumer who had been served a Kentucky Fried rat.

Legends are arguably the most common narrative form of folklore in American society, but they are equally popular throughout the world. Swedish, French, South African, Italian, German, Polish, and Israeli scholars and journalists have written books and articles on the proliferation of the most popular stories in their countries. In the early 1980s an international group of scholars formed a professional association devoted to research on contemporary legends. The group—the International Society for Contemporary Legend Research—meets annually, and its members sponsor the publication of both an academic journal and a newsletter. The latter, *FOAFtale News*, takes its title from an idiom coined by Brunvand after he noted the frequency with which such tales are verified through a friend of a friend (FOAF). Newspapers, television programs, and radio talk shows are also frequently identified as the sources for contemporary legends.

The innovative engineers of the information superhighway, the Internet, may have intended it to serve as a high-speed carrier of up-to-the minute news and other data. While no one will deny the speed at which information travels in cyberspace, the validity of that information is another matter. Many active Internet users receive cookie recipes in their e-mail messages or find them posted to a newsgroup. Often the sender explains that he or she is sharing the recipe as revenge for a friend who was duped into paying a high price to Neiman Marcus or Mrs. Fields cookie company to obtain the recipe. In part because of the volume and variety of contemporary legends that circulate through the Internet, a newsgroup (alt.folklore.urban) was formed that enables one to check the validity of suspicious stories. However, no evidence exists that this group's presence and popularity has in any way quelled the circulation of material; it may even have given it increased visibility.

Many academically trained folklorists and sociologists have learned to move back and forth between popular and scholarly audiences. In our academic articles, we debate matters such as the sociolinguistic properties of narratives and their historical antecedents. However, when journalists call us to find out if the story about urine being used as an ingredient in a trendy beer is true, they present a different set of concerns. And they usually begin with the one that is hardest for us to answer: Who started it? Once they determine that a text is traditional, they are eager for us to agree that anyone who would believe such a "ludicrous" story must be naive and unintelligent.

Sometimes media attention devoted to contemporary legends leads individuals to anticipate the demise of the genre. As more sophisticated means of sharing and disseminating information emerge, pundits have expected the disappearance of "mere" folklore. They reason that once people become familiar with the formulaic structure of rumors and legends, they will cease to be duped by them. But that has not been the case. Some people become adept at recognizing the rumors of *other* folk groups, but they often overlook the traditional beliefs that speak to their own concerns. Thus in the beauty parlor one might hear the story of a group of elderly ladies who mistake a well-known black celebrity for a mugger. In spite of their error, he treats the ladies to a meal, flowers, or a bottle of champagne. The listener may then go home and send a version of the story to another friend via electronic mail. Good stories demand to be shared. We agree with the anthropologist Barbara Myerhoff, who concluded her ethnography of elderly southern California Jews by stating, "Homo narrens, humankind as storyteller, is a human constant."[4]

FROM MISLEADING SALAD BARS TO EXPENSIVE COOKIES

But are these just charming stories that reflect how willingly some folks will spread attractively packaged misinformation? Let us consider several stories mentioned earlier. Many students assure us that campus officials are so concerned with eating disorders among students that they spray carbohydrates on the vegetables at salad bars. A junior at the University of California at Davis said she had believed this story; she knew that many of her peers at her own campus and friends at other schools did so as well. When asked if she knew of any invisible substance that could be placed on the raw foods displayed on salad bars that would have no taste or odor, but would increase the food's calorie count, she maintained that these considerations had not occurred to her. The text seemed entirely plausible to her, and she had complete faith in the veracity of the peer who first shared the story.

For many people outside of this student's peer group, the rumor seems far-fetched. Why do so many young college women believe it? The story sutures two of their overriding concerns. Certainly it reflects their preoccupation with weight control. It also suggests the hidden power of the university. In this case the power is used "benevolently" as campus officials attempt to protect the young women from themselves. For many students, the freshman year of college is the first time they control what they eat. No dining hall worker will urge them to add mashed potatoes to their plate. Unready for and perhaps somewhat afraid of the power that has been granted to them, young people willingly accept the notion that if they do make an unfortunate choice, someone is looking out for their well-being. The legend also appeals to those young women who may be inclined to diet but still desire pizza and burgers. By subscribing to the belief that the best available diet food has been altered, they rationalize succumbing to the other culinary offerings.

Whereas college students ponder the qualities of foods served to them in dining halls, middle-aged consumers are often vexed by desserts sold to them in restaurants. The Neiman Marcus cookie recipe has enjoyed a resurgence of popularity on the Internet. Probably the first contemporary legend about overpriced dessert recipes circulated in the 1960s. According to the story, the world-famous Waldorf-Astoria restaurant specialized in a red velvet cake, one of its most popular desserts. A customer, having enjoyed the dessert, asked for the recipe and agreed to paying the three-fifty she was told the recipe cost, only to find, when she received her bill, that the cost was $350, not the $3.50 she had assumed. Furious at the exorbitant price, she made the recipe available free of charge to all her friends and relatives and encouraged them to do the same. While this story once circulated by word of mouth, the contemporary version, in which it is usually the recipe for Mrs. Fields cookies or a Neiman Marcus dessert, sometimes is recited face-to-face but is just as likely to appear, complete with the tasty recipe, on Internet news digests.

Some individuals will immediately recognize the legend's logical flaws. After all, wouldn't the company have anticipated that it could not get away with charging an unreasonable fee for a recipe? Wouldn't someone have realized that customers could share the recipe? Further, wouldn't the company have the foresight to realize that this blatant exploitation would antagonize customers and damage the business's public image?

The Waldorf-Astoria, Neiman Marcus, and Mrs. Fields are all associated with high-quality, high-priced merchandise. The high-priced food recipe always refers to a fancy dessert; we know of no versions in which the wicked entrepreneur overcharges for a salmon croquettes recipe. For many people, indulging in a lavish, rich dessert such as red velvet cake or a chocolate-laced cookie requires some degree of rationalization. Desserts inflate a restaurant tab, and we could bake a batch of cookies for what Mrs. Fields charges for one. This leads to resentment toward those who have the gall to tempt us with these delectable morsels.

Of course, there is an element of truth to the core narrative that undergirds the story. Most adults realize that desserts serve no nutritional purpose. Elite shopping establishments often charge steep prices to compensate for the high overhead they must pay. Part of the story's appeal comes from the willingness of the abused consumer to turn the tables on the big corporation. When we pass the recipe along, we participate in the customer's revenge.

These two examples illustrate that even seemingly innocuous legends reveal much about how people cope with bothersome and distressing aspects of their day-to-day life. Rumors and legends address those aspects of life about which we receive mixed or ambiguous messages. Given that matters relevant to race remain charged and divisive in many corridors of American society, it is not surprising that rumors and legends that reflect racial misunderstanding and mistrust frequently circulate.

Unlike *Candyman*'s young protagonists, we are more seasoned and have been collecting and analyzing contemporary legends for decades. Several factors influenced our decision to join forces and write this book together. For over twenty years Fine has collected and analyzed rumors and contemporary legends. From the ever-durable "Kentucky Fried Rat" cycle, the persistent Pop Rocks warnings, the troubling "AIDS Mary" texts, and numerous others, he has endeavored to explain how people can find suspicious stories plausible. Fine has been less interested in debunking the stories themselves; rather, he examines the contexts in which they emerge in order to offer reasons for why so many people take them at face value. Turner has also been studying similar rumor and legend cycles for over a decade. Her specialty is those texts that circulate within African-American communities. She has researched stories of purloined Church's chicken, beliefs about athletic footwear manufacturers and their support of white supremacist regimes, notions that the AIDS epidemic is rooted in a genocidal experiment designed to diminish the black race, as well as other similar cycles. In *Whispers on the Color Line*, we focus our attention on those rumors and legends that reflect attitudes that blacks and whites have both about each other and about the world they face. Some people find it easy to believe that gang members have required the rape of a teenager as an initiation test for membership. Others may subscribe to the notion that the U.S. Army is using Ritalin to conduct experiments on African-American children who attend public elementary schools. The popularity of these texts indicates, among other things, how many dangers we face as citizens in an uncertain environment.

RACE AND RUMOR

The easy work of superficial integration has been long completed; blacks and whites have equal access to lunch counters, hotels, and elementary schools, and other social institutions are now integrated by law, open to all who can afford them. Yet the hard work remains to be completed, as full equality sometimes appears to be slipping away. A 1995 survey in *Newsweek* reported that 75 percent of whites—and an astounding 86 percent of blacks—say that race relations are "only fair" or "poor," and only 1 percent of whites and 2 percent of blacks feel they are "excellent."[5] Of course, these statistics do not suggest that the 86 percent of blacks who perceive race relations as unsatisfactory do so for identical reasons, or that the 75 percent of whites would concur with these reasons. Yet, thirty years after the heyday of the civil rights movement, we are haunted by the disturbing words of the 1968 National Advisory Commission on Civil Disorders: "Our nation is moving toward two societies, one black, one white, separate and unequal."

In many instances, efforts to improve this situation fail because blacks and whites misunderstand each other's past experiences and the impact those legacies have on their present lives. Many African Americans maintain that this lack of historical knowledge is one-sided. After all, until very recently "white" history dominated the classroom. When information about the past of African Americans was included, it was often presented from a nonblack perspective by white instructors. Some textbooks painted an "evenhanded," or even romantic, version of the institution of slavery. Others focused on a few laudable individuals such as George Washington Carver or Martin Luther King, neglecting how the average African American felt about his or her social position. Only in recent years has African-American history been incorporated into some educational systems in a meaningful and historically grounded way. However, many blacks seem uninterested in the history and concerns of whites. And though we as educators are loath to admit it, many individuals—white and black—dislike history altogether and move through life with a sense of the past dominated by artifacts of popular culture such as comic books, television shows, and movies.

On occasion people become aware of their lack of comprehension. One white Bostonian remarked, "I don't know if it's ever possible for me to understand what it's like to be black. I don't know if, not having been a black growing up in the inner city, I'd ever understand."[6] A black woman speaks similarly: "If you want to help me, you can to a certain degree. But don't try to understand me because you can't understand what it's like to be black any more than I can understand what it's like being a man."[7] Because white had been taken for granted as being "normal," until recently people rarely asked how it feels to be "white."

High-profile conflicts often remind members of one group that others perceive the world differently. In the 1990s the furor over the trial of the officers in the notorious Rodney King episode as well as the various responses to the O. J. Simpson trial forced many whites to realize that their views were different from those of African Americans. For blacks the statements made by whites claiming that racial discrimination had been eliminated and that affirmative action programs should be dismantled demonstrated how differently the two races cast the events of the recent past.

With all this cultural baggage, can we ever understand each other? Do we have the skills necessary for sharing experiences? Most of us have few friends of a race different from our own. Race is often seen as an unbridgeable chasm. All too often, even those eager to expand their networks will find these desires to transcend racial boundaries backfiring. Ruth Frankenberg, an American Studies scholar, put the matter bluntly: "Too often, I witnessed situations in which, as predominantly white feminists, workplaces, classrooms, or organizations tried to move to more multiracial formats or agendas, the desire to work together rapidly deteriorated into painful, ugly processes in which racial tension and conflict actually seemed to get worse rather than better as the months went by."[8]

How can a study of rumor and legend reduce the kind of breakdown described by Frankenberg? In this and so many other instances, participants want to avoid racial tension and presume that others do as well. But they often underestimate the extent to which different worldviews can collide. Blacks and whites genuinely interested in interracial cooperation need to understand some of the truths believed by those outside their own group. Rumors and legends provide insights into "the Other" for several reasons. As we shall demonstrate, these texts emerge about a wide array of topics. From sex acts to business transactions, from fashion to food, from heroes to heroin, rumors and legends cover every charged topic. Children circulate texts about toys and candy; teenagers share stories about sex, drugs, and rock and roll; young professionals commiserate over the hazards of the work world; parents share their concerns about threats to the sanctity of the family; senior citizens articulate their anxieties about matters relevant to health care and physical safety. In other words, we use rumors and legends to increase our understanding of every age-group. Although many argue that well-educated professionals are not taken in by rumors and legends, our research indicates these beliefs span all class divisions. A Fortune 500 executive might not believe that anyone ever put a cat in a microwave oven, but he or she might easily succumb to the notion that black drug abusers are leaving dirty needles in the change boxes of pay phones.

Rumors and legends can be used to demonstrate how differently blacks and whites perceive contemporary society, but they also prove just how similar we are. Some African Americans believed that the Liz Claiborne company was using its profits to support white supremacist groups. Some nonblack informants reported that the company was underwriting satanic cults. Clearly this company was judged to be conducting business in a way that disturbed some of its customers. Members of all ethnic groups found themselves on common ground with their perceived dissatisfaction even if the precise causes varied.

RACISM AND PARANOIA

As sociologists Joe Feagin and Melvin Sikes noted, in speaking of black "paranoia," "One more aspect of the burden of being black is having to defend one's understanding of events to white acquaintances without being labeled as racially paranoid."[9] Likewise, whites have similar concerns, as in the plaint of a white teacher, troubled by her mixed thoughts, who confides, "Though I was brought up not to be prejudiced, I hate to admit that I am. I don't like my thoughts and feelings."[10] Or consider the remarks of a white cabdriver who finds that his brain is a racist turncoat: "When traffic's beginning to close in on me and I'm behind in my money, I'm really uptight. There's a black driver in front of me, the word 'nigger' will come into my head. . . . These sinister forces are buried deep inside you."[11]

How can we control those invading words and buried forces? When we attempt to explore controversial issues, we may be forced to beat a hasty apologetic retreat. This realization of enforced silence on many topics of racial contention leads African Americans to suspect racism even without evidence. This in turn leads whites to see African Americans as paranoid. Whites are prone to deny the "counterknowledge" or "blackstream" knowledge that African Americans find plausible.[12]

Somehow we must force ourselves to bring to the table a set of uncomfortable beliefs and recognize how these beliefs came about and why they remain plausible. These are not the beliefs of them, but of us. To have a dialogue is to accept these beliefs as ours and, if not embrace them, at least recognize that they are historically grounded, plausible, and not easily discarded. In this we agree with Studs Terkel, who writes:

It might be best for these things to actually be put on the table. If this tumor is to be drawn from the guts of the people, you can look at it and say this is the nature of it. You can't make the correct diagnosis if you pretend it doesn't exist. I think there's been an unhealthy trend in America for a long time not to discuss race. It was governed by a taboo in which people had to be very careful what they'd say or how it might appear.[13]

What happens when we dare not speak these beliefs? What happens when we deny—to ourselves and others—that we hold them because we have come to accept that they are morally illegitimate? We believe that two responses are common. First, we become ashamed; we withdraw from dialogue. No one wishes to admit to holding unacceptable beliefs that may undermine one's public identity. While we are not ready to assert, as does sociologist Frederick Lynch, that this constitutes "the New McCarthyism,"[14] we do believe that tabooed discourse ultimately harms a free society. Former New York mayor Ed Koch noted that many whites fear that "if they talk honestly they'll be called a racist." Journalist Ellis Cose, in turn, worries that blacks fear that if they express their honest views they will be penalized for speaking out against racial inequality.[15]

Second, following from this, we become too willing to accept claims of "actual happenings" that support these hidden beliefs. We cannot speak directly, but surely we are able to shake our heads as we report "the facts"—facts that accord with our unacknowledged beliefs.

This leads to the concern that any incident may come to typify race relations and can then be used to "demonstrate" that one's prejudices were correct after all. Thus, targets of discrimination are always wary. One of Turner's most vivid recollections is of a time when she was about eleven years old, in 1966, and her family's household was mesmerized by the terrible news that eight student nurses had been found murdered in a Chicago hostel. Her parents, neighbors, and other relatives followed the case with dismay, in part because of the despicable crime, but especially because they were eager to determine the race of the killer. Turner recalls her mother praying that the assailant not be black. The early 1960s had charted numerous civil rights successes. The Turners and countless other black families believed that if a black man had committed this crime, all the good work of the civil rights activists would be undone. A collective sigh of relief came when Richard Speck, a white man, was arrested. But similar incidents occurred throughout Turner's childhood, and even today, when she hears of a gruesome murder or kidnapping, she sometimes finds herself thinking, "I hope it doesn't turn out to be a black man." Fine's recollections of the Speck case did not touch on the question of race, although for his parents at an earlier period, similar issues concerning religion were real, as incidents (real or rumored) could generate a wave of anti-Semitism.

We search for images or stories that confirm our beliefs, and often we can be loose about the standards of evidence that we demand. As folklorist Alan Dundes has argued, persuasively we believe, by transforming unacceptable impulses into a narrative that is claimed to have actually happened, we are able to express the inexpressible. This is what legend and rumor are all about.[16]

Let us emphasize that rumors do not emerge only in times characterized by "official" tolerance. Hostile racial rumors have been with us as long as blacks and whites have shared these shores, and no doubt Indians and Pilgrims had their rumors about each other's motives. Yet conditions of tolerance may be particularly pernicious for those who wish to confront false belief. At least with intolerance the beliefs are publicly acknowledged. Under conditions of toleration, a patina of moral disingenuousness covers one's belief. In some ways it is better to confront the admitted bigot or paranoid than to confront those who aspire to appear reasonable and broad-minded.

We address the response of retreat in the final chapter when we discuss what is needed to overcome a dishonest discussion of racial issues. As scholars of rumor, our focus is on understanding what these "actual happenings" that never happened—these "rumors" and "contemporary legends"—tell us about the state of race relations in contemporary America.

RUMOR IN BLACK AND WHITE

As we describe in chapter 2, rumor has a fairly precise definition, referring to information that is spread without "secure standards of evidence." Like many concepts used by the general public, however, rumor has multiple meanings and connects to another concept, the contemporary legend. In general rumor is said to refer to short, nonnarrative statements of belief, whereas contemporary legends—"solidified rumors"—involve narratives of belief containing motifs linked to modern life. We refer to both the literature on rumor and that on contemporary legend in this book, using the two terms to refer to what are, insofar as discussion of race is concerned, essentially overlapping phenomena. However, our discussion extends beyond rumor and legend to include a broad understanding of racial talk.

An additional concern is with what we label as "truth claims"—statements about the world that are to be taken as true—particularly when these claims are not based on evidence to which others have access. For instance, in chapter 7, which describes instances in which a "crime victim"—such as Susan Smith or Tawana Brawley—claims to have been attacked by a mysterious (male) member of another race, we address a cluster of claims that ordinarily might not be considered rumors in that the tellers presumably recognize that their statements are false. In one sense, these are "lies," yet to their audiences they make the same sense as popular rumors. These are communications that make "cultural sense" but are not backed by definitive and shared evidence. While these claims of personal attack do not fully qualify as rumor (before the truth comes out, they are personal experience stories; after the truth emerges, they are lies), they have some of the qualities of rumors in that they take our hidden assumptions and incorporate them into public talk. Rumor is a convenient label for a type of talk that claims factual status for beliefs.

This volume may prove difficult for some readers for several reasons. First, in our analysis of rumor, we do not emphasize whether stories are true or false. Rumors are "truth claims" that are accepted if they are deemed plausible. In a society in which some people entertain the notions that Elvis is alive, that Paul McCartney is dead, and that men have not walked on the moon, definitive proof is hard to come by. The power of rumor is that it is seen as something that could have happened. It is talk or writing that has a "cultural logic." The assertions that the Ku Klux Klan does not own fast-food chains or that gangs are not targeting white virgins may be true enough, but the denial of these claims does not address the reason they were believed as something that might have happened. To disprove that the Klan owns Church's Fried Chicken does not mean that next week we will not have to confront the claim that the Klan owns Popeye's. To focus on the truth or falsity of a rumor ignores the source of its psychological power, as a means of representing aspects of society that cannot be easily expressed.

Second, it is not helpful to throw around insults such as "racist," "white-hater," "anti-Semite," "paranoid," and "bigot." Perhaps it makes one feel better to differentiate oneself from bigots, but it does not solve the problem. Further, to the extent that we become convinced that we are racists or bigots, most of us will be less inclined to reveal this flaw to others, thus avoiding meaningful contact. To use labels such as "paranoid," "racist," or "bigot" too broadly closes discussion, rather than enlarging it, and effectively makes talk self-conscious.

Our collective unwillingness to recognize our own racial beliefs contributes to rumors about race being so pervasive and so plausible. Every month, it seems, we learn of another rumor that suggests that blacks have much to fear from whites and, equally, that whites have much to fear from blacks. Every month another topic of public concern emerges that directly or indirectly addresses these partially hidden racial concerns. Of course, every month there are genuine racial incidents, but the absolute number of such incidents is substantially smaller than what the fervid rumor mill would have us—both blacks and white—believe. For instance, during the 1994–95 academic year, in which this book had its gestation, the following diverse events occurred, each linked to rumors and folk beliefs about race: (1) the story spread that the Klan was selling crown-shaped air fresheners to African Americans, (2) a white woman in South Carolina claimed that a black man kidnapped her children, (3) a scholarly book claimed that blacks had lower—and unchangeable—IQ scores, and (4) O. J. Simpson was acquitted of murdering his white ex-wife. Consider each of these events.

1. A flyer circulated in the African-American community in Richmond, Virginia, stated that a representative of the Ku Klux Klan appeared on a television talk show to thank the black community for purchasing crown-shaped auto air fresheners from a company that contributes money to the Klan. According to the report we received, sales of these air fresheners have subsequently declined precipitously. The distributor of these products—blameless as far as we know—vehemently denies any link to the Klan and wonders what has happened to his financial security. As we note in discussing rumors about corporations, this rumor is merely another transformation of rumors about Klan involvement in businesses that market products to the African-American community.

2. In October 1994 the United States was shaken by a "victim's" claim that a black man had kidnapped the young children of a white woman in South Carolina. Susan Smith eventually admitted to the murder of her two sons, but not before search parties were dispatched and the story was widely disseminated and discussed. White Americans had little difficulty believing that her original claim was plausible; after the confession, blacks emphasized that this acceptance occurred without any evidence other than Smith's flimsy alibi. Many blacks, however, were always suspicious about the likelihood of a carjacking—a crime associ-

ated with urban American streets—taking place in small-town South Carolina.

3. Both of these "truth claims" occurred against the backdrop of the "serious," "academic" debate over Richard Herrnstein and Charles Murray's book, *The Bell Curve*, which describes the biological basis of intelligence. The book presented evidence that the IQ test scores of African Americans were significantly lower than those of European Americans, and that no policy that the authors could imagine appeared likely to eliminate the difference. Although our colleagues in sociology and black studies immediately identified inherent flaws in Herrnstein and Murray's argument, everyone continued to talk about their book.

4. Finally, during 1995, the murder trial of O. J. Simpson wound its way through court and attracted much attention. Even if we wished to ignore claims that invoke the violence of blacks and the bias of white institutions, this "trial of the century," with blasts from prosecutors and defense attorneys, kept these issues on newscasts and front pages.

Each of these public topics, occurring within a short time span, chilling and dispiriting though they surely are, depends on a set of beliefs that in turn depend on a "cultural logic." These truth claims "make sense" given the way in which blacks and whites understand their world. Before we examine these claims dispassionately, we must understand the dynamics of rumor and how rumor reflects popular belief.

In examining those rumors that deal with racial topics, we find that three basic patterns emerge: mirror rumors, Topsy/Eva rumors, and formula rumors. *Mirror rumors* are those rumors that are identical when spread in the black and white communities except that the racial label is altered. The rumors that presage racial conflict (in contrast to riots or rebellions precipitated by one group) often seem remarkably similar, with only the race of the protagonist altered. Rumors about a brutal, bloody castration in a shopping center rest room speak of a white youth being mutilated when they are spread within the white community and of a black youth being harmed when repeated in the African-American community.[17] When a stabbing occurred at South Boston High School during the school busing controversies of the mid-1970s, the race of the youth who was reported stabbed depended on the race of the teller and the audience. These rumors typically refer to highly salient events, which have similar meanings for both races.

The second class of rumors—what we term *Topsy/Eva rumors*—describe the identical topic but are transformed to make cultural sense depending on the community in which they are spread. This label refers to a popular folk doll that supposedly was inspired by the best-selling nineteenth-century novel *Uncle Tom's Cabin*. The book featured two young girls: Little Eva, who is white, well-dressed, blond, and blue-eyed, and Topsy, who is black, poorly dressed, kinky-haired, and dark-eyed. Held one way, the doll resembled Eva, but when it was flipped upside down, Topsy appeared. The two figures were different in more than the color of their skin, but they fit together and were meant to be seen as parallel despite obvious cultural differences. Those similar yet culturally distinct rumors that travel separately through black and white communities resemble the Topsy/Eva doll in that a similar story is shaped to fit the worldview of each group: each version "makes sense" to its audience.

Thus, the specifics of the many rumors and "facts" surrounding the Rodney King beating depended in considerable measure on one's race, with whites emphasizing the violence and crazed behavior of the black motorist, and rioters and blacks focusing on the violence and crazed behavior of the white police. Although these rumors and charges were not precisely symmetrical, they were attempts to process an identical reality through different lenses. The classic example of this process is reported in folklorist Janet Langlois's discussion of the rumors surrounding what became known as the "Belle Isle Incident," which sparked major civil unrest in Detroit in 1943.[18] Several unsubstantiated stories triggered very real racial violence. Mirror rumors claimed that a woman and her baby were accosted by members of the other race and were thrown off a bridge. Other rumors spoke of interracial rapes. Still others described the action of the police and political authorities in handling the disturbances. The political rumors were not identical, but they were parallel in that both groups attempted to make sense of similar claims in light of their own situations and the particular form of their concerns.

The third set of rumors—*formula rumors*—do not explicitly rely on the same events. Some stories "make sense" with a black protagonist, others with a white protagonist. Publicly held stereotypes direct the content of the rumor. We could, if we wished, suggest in our rumors that gang members were Pakistani-American, or that government officials were Dominican-American, but the narrative would lose power as a result. Telling a "good story" depends on the knowing and skilled use of stereotypes. Thus, we find that whites are frightened by black street violence but not by black corporations attempting to poison them. Within the African-American community, white corporations and the white-dominated governmental structure provide the greatest threat.

These three classes of rumor patterns remind us that in some regard our fears and anxieties about each other are similar in content, whereas in other instances they are distinct, relying on historical circumstance and cultural beliefs. In either event, we use rumor to make sense of the risks we face in a dangerous and uncertain society.

THE PLAN OF THE BOOK

In this book we set ourselves several fundamental goals: (1) to explain the dynamics of how rumors work and reveal otherwise unspoken aspects of society; (2) to present an overview of the beliefs that blacks and whites maintain about each other, both currently and historically; (3) to place these beliefs in context; (4) to provide a background that permits us—both black and white—to understand the dynamics of racial rumors, hoping to provide yardsticks by which we can evaluate the likelihood that a particular claim is likely to be true; and (5) to provide a basis from which an honest racial understanding is possible, based on discussion without pretense but grounded on fundamental, if imperfect, goodwill.

We gathered our data both from our own fieldwork and from the research of other scholars. To provide context for readers unfamiliar with our earlier research, we also have incorporated background material from our own previous works. We do not believe our present goals and the kinds of beliefs we are scrutinizing are particularly enhanced by statistical analysis. Readers eager to know just how many whites believe Liz Claiborne supports satanic cults or how many African Americans believe the Voting Rights Acts of 1964 is due to be rescinded will be dissatisfied. This type of quantification would be nearly impossible to provide, and it would not help answer the more interesting "why" questions.

We realize that, by focusing on blacks and whites, we are simplifying contemporary racial and class dynamics. We encourage other folklorists to use our research as a foundation for subsequent efforts. We find that many individuals who are willing to acknowledge that contemporary folklore is alive and well assume that it operates in the domain of undereducated people. Our fieldwork suggests otherwise. For example, we found numerous well-educated people who immediately believed and circulated the "Lights Out" gang rumor we will analyze in a subsequent chapter.

In chapter 1 we present an example of a rumor complex that infects black and white discourse: rumors about racial disturbances, particularly focusing on the riot or rebellion in Los Angeles in the aftermath of the first Rodney King verdict. This complex reminds us that violent racial disturbances are virtually always preceded by rumor, fueled by rumor, and then interpreted by rumor. These rumors appear, in different forms determined by circumstance, in both the black and white communities, depending on the location and instigators of the violence.

In chapter 2 we turn to a consideration of the models that scholars have developed to understand rumor and contemporary legends. Over the past century, rumor has been explored by psychologists, sociologists, anthropologists, political scientists, historians, and folklorists. Each discipline places its own spin on the meaning and course of rumor; when taken together, these interpretations provide an adequate understanding of the conditions under which rumors will spread and the roles they play in communal life. Rumors may serve functional needs for a society, or they may serve strategic interests of individual narrators.

Both blacks and whites believe that large corporations do not have people's interests at heart and pose a danger to the community, as we describe in chapter 3. Whereas African Americans are prone to attribute corporate threats to a long-standing racial animus, white Americans are prone to define corporations as motivated by greed, sometimes linked to political extremism or religious cultism. Many stories claim that the Ku Klux Klan or a related organization controls corporations, with the explicit goal of swindling, sterilizing, or even murdering African Americans. In contrast, militant pro-life organizations, exotic cults such as the Moonies, or devil-worshiping sects are often identified by whites as the real power behind several large corporations.

As we present in chapter 4, rumors and contemporary legends tie mistrust not only to corporations but also to the government. Again, perhaps because they are largely excluded from the inner workings of government, blacks are more prone to see the machinations of government as being explicitly targeted against them. Whites' fears and dislike of government, equally robust, tend to be race-neutral, with the exception of stories of governmental discrimination in favor of African Americans in affirmative action, voting rights, and welfare policy. While many blacks see charges of preference as ludicrous, governmental policies of redress are transformed into ideas of advantage.

Since the first contact between sub-Saharan Africans and Europeans, stories about the sexual conduct of the "other" group have abounded. In chapter 5 we address the set of beliefs that assert the presence of immorality and sexuality, most particularly in white beliefs about African Americans. Following from Joel Kovel's argument in *White Racism*, we suggest that the image of sexuality is a central template by which whites interpret the cause of "pathologies" within African-American communities. The legends and folk beliefs are particularly potent in those cases in which white womanhood is threatened. Today many of these rumors are suppressed, but they continue to emerge at the margins of discourse.

Attitudes about crime are often cited as an obstacle to the integration of black and white communities. When asked, many whites claim (perhaps sincerely) that they bear no animosity toward African Americans; they are merely concerned about the association of blacks and criminal activity. In recent years, the issue of gang violence has become a polite stand-in for the fear of young black males. While "gang" ostensibly has a race-neutral reference, in reality, as we describe in chapter 6, it is directly linked to issues of race and class, a handy euphemism for a society that demands rhetorical tolerance.

The related cases of Susan Smith and Tawana Brawley remind us that even "personal experience" stories can be manipulated to fit cultural models. In chapter 7 we turn from the consideration of rumors per se to examine truth claims that operate much like a rumor: the motivated lie, focusing on the false accusations in which members of one race allege that they have been assaulted by members of another, gaining sympathy and escaping blame. In this, Susan Smith and Tawana Brawley are sisters. Little attention has been paid to false accusations, but because, on the surface, they appear to be true, they are rhetorical dynamite and serve as an intensification of rumor. By looking at instances in which blacks and whites make charges, we explore the dynamics by which belief fits into cultural categories.

Finally, in chapter 8 we describe the implications of our findings. We outline some techniques for judging the likely factual content of racial rumors, suggest some responses when faced with these troubling stories, and present guidelines for what we hope will be a fruitful conversation between the races.

As authors, we come from distinct backgrounds that illustrate the reality of race in America—not typical, but representative of some racial themes. Our personal histories make a difference in how we interpret the world, even if we attempt to transcend part of this background. We recognize that the issues that characterized American society in our formative years have changed mightily since that time.

Gary Alan Fine was raised in comfortable circumstances in New York City, the child of a father who was a Freudian psychoanalyst and a mother who was a full-time housewife. His family hired domestics— African Americans and others—to help with child care, cooking, and cleaning. He attended private schools with only a handful of black classmates, who themselves often were from privileged backgrounds. Further, and not least important, his parents, well-educated Jewish Americans, were liberal Democrats who contributed to the National Association for the Advancement of Colored People (NAACP) and other like-minded groups. Indeed, his first memory of a racial incident concerns a black playmate from first or second grade. According to the policy of the Park Avenue apartment building where Fine lived, blacks were required to ride in the service elevator. In one of those small civil rights victories of the 1950s, his mother insisted that his schoolmate be allowed to ride in the main elevator. She won that battle but did not push to change the rules for black adults. Today we might view such efforts as patronizing, but at the time they took some courage. Like many of the time, her hope, which she instilled in her children, was that someday skin color simply would not be noticed.

Patricia A. Turner's background was dramatically different. She grew up in a rural area of New York State. Her mother did not have a domestic; she was a domestic. And Turner herself worked as a domestic during high school and college vacations. Neither of her parents graduated from high school. A combination of her earnings, scholarships, and affirmative action programs financed her college and graduate school years. Her parents' lives were consumed by meeting the family's basic needs. They did not join the NAACP or any similar organizations, and often they did not vote.

A passion for folkloric discourse brought us together. By talking and arguing about all manner of things, we have come to the understandings that undergird this book. Ignoring the warning to folklorists in *Candyman*, we moved forward.

We have no illusions that we have presented the last word on the subject; indeed, if we have, that would negate the possibility of a vigorous dialogue. Perhaps most dramatically, we are painfully aware that in examining only blacks and whites, we are addressing just a portion of the American mosaic. Hispanics, Asians, American Indians, and others are targets and sometimes originators of rumors and beliefs. We are sadly aware that some readers may consider us to be racists, apologists, naive scholars, or fools; these labels are mantles we do not choose, yet we believe they are ones we must not fear. This book should serve as the beginning of a challenging, painful set of racial understandings; yet its challenge and its pain must not prevent us from beginning.

ONE

Rumor in the Life
of America
Riots and Race

We interrupt this program to announce that the Simi Valley
jury is about to announce its verdict in the trial of the four
Los Angeles police officers who have been accused of having
assaulted Rodney King. . . .

April 29, 1992, had been an ordinary day in the life of America until
midafternoon, when network news bureaus broke into the talk shows
and soap operas with a long-awaited announcement from Simi Valley,
California. An affluent enclave, unaccustomed to widespread public
scrutiny, Simi Valley was the suburban community where four white
officers from the Los Angeles Police Department were acquitted by a
jury consisting of ten whites, one Asian American, one Hispanic, and
no African Americans. Charged with assaulting an unarmed African-
American motorist named Rodney Glen King, the officers had stead-
fastly proclaimed their innocence.[1]

Most Americans were first introduced to the officers and King thirteen months earlier when a grainy but graphic videotape documenting
King's arrest was first televised. Television news may have been the first

source of information about King and the LAPD, but other major news outlets—radio, newspapers, and magazines—also tackled the event as the first prominent incident concerning race relations in the 1990s. As journalists reported on the incident, they constructed narratives consistent with the evidence they accumulated. In seeking and sorting information, they made choices about what questions to ask, whom to interview, and what to include in and exclude from their reports. These choices were influenced by the journalists' professional sense of what would make their version of this story attractive to the public. As people watched, listened to, and read these accounts of baton-wielding cops and a large-framed black man, their interpretations were influenced by their personal values and experiences.

As major media outlets constructed and disseminated their versions of the Rodney King incident, people ignored, amended, or revised these accounts and then shared their own interpretations. These informal exchanges fused with information garnered from more formal channels to provide the fodder for numerous rumors. As we point out later, domestic crises in general, and riots in particular, have always been accompanied by a plethora of rumors that are especially difficult to analyze. We must rely on recollections from informants after the incident has ended. More than we would like, we must rely on print media and other secondhand sources. Yet, because of its importance as a marker of race relations in America, we begin with some of the texts surrounding the LAPD/Rodney King incident. As the first significant rumor-generating event of the 1990s, it provides a useful starting point, demonstrating how familiar racially influenced stories emerge in contemporary America and the ways in which new aspects of race relations affect these traditional stories.

The initial reports of the beating generated many emotional responses. For the most part, the major media shaped the story into a familiar one about blacks and whites. And, indeed, since the trial had focused on white police officers versus a black motorist, it is easy to understand why these terms were chosen to frame the trial's aftermath.

But unlike many earlier urban upheavals, the LAPD verdict generated immediate and violent responses from members of several ethnic groups. In May 1999, seven years after the event, a columnist in an Asian Pacific newspaper recounted the enormous financial, social, and cultural toll it placed on Korean Americans, who commemorate the day as "Sa-ee-gu" ("April 29" in Korean).[2] Thus, while we can talk about how rumors surrounding the assault and verdict resonate with discourse that accompanied other urban upheavals, we must note that the black/white dichotomy oversimplifies the racial reality of the 1990s.

Whether one calls the aftermath a riot (as whites are prone to brand it) or a rebellion (the preferred label of many African Americans), the financial and social costs were enormous, and another painful chapter was written into the history of American race relations. By the time the disturbances ended three days later, more than ten thousand blacks and Latinos had been arrested in this "multiethnic riot."[3] One estimate placed the number of active participants at about forty-five thousand, with another hundred thousand sympathetic onlookers. These numbers are twice as great as the estimates for the Watts riot of 1965, which had an affected region that was at least twice as large.[4] Forty-five people had been killed, and nearly twenty-four hundred were injured. More than six hundred arson fires had been set, and insured losses were said to reach $1 billion; uninsured losses could not even be calculated. Some twenty thousand people were put out of work, at least temporarily.[5] As the news of the bedlam was reported, scattered violent outbreaks developed in other major American cities.

INTERNAL NEWS

Rumor, particularly as it emerges during crisis episodes, is frequently described by metaphors associated with riots, notably that of an out-of-control fire. The expression that "rumor spreads like wildfire" is a cliché. Scholars have long noted that rumors often *fuel* riots. We also hear of rumors spreading, erupting, and igniting. The metaphor is tenacious and appealing in part because the rumors that emerge during crises can do as much damage as fire.

Reports of violence after the Simi Valley verdict made clear that much of the crowd behavior was fueled by a set of internal rumors that heated the situation and led to decisions being made without clear and compelling evidence. Even the extent of the violence was exaggerated, with the number of arson fires initially reported at more than five thousand, and arrests at nearly twenty thousand. These figures made the riots seem even more dangerous and widespread than they were and further inflamed public fears.[6] The rumor that a third of those arrested were illegal aliens exacerbated tensions over immigration, contributing to the desire to "crack down" on undocumented aliens and permitting the deportation of many.[7] Accounts pictured frantic parents searching the streets for their missing children, possibly "victims" of agents of the Immigration and Naturalization Service.[8] Fears that the riot would permit the authorities to crack down on gangs and illegal immigrants were rampant throughout the affected communities.

While the crowd was not a single entity, the small groups that constituted the mass had only limited information to act upon, and much of that information they mistrusted, sensing the media were part of the city's power structure. Firefighters, seen as being in league with the police, were jeered and attacked with rocks and bottles. People heard that others were looting, and there was a strong desire not to lose out, given the emotional tenor of the moment, especially when word went out that the police were not responding. What began as an angry political protest became a poverty riot, as stories spread about the best places to gather food and other goods. The riot, seemingly chaotic to outsiders, was directed by internal information channels as rival gangs joined ranks, creating a new social structure.[9]

Spread by rumor, conjecture, anger, and in some cases an opportunity to profit, the disturbances provided one of the more dramatic, if ultimately ineffectual, challenges to a white power structure and eventually led directly to the replacement of the controversial white chief of police, Daryl Gates, by the black police chief of Philadelphia, Willie Williams. Nonetheless, tensions between Los Angeles elites and minority residents remain charged, and new rumors still emerge. Claims were made that the police arrested people in poor neighborhoods who were innocently sitting in their living rooms, unable to produce a sales slip for their TV or couch,[10] or that a man caught with a packet of sunflower seeds and two cartons of milk was held on $15,000 bail.[11] All the old accusations of racist behavior by the LAPD and the Sheriff's Department were revived. Residents claimed that a white racist group, known as the Vikings, had been organized inside a sheriff's station in a predominant minority suburb, contributing to a string of police abuses, perhaps including murder and torture.[12]

Old injustices, barely healed, like the shooting of an unarmed black teenager, Latasha Harlins, by a Korean grocer in Los Angeles, were pointed at by some African Americans as exemplifying the unfairness of the system and justifying their anger toward the courts and toward Koreans. The Harlins killing served as a template to justify violence. Journalists were repeatedly told during the disturbances, "This is for our baby sister. This is for Latasha."[13] Many African Americans draw attention to controversial police practices. The deadly choke holds, previously practiced by the Los Angeles Police Department, were alleged to have killed at least fifteen suspects over the years. The police department denied these claims and admitted only one death, and police asserted—with some measure of irony—that the outlawing of these choke holds left the police few options and thus contributed to the beating of Rodney King.[14]

Residents of the poorer areas of the city claimed that the curfew during the riot was enforced unfairly. One observer argued that while many homeless people were held on $8,000 bail, a "group of city attorneys threw a wild party on the fourth night that lasted far beyond curfew. Then on Monday morning, they came into court and sanctimoniously asked the judge for three-day sentences for hapless curfew arrestees."[15] Further, injured police and firefighters were said to be taken to the better hospitals because of their race, whereas blacks and Latinos were said to be taken to poorer neighborhood hospitals. As one man remarked: "All the people of color that was injured, they took 'em over to Daniel Freeman [Hospital]. . . . But that white fireman that got shot, they took over to Cedars Sinai. You see what I'm saying?"[16]

EXTERNAL VISIONS

Just as rumors propelled the actions of those within the confines of the strife-ridden community, so did individuals beyond the immediate reach of the rioters take unsubstantiated information seriously. In the greater Los Angeles area, many residents altered their plans based on rumors about the South Central neighborhood. In the rest of the state of California and throughout the United States, rumors circulated about the potential damage by the rioters themselves or those sympathetic to them.

During the days following the announcement of the not-guilty verdict in the trial of the LAPD officers, white southern Californians became frightened by the violence dominating their screens. The televised beating of white truck driver Reginald Denny in South Central Los Angeles provided a visual counterpoint to the King videotape, sparking the fears of whites. Conservative journalist Patrick Buchanan, interviewed on CNN, saw the uprising as "an orgy of rioting, arson, murder, and lynching."[17] Buchanan used the images of an orgy and lynching, in effect, to sexualize the rebellion and to historicize it in light of African-American stereotypes, much as the Los Angeles police did in referring to "Mandingo blacks," "mo fos," and "gorillas in the mist."

In some ways, the fact that southern California was the site of the riot was deeply ironic. The City of Angels is home to some of America's most successful and visible celebrities, including very wealthy and prominent African Americans. It is also, as the riots graphically demonstrated, the locus of some of the nation's worst urban poverty. Some of the nation's wealthiest citizens live in close proximity to some of the poorest residents, as evidenced by the rioting in the seedier reaches of Hollywood. Yet when one considers the housing patterns of the city as a whole, Los Angeles is "hyper-segregated."[18] To be sure, this dynamic exists in other cities as well, but in Los Angeles much of the wealth is highly visible and public, controlled by members of the entertainment industry. These are not the anonymous superwealthy, but many are famous and are people "everyone" feels they know.[19] The image is that Los Angeles is where one can live out one's dreams, which is a theme of popular films. Although Hollywood producers, directors, actors, and musicians often strongly affiliate politically with the "underclass," frequently the support goes little further than feel-good rhetoric and fund-raisers. The apparent hypocrisy of those skilled at saying "the right thing" is not lost on their less-privileged neighbors.

In preparation for her acclaimed one-woman performance based on the LAPD/Rodney King debacle, *Twilight Los Angeles, 1992,* the African-American playwright Anna Deavere Smith interviewed a range of local residents about their fears and attitudes. One of those interviewed was Elaine Young, an affluent white resident of Beverly Hills. Young acknowledged that she, like other Angelenos of her station, gravitated to the world-renowned Beverly Hills Hotel after viewing the televised violence that was erupting within miles of her palatial home. Inconvenienced by the fact that many Los Angeles restaurants had opted to close until the turmoil subsided, Young reasoned that the hotel, long a sanctuary for her, would be obligated to serve meals. Defending her impulse to seek shelter at a five-star hotel, she claimed to have lunched there almost every day for thirty-six years. When she was called upon by a television interviewer to comment on the closing of the hotel's Polo Lounge, she noted that she and many of her acquaintances sought refuge in the hotel. According to Smith's poetic rendition of Young's remarks:

So that was the mood at the Polo Lounge
after they talked about how bad it was
and maybe they would come back after an hour
but then they tried to go on.
"Here we are
and we're still alive,"
and, you know,
"we hope there will be people alive
when we come out,"
but basically,
they would come there every night.
And I finally went there for three nights
and stayed till two or three in the morning
so I wouldn't be alone.[20]

Young was dismayed when her comments were assailed and ridiculed by a man who saw the televised interview. She surmised that his disgust at her confession stemmed from the belief that she "was being flippant." Defending her actions, she said,

It was like
people hanging out together,
like safety in numbers.
Nobody can hurt us at the Beverly Hills Hotel
'cause it was like a fortress.[21]

Clearly, the rich and famous felt vulnerable and uncertain, worrying if there would be a Los Angeles to which they could return. During the early hours of the uprising, it was by no means clear how lengthy and deadly the rioting would be. It was easy to give credence to the belief that wealthy white neighborhoods would be targeted. Waiting times in lines at gourmet markets were said to be two hours long, and the rooms in the best resorts on the California coast were said to have suddenly filled up.[22] Whites patrolled their estates with guns and worried about the extra sets of house keys they had given to their maids.[23] Similarly, in New York rumors swept wealthy areas, leading stores such as Saks and Lord and Taylor to close early, and white shoppers to warn each other to leave the city as rapidly as possible to avoid the potential riot—a disturbance that never transpired.[24]

To Young and those like her, the riots seemed to augur a frightening shift in power; the threat to the status quo was all too close to home. Yet as in many contemporary riots, the primary victims in this case were residents of impoverished neighborhoods and those businesspeople who served them. In some ways the events of the spring of 1992 represented community self-mutilation. Businesses were attacked by customers who patronized them. Consumed by frustration over the steady economic deterioration of their communities, the lengthy recession, persistent un-employment, and the power structure's apparent indifference to the de-cay, men, women, and children simultaneously expressed their anger and despair and declared a holiday from self-restraint.

All this was read by middle-class and wealthy Angelenos through the eyes of the media, and the information provided was transformed into fearful rumors. No transcripts exist to provide a record of the conver-sations that took place in the Polo Lounge, but they most probably echoed those going on throughout the nation as viewers searched for explanations of what was happening, why it was happening, and what would happen next. If people were truly overcome with anger at the white political and economic system, why hadn't they directed their hostility outside their own community? Would that occur tomorrow? Situated in a plush hotel, guests feared that the rioters would come after them.

These fears and associated rumors did not end after the riots sub-sided. Before long, a tenacious rumor was circulating, alleging that mi-nority gangs intended to go after the affluent suburban enclaves, known to Angelenos as the 3 B's—Beverly Hills, Bel Air, and Brentwood. In most versions it was alleged that if the four white police officers were acquitted after the second (federal civil rights) trial, "gangs" intended to attack and destroy the 3 B's.

This rumor spawned by the LA riots was no doubt fueled by a very public truce between the notorious Crips and Bloods, two powerful rival street gangs. Angelenos were persuaded that large numbers of minority youths are gang members. For instance, then district attorney Ira Reiner suggested that 47 percent of all young black males in Los Angeles County were active gang members.[25] Following the demolition of so much of South Central, the gang leaders pledged to eliminate their differences and work together. Their truce was televised, and numerous images were depicted of smiling "gangbangers" wearing T-shirts pronouncing the new allegiance. Cameras recorded the ceremony as the Crips and Bloods shook hands, embraced, and spoke of the importance of moving in a new direction. But which direction? Perhaps the era of "gangbanger" had ended, replaced by that of "liberation fighter."

Most media outlets reported the truce as good news. Perhaps the violence connected to gang life might be nearing an end, lifting the state of siege in which many poor residents lived. Maybe money spent for drug enforcement could now be directed to education. Perhaps no more innocent children would die in the crossfire volleys of drive-by shootings. But if the gangs were not planning to shoot each other, who would they target? Many members of the public and the police worried that this was a prelude to collective action. Public programs offering to trade guns for tickets to sporting events resulted in the collection of just a handful of the weapons law enforcement officers knew to be owned by gang members.

The claim that combined gangs would pillage the 3 B's is a classic folk formation. First of all, as has been noted by folklorist Alan Dundes, the number three holds a particular resonance for Americans, and many narratives contain references to three. Also, many contemporary legends exhibit the kind of easily interpreted code evident in these texts. Many rumors trade in tragic predictions, based on formulas.[26] Southern Californians could easily figure out the communities identified as the 3 B's.

The 3 B's and other rumors that emerged following the riots suggest that many people did not interpret the truce announcement as genuinely good news. The only thing worse than having gang members shooting each other was having them shooting us. Rumors developed in which most individuals could position themselves or a group they belonged to within the "us." A related account, spread from the Los Angeles Sheriff's Department, suggested that the Crips and Bloods, operating under the direction of "Muslims," were planning an assault on a police station and attacks on individual police officers on their way home. A crudely drawn leaflet proclaimed "Eye for an Eye—Let's Kill Two Cops."[27] A student at the University of California at Davis (in northern California) reported that her sorority sisters on the volleyball team were scheduled to compete in Santa Monica (in southern California) on the weekend following the first verdict. She reported, "Thousands of sorority women come from schools all over the western U.S. to play volleyball and party at the beach. Our sorority's ISVT representative has heard that groups of blacks have targeted many 'white' communities for rioting if the LAPD officers are acquitted, and Santa Monica is one of them."[28] Members of her sorority, who had been looking forward to this annual spring frolic, seriously considered skipping the 1992 event. Hearing that Santa Monica was one of the targeted communities placed them within the "us."

RIOTS AND THEIR RUMORS

Dramatic as the Los Angeles violence was, it would be a mistake to assume that it was unprecedented. Race riots and rebellions—sometimes led by whites and sometimes by blacks—have long been part of American history, occurring for almost three centuries and in virtually every major city. In nearly every instance these riots were spread and often sparked by the presence of rumors; the behaviors of April and May 1992 fit this pattern.

In many ways rumors during riots link a set of "truth claims" to racial misunderstandings. In situations of disorder, tension, passion, and anger, people are hungry for any and all information that sheds light on their circumstances. In the potent phrase of the sociologist Tamotsu

Shibutani, people are willing to accept "improvised news"—information that in other, less ambiguous or less threatening circumstances they might reject. The examination of rumor during periods of societal tension has long been central to rumor scholarship. The desire to curb—or at least to understand—rumor in times of war and domestic disturbance impelled much important scholarship. Experts believed that "false" information inflamed situations and disrupted the smooth organization of society. In much early writing on rumor, the rumormonger was the enemy—either explicitly an enemy agent who deliberately attempted to provoke disorder, or implicitly a bigot whose values were at variance with those of the broader culture.

Perhaps this theme can best be seen in the earliest of the classic social scientific writings on rumor, *The Psychology of Rumor* (1947), by Harvard University social psychologists Gordon W. Allport and Leo Postman. Allport and Postman's research originally developed from the studies of Robert H. Knapp, who was working for the Massachusetts Committee of Public Safety in the early days of World War II. At that time the primary concern was the use to which rumor might be put by hostile agents in the service of the wartime enemies of America.

The presence of racial tension was a primary point of division in the society upon which a malicious rumor could play. People were ready to believe many things about racial outsiders. Allport and Postman note, "Although rumor spreading is at all times a social and psychological problem of major proportions, it is especially so in times of crisis. Whenever there is social strain, false report grows virulent."[29] Allport and Postman were not interested only in rumor in times of war; writing in the immediate postwar era, they also were interested in how rumor inflamed race relations and increased prejudice.

In their research, which is described in more detail in chapter 2, Allport and Postman dramatically demonstrated through a series of clever experiments how prejudice could influence the recall and presentation of a rumor—a distortion that they assumed would be greater during periods of tension. Their research underlines one crucial dimension of the LAPD verdict. As noted previously, most people "read" the videotape as showing an attack on a powerless black man by white men in authority. In contrast, members of the jury, influenced by the logic supplied by talented defense attorneys, saw a completely different picture in the tape. Visual evidence is not merely present but needs to be interpreted, a point artfully made by the social psychologists Albert Hastorf and Hadley Cantril in their examination of how fans of two rival football teams interpreted the events of a controversial game.[30] Jurors became convinced that Rodney King was in control of the situation and that the police were acting out of legitimate fears for their safety, basing their actions on professional standards.

A second important study of rumor also stemmed from a concern with prejudice and war. Sociologist Tamotsu Shibutani's *Improvised News: A Sociological Study of Rumor* (1966) originated in his personal experience as a Japanese American during World War II.[31] He examined rumors among Japanese Americans in the San Francisco area, who were suddenly suspected of being enemy agents, and then examined rumors during confinement in relocation centers. Shibutani's concern was to trace how rumor emerges in periods of ambiguity and how it attempts to solve that ambiguity. Shibutani argued, hopefully, that rumor is problem-solving behavior. Again, it is the social strain—for Shibutani, as for Allport and Postman, a racial strain—that provides the impetus to rumor formation and spread. Situations in which people tend to mill about often provide openings for rumor to emerge.[32] In such settings, defenses that prevent interaction among strangers tend to melt away, and because of the need for information, people are more accepting of what they receive. In normal conditions we are likely to have fairly high standards of judgment, but any knowledge will serve in a storm.

The series of destructive racial riots of the 1960s gave rise to a concern with rumors in times of civil disturbance. In 1975 Terry Ann Knopf, a staff member at the Lemberg Center for the Study of Violence at Brandeis University, presented what she labeled "riot process theory" in her book *Rumors, Race, and Riots*. After describing the history of riots in the United States and their linkage with the presence of rumors, Knopf suggested that rumors in times of social strain develop through the crystallization of hostile beliefs and the reality of group conflict rather than being grounded in the manipulation of social agents, chance, or cultural images. The hostile belief system provides a fertile base in which rumors can be formed. This model, drawing on sociologist Neil Smelser's value-added theory of collective behavior, emphasized the social conditions that led up to the riot itself. Knopf suggested that rumors translate a hostile belief to a fact and, in the process, intensify the belief.[33] These rumors are typically tethered to an ambiguous event that can be made meaningful through the linkage to an actual happening— even if the meaning of that event is transformed through rumor. Knopf found that prior to many riots, rumors increase in number and virulence, often connected to pending issues that deal with racial concerns. Of course, counting rumors is an uncertain art, and after the riot, rumors may be more memorable; thus, the conclusion may be biased because rumors in normal circumstances are often ignored. From Knopf's perspective, a precipitating event, open to multiple interpretations, provides the spark that ignites violent behavior. Often rumors in black and white communities, though not identical, will have similar thematic content (the Topsy/Eva phenomenon, described in the introduction) in that they relate to the complementary aspects of a hostile belief system.

RUMORS OF VIOLENT PROTEST

As Turner has documented in *I Heard It through the Grapevine*, since the first European slave traders shackled their African captives in the bowels of their ships, there have been rumors that blacks will rise up in rebellion. These rumors recognize the oppression that blacks have suffered, and, as a result, they have a compelling plausibility. One might almost wonder why there have been so few violent protests, not so many. These assertions ask, in effect, if you were brutalized, what would you do? It is not surprising that many whites hold tightly to the protection offered by the Second Amendment because of their fears of racial violence. They suspect that if they were treated as blacks have routinely been treated, they would rise up in armed revolt against their oppressors. It is only slightly too cynical to suggest that the debate over gun control involves an argument between those who believe that whites need guns to protect themselves from an oppressive government and marauding blacks and those who feel it is necessary to get guns out of the hands of poor and minority communities, so that they cannot rise in rebellion.

According to the 1968 report of the National Advisory Commission on Civil Disorders, better known as the Kerner Commission report, 66 percent of the riots the commission examined could be attributed to the presence of rumors. Knopf discovered that in one-third of the cases of racial disturbances that she examined (excluding the rioting after the assassination of Martin Luther King), rumor intensified a racial incident.[34] This relationship was particularly salient for serious disturbances, where fully 67 percent were linked to rumor. Further, a previous increase in rumor was noticed in those localities where rumors circulated after the assassination of King.[35] The intensification of rumor permits an incident to become the grounds for violence.

One incident in which rumor was directly implicated in racial violence was the shooting in 1989 of Yusef Hawkins, a black teenager, in the Bensonhurst neighborhood of Brooklyn, a white, working-class area. At the time of Hawkins's murder, several rumors were spreading. One suggested that a local white girl was dating a black boy. Even more significant (and possibly related to the first rumor) was the allegation that a band of blacks would be entering the neighborhood to cause trouble. Not knowing this background, Hawkins and some friends had the misfortune to be walking through Bensonhurst to inspect a used car. They chanced to walk by a group of armed white young men, who assumed they were part of the impending invasion.[36]

Such racial violence is by no means a recent phenomenon. As early as 1741, weakly substantiated rumors led to brutality when a Spanish vessel with a black crew arrived in colonial New York. New Yorkers planned to sell part of the crew at a slave auction. New York already had a large slave population; one out every five New Yorkers was black.[37] At this time mysterious fires broke out, damaging the governor's house and the king's chapel. Rumors swept through New York that the captured blacks had set the buildings on fire for revenge. Some even felt that the black population was planning to burn down the entire city.[38] Tensions were exacerbated, then as now, by the willingness of some white women to cohabit with black men. As a result of evidence stemming almost entirely from rumors, thirteen black men were burned at the stake, seventeen were hanged, and four whites (including two women) were hanged.[39] These circumstances from almost three centuries ago are remarkably similar to those that have emerged in conjunction with twentieth-century riots.

The eminent African-American sociologist W. E. B. Du Bois predicted that the twentieth century's paramount problem would be the color line. Throughout the century, relations between white and black Americans have been marked by persistent tension interrupted by periodic cataclysms. The eruptions occur when the tenuous racial equilibrium becomes disturbed by economic, social, or cultural shifts, unexpected at the time, although clear in retrospect. These are the same circumstances that contribute to the emergence of rumors. As a result, rumors and riots have gone hand in hand throughout the century. Despite this, some aspects of race riots have changed markedly. The early race riots of the twentieth century were quite distinct from those of the past several decades. During the World War I era, most race riots were characterized by brutal attacks of whites on blacks.

One of most dramatic of these occurred in East St. Louis, Illinois, in 1917. This industrial city was experiencing profound changes as whites increased their union-organizing activities. In order to diminish the unions' power, business leaders stepped up their efforts to attract black laborers from the rural South. Much to the dismay of the white laborers, blacks were willing to work for less money. Trouble began following a labor rally during which a series of white speakers denounced the attempts made by business leaders to "colonize" the city with cheap black labor. As the meeting dispersed, a series of rumors spread through the crowd. One alleged that a black man had just killed a white in a hold-up attempt. Another indicated that a white woman had just been insulted or shot. Responding to the tenor of the meetings and the rumors, clusters of whites began assaulting those blacks they encountered. Over the next several days, tensions remained high as stories of blacks buying large caches of firearms and smuggling them into their neighborhoods abounded. To be sure, blacks and whites alike were bringing in guns, but at bridges the vehicles of black drivers were the only ones being inspected. As Elliot Rudwick has pointed out, the one-sidedness of the first episode, caused whites to fear massive retaliation by the blacks.[40]

After more than a month of skirmishes fueled by rumor and speculation, rioting resumed. The renewed violence began after a car filled with whites fired random shots into black homes. Several minutes later a similar car, driven by a policeman, cruised the same street and was fired upon by local residents. Eventually nine whites and approximately thirty-nine blacks were killed.

For similar reasons, relations between blacks and whites were also charged in Chicago in 1919. The African-American population in that city had more than doubled during the preceding decade. Affluent white businessmen used the increased black labor supply to contain union strength. Suitable housing units were in short supply, and the mass transit system was overburdened. The trouble began at a beach when an adolescent African-American bather, Eugene Williams, strayed across an unmarked color line from the black to the white section of the water. White bystanders began throwing rocks, and the young man panicked and drowned. The news of Williams's death spread quickly, as did stories alleging that a white police officer refused to arrest the white assailant who threw the rock that felled the young African-American man. In the next several days, rumors emerged, including ones that would recur in Detroit some twenty years later, alleging that a woman and her infant had been brutally killed by members of the opposite race. Mobs of people looked for lone members of the opposite race and attacked them brutally.

The Detroit race riots of 1943 are striking for the similarity of the rumors that stimulated each side into action. Just as was the case in Chicago and East St. Louis, violence erupted after prolonged racial antagonism and industrial strife. In the World War II years, white Detroiters were disturbed by the marked increase of southern blacks being lured to the Motor City to take jobs in war-related enterprises. Filling jobs, of course, meant that these southern blacks would have to live in the city, riding public transportation and enrolling in schools. In their efforts to lure blacks northward, recruiters depicted Detroit as much more racially hospitable than proved to be true. Hence both whites and blacks were angry and frustrated. Whites feared the encroachment of blacks, and blacks felt that they had been deceived. As folklorist Janet Langlois points out, "Order deteriorated on Sunday June 20, 1943. Spasms of violence permeated the city. As a result, twenty-five blacks and nine whites were killed. Fifteen of the blacks were killed by police. Three-fourths of the nineteen hundred people arrested were black."[41]

After the violence subsided several days later, political authorities sought an explanation for the events. What had led generally law-abiding citizens to take up arms against each other? To be sure, the racial tension and labor policy of the previous years were the crux of the problem. But why, on that particular day, did an uneasy coexistence disintegrate? Many rumors circulated through the crowds. In interviews with whites, investigators learned that word had spread that blacks had accosted a white woman holding a child and threw them both from the Belle Isle bridge. Investigators heard the same story from blacks, except in this version the woman and her child were black, and the assailants were white. The river produced no corpses of any gender, of any age, of any race.

In urban areas with long-standing black populations, festering racial animosity contributed to domestic upheaval. Unlike East St. Louis in 1917, Chicago in 1919, and Detroit in 1943, Harlem in 1935 had been the home to a sizable black population for decades. On a particularly hot day, a sixteen-year-old African-American male was caught shoplifting an inexpensive pocketknife. Shortly after he exited through a rear door with the police, an ambulance arrived at the front of the store. A rumor circulated through the crowd that he had been killed for shoplifting. The next day blacks vented their anger by attacking white-owned businesses. Although there was widespread property damage, no loss of life occurred.

The backdrop of World War II also played a role in the Harlem riot of 1943. Many Harlem residents were dismayed by the treatment of black soldiers who were writing back from southern training camps about the blatant Jim Crow segregation they were experiencing. Excerpts from such letters were often printed in Harlem's black newspapers. When a fracas broke out between a white policeman and a black military policeman in a Harlem hotel, conditions were ripe for violence. The black MP was shot in the shoulder but not killed; nevertheless, word spread that a white policeman had killed a black soldier. In the violence that erupted that night, six persons were killed, over five hundred were injured, and millions of dollars of property damage resulted.

The domestic dissonance stimulated by war also contributed to rumormongering among whites. Throughout World War II, many whites believed that blacks would rebel through the establishment of "Disappointment Clubs," "Eleanor Clubs," "Bump Clubs,"[42] or "push days." Whites believed that black women were deliberately bumping them while shopping at urban department stores. According to one white woman reminiscing about her days in Detroit during this period:

> When I was in high school we'd go downtown shopping. And I remember one day specifically I was going into the big department store, and they had the revolving door. And as I got in this great big fat Black lady got in with me and I could hardly breathe, and I got through, and I thought, "Wow, that was crowded," and I found out afterwards that they had something called "push day," where,

that day of the week, anyone who was white who was downtown, they would do something to harass them. And until then, that had never been a problem. And it wasn't too long after that the Belle Isle race riot occurred.[43]

Because of the tensions of the war, both the Federal Bureau of Investigation and local police departments felt it necessary to investigate these white beliefs, but their investigations produced no evidence of conspiracy. Perhaps the danger to the community from the Axis powers reminded white Americans of how dependent they were on the patriotism and good faith of those they had oppressed over the years. The bump or push rumor symbolically harkened back to beliefs in sabotage by house Negroes. These stories also reminded whites of the days when blacks were not allowed or did not have the resources to shop at the same stores as white consumers. Mass integrated shopping was depicted as having social costs, just as contemporary rumors reveal worries about interracial castrations in the rest rooms of large shopping centers.[44]

Rumors about Disappointment Clubs even more graphically underline this anxiety about wartime social change. Supposedly, members of this club would answer advertisements for employment and promise to report for work, but then never showed up. This rumor, spread in the shortage years of World War II, commends whites for their willingness to hire African Americans, while simultaneously condemning African Americans for their laziness, ungratefulness, and sabotage. It also reflects a growing awareness of the economic power some blacks were enjoying because of the economic dislocations of the war.

A third set of rumors from the World War II era were more explicitly political, inspired by the activism of First Lady Eleanor Roosevelt.[45] According to the Eleanor Club rumors, black housekeepers were organizing in an effort to have "a white woman in every kitchen by Christmas," and they would break dishes and quit their jobs immediately if anything was said in the household against the First Lady.[46] No evidence was ever found to attest to the existence of these clubs, yet they coupled a recognition of the dependence of the white community on African Americans with distaste among conservative whites for the activist First Lady.

These rumor cycles reflect a preoccupation with the possibility of black conspiracies. While it is easy to understand that slave traders and plantation owners believed that their captives were forever plotting revenge, it is striking that white housewives could imagine that black domestic employees, often thoroughly overworked, were planning how and when to bump white strangers. Whites believed that black women were organizing to sabotage their employers or punish them for their political beliefs, social condescension, or affluence. It is ironic that the "enemies" in these texts are black domestic workers. During most of American history, these have been among the least powerful and most impoverished of American citizens. World War II, straining every aspect of American society, was perceived as empowering the most docile of Americans.

In terms of racial tension and riots, no recent decade stands out as clearly as the 1960s. The hundreds of episodes of civil disobedience from that decade that are commonly characterized as riots conform in many ways to those that came before and those that have erupted since. Like the Harlem riots of 1935 and 1943, the 1960s riots were characterized by massive property damage. As was the case with earlier disturbances, riots in the 1960s were often triggered by stories about heinous assaults on the body of a black person. These attacks were often perceived as the "proverbial last straw."[47] Such incidents solidified African-American dissatisfaction with postponed promises of social and economic equality.

The Bensonhurst and Harlem riots of 1964 began after a conflict between a white policeman and a fifteen-year-old African American resulted in the young man's death. Descriptions of the incident are riddled with contradictory statements. According to some witnesses, the officer unnecessarily discharged his weapon at the youth. According to the policeman, the youth was lunging at him with a knife. Some people reported that after shooting the young man, the policeman kicked his body as it lay on the sidewalk. The violence that ensued lasted for six nights. Civil rights organizations and law enforcement authorities endeavored to restore peace, but their efforts were continually undermined by the eruption of new rumors that antagonized both sides. Black New Yorkers were angered by stories of gross police misconduct; white New Yorkers heard stories about capricious looters who were taking advantage of the melee to do their back-to-school "shopping."[48] According to some estimates, as many as four thousand black New Yorkers participated in the vandalism, the attacks on police, and the looting and burning of businesses.

A year later and a continent away, black Californians took to the streets of Watts in much the same fashion as their counterparts in Harlem, a week after Lyndon Johnson signed the Voting Rights Act. Once again a relatively minor incident served as the triggering episode. As white police officers attempted to arrest a black youth for reckless driving, a crowd began shouting in protest. Soon the shouting became violent, and then rumors began to proliferate. One claimed that a pregnant African-American woman had been arrested and brutalized by the police.[49] Blacks were warned that a force of two thousand white men was about to march into Watts. Other rumors that frightened whites and police alleged that blacks were arming themselves with machine guns and conducting makeshift classes on how to make Molotov cocktails from hollowed-out eggshells.

Experts claim that the Watts riots left thirty-four people dead, more than a thousand injured, and nearly four thousand arrested. Property damage was estimated at $182 million.[50] For the next two decades, the scars left by the massive property damage were evident to residents of the area. In response to the Watts riots and the following 329 riot-rebellions in 257 cities during the next three years, Lyndon Johnson appointed the Kerner Commission to study civil disturbances.[51] Charged with identifying the underlying causes of riots and offering solutions to the problems, the commission appointees noted that minimal employment possibilities, substandard educational opportunities, dilapidated housing, and persistent racism lay at the heart of the civil disobedience of the 1960s. Their report painted a pessimistic portrait of a nation with two separate and unequal societies that, while it did not result in massive rioting in the following twenty years, did suggest the sad fate of many inner-city neighborhoods.

CONCLUSION

The role of rumor in generating, perpetuating, and channeling riots reminds us just how important this seemingly insignificant form of talk can be. Under some circumstances, rumor can kill. This alone makes the understanding and control of rumor significant to all people of goodwill. Given that many of the most troubling rumors that we must face today deal with racial beliefs and misunderstandings, this suggests that blacks and whites must discover ways to transcend the willingness to accept beliefs that seem so plausible. This is particularly important because during times of civil disturbance rumor must be responded to rapidly and without certainty.

As noted earlier, some individuals may manipulate information and spread rumor to advance their political agendas or achieve personal gain. If one sees oneself as being in the midst of a revolutionary struggle, the use of disinformation may be justified for the cause, despite the dangerous ends. Fortunately, the images of rebellion and revolution are not widely shared today, even by those who call for change and who feel most aggrieved. Still, it is worth remembering, particularly when considering rumors and riots, that individuals may have different motives for spreading information.

In the next chapter, we present a model that we label the folklore diamond. This model suggests that the social structure of society affects the personal needs and performance dynamics of rumor tellers and audiences, and that these personal needs and performance dynamics shape the content of rumor. In the case of a riot, these connections are readily apparent. Ultimately the structural characteristics—particularly injustices and inequalities—of society lead to the motivations for information diffusion. The conditions of riots and violence promote rapid information diffusion without great concern for the accuracy of the information. Much may be believed that might not be accepted under circumstances of greater calm. In tense situations, individuals struggle for knowledge, knowing that what they learn might be simultaneously important and ambiguous. These features lead, then, to the particular content of information that will be spread, believed, and acted upon. Although rumors in times of riot are more immediately dangerous than other forms of racial rumors, they are not the only type of hearsay that provokes racial hatred and mistrust.

TWO

How Rumor Works

This guy picked up a girl at a bar and took her to his apartment, and the next morning she was gone. He went into his bathroom, and written in red lipstick on his mirror was "Welcome to the world of AIDS." At first he thought it was a prank, but he called the police, who told him, "We didn't want to worry people, but that's the seventh time that happened this year, and one of them tested positive."

This is a strange, true story about a woman being bit by a snake. The woman was taken to Norwood (Mass.) Hospital because of a bite on her arm. It was diagnosed as a snakebite, and it wasn't understood how she got it. She was asked to report her doings during the day, and she reported that she had tried on coats at Sears. The coats she tried on were then searched, and in one coat was found a snake in the sleeve lining. This coat was made in Taiwan, and somehow the snake got in the lining of the coat.

Rumors surround us. Their content is as diverse as their style and the conditions under which they are performed. These two rumors, although not explicitly about race, dramatize that rumors address things that we care about—in this case, about sex, crime, and business, and hanging over each is the fear of death. Whether the danger derives from strangers (clothing made by people of color from distant lands) or from those with whom we are intimate (and who secretly are immoral), we need to be alert to those who stand outside social and cultural boundaries.

This chapter addresses the processes by which rumors operate, drawing upon social scientific research. Those readers most interested in the dynamics of racial tension may wish to skip to chapter 3, although we present general information here that provides a basis for understanding the examples in the remainder of the book. Further, many of the examples in this chapter, often classic accounts from the scholarship on rumor, although not explicitly concerned with race, deal with the same broad concerns.

People use the label "rumor" to refer to brief, unsubstantiated bits of information. Perhaps the news comes from a friend and concerns a juicy intimate matter such as an unplanned pregnancy or a nasty divorce. Yet shared knowledge is not always negative. Friends are as likely to share news about a pending engagement or a financial windfall. Coworkers often swap information, as workplaces readily breed rumors. A trusted colleague might share secondhand information about a new downsizing plan or a boss's unorthodox work habits. Beyond our homes and our workplaces, most of us belong to several communities, such as our preferred churches, clubs, and coffeehouses. We eagerly consume any information that affects us and those we know. The willingness to gossip suggests that we "care" about the target. Despite our preconceptions, research suggests that most "gossip" is positive or neutral in tone. When unable to confirm information, even official news sources report rumors about local, national, or world events such as economic trends, terrorist attacks, or confusing civil disturbances. Events that capture public attention, such as schoolyard mass murders or corporate toxic spills, are ripe for the proliferation of rumor, as more information is demanded than is available.

When we find rumors credible, we share them. Our assessment of credibility is linked to our respect for the source and our knowledge of the topic. If a friend's sister whispers that our friend just received a small velvet box from her longtime beau, we assume a happy announcement will come soon. Few can resist the temptation to share the "news" of a friend's betrothal in advance of the formal announcement. If we learn that a new boss has a pet peeve, we share this valuable information with friendly coworkers. Similarly, if we know someone who is contemplating buying a car or a house, we will share rumors about changes in interest rates. It is unlikely that we will tell our boss about the possible engagement of someone she does not know.[1] A rumor about a family member will only be spread within the family. Hearsay from our job will probably be of little interest to those with whom we worship.

While personal texts often come to mind when people think about rumors, in this book we emphasize public texts that depict well-known people, institutions, and social categories. We describe rumors about restaurant chains rather than one neighborhood eatery. Instead of probing whether a certain doctor provided inadequate care for a particular patient, we examine rumors about whether a racial group has been ill served by the medical establishment or whether health maintenance organizations have policies that do not serve the interests of their clients. The personal and the global intersect in the telling of these rumors.

How is it that people learn what "everybody knows"? If talk is cheap, the information on which talk is based—true or false—can have considerable value. To appreciate the power of rumor, we need a concrete definition. One of the simplest and, for us, most appealing definitions is that a rumor is a claim about the world that is not supported by "authenticated information." It involves "unsecured," "unverified" information.[2] For tellers and audiences, the stories about the deliberate spread of the HIV virus and the snakes in clothing remain unverified, no matter what the claims might be. Even if the audience does not believe that the rumor is factually correct, it is presented as something that could be believed; it is a *truth claim*. Rumor is *deliberate communication*—often spread in face-to-face conversation, sometimes spread through written material, and now frequently spread through the mass media and other modern information technology such as fax and the Internet. By speaking of a rumor as a truth claim, we refer to the fact that it claims to present an accurate picture of the "real world."

"Is it true?" is the standard query following the articulation of a rumor. In today's world, where so many "truths" are routinely debunked, people often assume that such narratives are false unless proven otherwise, *if* and *when* they recognize the narrative as rumor. Jan Harold Brunvand, a leading student of rumors and contemporary legends, describes them as "true-sounding but utterly false."[3] Another scholar announces that "rumors have no foundation, and that is perhaps their most basic definition."[4] Yet others recognize that some rumors may turn out to be fully accurate. As the French rumor scholar Jean-Noel Kapferer writes, "Rumors are bothersome because they may turn out to be true."[5] Further, some rumors may be factually incorrect in the specifics of their claims (their superficial truth) yet reveal fundamental truths about the nature of the cultural order. Are these rumors true or false? These rumors contribute to our cultural knowledge, while misleading us about the factual conditions of our existence.

Judging the truth of some rumors is quite simple, but assessing the validity of others is nearly impossible. Doctors are able to determine whether an individual is infected by the HIV virus, and herpetologists are adept at determining the species of snake they examine, even if discovered in an overcoat. On the other hand, recall how difficult it has been for those who wish to dispel the numerous rumors about the assassination of John F. Kennedy. Can we ever say for sure that some women do not attempt to infect some men with the HIV virus or that dangerous insects or serpents are transported from overseas? While one should never dismiss the truth or falsity of a rumor as irrelevant, we must recognize that it may be equally important to know if it is *assumed* to be true or false, and to ask about the conditions that make a particular rumor plausible for its audience. In the case of rumors about race, this is of considerable significance. Judgment of the plausibility of rumor represents a complex combination of evaluations of the cultural fit (or resonance) of the content and evaluations of the narrator. What people believe is true reflects how they perceive themselves, their associates, and the conditions under which they live.

The potential power of rumor to provoke mass violence and hysteria is clear. Sometimes communities have been completely disrupted by rumors. The literature on what is called mass psychogenic illness or hysterical contagion—illness based on beliefs about fictional and unobservable toxic agents—is extensive.[6] These episodes often occur in periods of stress, in which groups believe that they smell a strange or unpleasant odor, which they assume to be poisonous. Nausea, dizziness, shortness of breath, weakness, or headaches are the primary symptoms. These symptoms, which are so general that their cause is hard to determine, spread rapidly, and word quickly circulates that poison is in the air. In one well-documented case, workers in a southern dressmaking factory believed that they were being bitten by a tiny June bug, but no such bug was ever found.[7]

An even more dramatic case is recounted in the "Phantom Anesthetist of Mattoon."[8] A resident of Mattoon, a small town in Illinois, believed that a prowler had opened her bedroom window and sprayed her and her daughter with a paralyzing gas. Although the police arrived rapidly, they could find no trace of an intruder. The following day, a front-page headline in the local newspaper read "Anesthetic Prowler on the Loose." During the next week, report followed report of prowlers and gassers. Yet despite a massive effort and some "sightings," the perpetrator was never found. Nevertheless, the belief was real. One newspaper wrote:

> Groggy as Londoners under protracted aerial blitzing, this town's bewildered citizens reeled today under the repeated attacks of a mad anesthetist who has sprayed a deadly nerve gas into 13 homes and has knocked out 27 victims. . . . Seventy others dashing to the area in response to the alarm, fell under the influence of the gas last night. . . . All skepticism vanished and Mattoon grimly conceded that it must fight haphazardly against a demented phantom adversary

who has been seen only fleetingly and so far has evaded traps laid by city and state police and posses of townsmen.[9]

In time, the episode ended as mysteriously as it started. Calls to the police eventually stopped. No anesthetist was ever discovered. Can we say that one did not exist? The problem of combating rumor is that it is impossible to prove a negative. Yet this instance of hysterical contagion demonstrates the power of rumors within a community.

The negative connotations of rumors are not surprising considering the harmful effects that a false rumor can have. Further, these concerns are not limited to the modern world. Shakespeare wrote in *Henry IV*:

> Rumor is a pipe
> Blown by surmises, jealousies, conjectures,
> And of so easy and so plain a stop
> That the blunt monster with uncounted heads,
> The still-discordant wavering multitude,
> Can play upon it.

Reviewing his experiences in World War I, General Smedley Butler of the U.S. Marines claimed, with some hyperbole, "I'd rather fight an entire army than battle an idle rumor."[10] At least in fighting an army, one knows where one stands. The 1968 report of the Kerner Commission, established by Lyndon Johnson in response to a series of deadly race riots, concluded that "rumors significantly aggravated tensions and disorder in more than 65 percent of the disorders studied."[11] While riots develop from real grievances, beliefs are also important stimulants.

Shakespeare, Butler, and numerous other social commentators focus on the rumor itself and too often ignore that it is an outcome of a social situation. Rumor does not stand alone, and it is only rarely the product of a vicious mind. As the sociologist Tamotsu Shibutani noted in his influential book, *Improvised News*, rumor is part of collective sense-making. Shibutani emphasizes that rumor is a "form of communication through which men [and women] caught together in an ambiguous situation attempt to construct a meaningful interpretation of it by pooling their intellectual resources."[12]

Rumor is, from this perspective, a form of problem solving, permitting people to cope with life's uncertainties, surely a more hopeful image than that of immoral mischief. Shibutani insists that people have a healthy desire to find meaning in events.[13] The vigor of organizational grapevines is a sign that workers care about their colleagues and the conditions of their employment.[14]

One's approach to rumor—as pathology or as problem solving— often depends on the class of rumor one studies. When one examines riots, panics, wartime stress, and natural disasters, it is not surprising that rumor would be seen as undesirable. Similarly, using rumors to enrich oneself economically has been made illegal. The New York Stock Exchange enforces a rule forbidding the spread of rumor on the floor of the stock market even when fraud is not intended. One can imagine the effects the rumor of a quarterly loss might have on the value of a stock, much less the effects of a report of a major governmental policy announcement or an assassination attempt. Rumor may involve intentional deception as well as misguided beliefs. Here the role of a government's propaganda arm comes to mind, especially in wartime. The false claim that the Iraqis were disconnecting premature Kuwaiti babies from their medical tubes was designed to inflame the citizens of Kuwait and the United States, and it was highly likely that at least some of the government agents that spread the rumor knew it to be false. The goal was to demonize an enemy at any cost.

In contrast, some rumors promote solidarity and shared concern. At times rumor can permit a community to discuss ongoing anxieties and events. By focusing on a common issue, people engage in collective problem solving. Although the outcome of this discussion may be negative, at least people are talking. A problem in racial rumors is that the communities in which the rumors are spread are not broad enough; whites are unlikely to share claims about blacks with blacks. African Americans are just as likely to keep private what they "know" about white institutions. This is what the sociologist David Maines speaks of as "racialized pools of knowledge."[15] In these circumstances, sadly characteristic of racial contact, the potential benefits of problem solving are short-circuited by the segregation of talk, in practice, if no longer by law.

THE LIFE CYCLE OF RUMORS

If "Is it true?" is the most frequently asked question about rumor, then "Who started it?" is second. A challenge of studying rumors is that their origins are lost in the mists of time. We often cannot determine where rumors come from and when they begin. Still, four general patterns can be recognized: intentional deception, misunderstanding, transformation, and suspicion of incongruous details.

INTENTIONAL DECEPTION

Some rumors are started maliciously by those who believe they can benefit from creating a story that sows discord. The saboteur in wartime is such a shadowy figure, as is the venal business competitor or the unscrupulous politician. Indeed, as mentioned previously, governments often find themselves in the business of creating rumors to undermine the confidence of an enemy. We have little evidence of actual cases of this, although it is clear that during World War II enemy broadcasters, perhaps most notably "Tokyo Rose" (a name given to several Japanese women broadcasters), attempted to affect troop and public morale by spreading discouraging stories.[16] In political life, rumors are sometimes planted, giving rise to whispering campaigns.[17] The fact that such rumors sometimes backfire suggests the danger of trying to direct public attention. One element of the Watergate scandal (the "dirty tricks") consisted of Nixon operatives attempting to spread discrediting rumors about the Democrats. Further, the agenda for COINTELPRO—the government group established to undermine the Black Panther Party—included rumor as one of its strategies for creating dissension.

While businessmen who have been harmed by a rumor often blame their competitors, few of these rumors were started maliciously. Nevertheless, some competitors are only too happy to take advantage by spreading rumors, as did a few Amway distributors who shared the classic rumor that Procter and Gamble was owned by the Church of Satan, or the beer distributors who announced that the bright yellow color of Corona Beer was from the urine of Mexican brewery workers. In cases of sabotage the identity of the rumor creator must be hidden if the rumor is to have the desired effect.

MISUNDERSTANDING

A second origin of rumor is more innocent. Perhaps a remark made in jest is heard by a listener who did not recognize the humor. One friend might tease another, asserting that McDonald's adds red worms to its meat, and the remark is overheard and then spread to others who were unaware of the speaker's intention. In "put-ons" we pretend that something is true even though we know that it is both false and implausible. Typically at the end of the conversation the victim learns of the deception, but if others are eavesdropping, a juicy rumor may result. Perhaps the widely known contemporary legend of the rat sold as a piece of fried chicken originated in this way.

TRANSFORMATION

A third possibility—that of transformation—is most closely connected to formal rumor theory. From the earliest writings on rumor, alterations in content, notably exaggerations, have been seen as central. What starts as innocent information becomes misremembered or repeated out of context. From truth comes rumor. When "soft" bubble gum was first marketed, the rumor spread that its softness was caused by "spider legs" (or, in some versions, "spider eggs"). Perhaps this rumor originated in a fifth-grade classroom where a teacher attempted to explain that to ensure safety, government health officials place a strict limit on the number of insects that can get into any food product. Even your bubble gum may have a few spider legs, she might have said. Could this hypothetical remark have started a rumor that swept through schools? Under some circumstances, innocent information can be transformed in odd and grotesque ways.

An example of this process is reported in the classic work *A Rumor in Orléans*, by the French sociologist Edgar Morin.[18] This study described the "mysterious disappearance" of young girls in the French city of Orléans; they allegedly were drugged and imprisoned by Jewish boutique owners in fitting rooms and then shipped to foreign brothels. The Jewish owners had supposedly bribed local police and political officials to let them get away with these crimes. In fact, no women had disappeared, and there was no white slavery ring. One possible explanation for the emergence of the rumor was a fictional kidnapping plot reported in a popular French tabloid magazine, *Noir et Blanc*. This account merged with resentments in Orléans toward Jewish shopkeepers. Fiction was transformed into fact through the alchemy of hostility. This rumor probably would have vanished rapidly had the public not believed that Jewish merchants were unscrupulous. If color is one basis of malicious rumors, it is not the only one.

SUSPICION OF INCONGRUOUS DETAILS

Some consumer products or political events make us particularly susceptible to rumors. Product packaging, pricing, advertisements, and names may have unintended effects on consumers. Just as products with unusual textures, such as the soft bubble gum, stir speculation, so, too, do other incongruous products or events. In interviews with those who believe that Church's Fried Chicken was owned by white supremacists, informants pointed to the firm's name—Church's—and the implications of buying fast-food fried chicken from "churches." Likewise, health care workers explain how difficult it is to provide certain drugs and services to African-American clients. In northern California, many HIV-positive black patients refuse to take AZT, a drug that health care workers give them for free, believing that something in it accelerates the rate at which full-blown AIDS develops in black men. The fact that AZT may be one of the few things these men have ever been given for free arouses their suspicions.

THE SPREAD OF RUMOR

Many rumors are spawned, but only a few survive. As the French anthropologist Claude Lévi-Strauss commented, some things are "good to think"—that is, they connect to a powerful "cultural logic" that makes sense to narrators and audiences. Plausibility is key. Rumor permits us to project our emotional fantasies on events that we can claim "really did happen," protecting ourselves from the implications of our beliefs. Can we be blamed for reporting the "news"?

The psychological dimension of rumor is tied to the intentions or motivations of the tellers. What emotions or goals are being satisfied by transmitting a rumor? Although several researchers have attempted to classify the motivations of narrators,[19] the model that remains most influential is that of Robert H. Knapp, who worked with the social psychologist Gordon Allport, during World War II. Knapp placed rumors into three broad categories—pipe dreams, bogey rumors, and wedge-driving rumors—reflecting the prime emotions of hope, fear, and anger.[20]

Pipe-dream rumors are a form of public wish fulfillment. They proclaim that good times are just ahead, and that evil will be vanquished. Rumors about technological breakthroughs have this quality, as, perhaps, do the rumors—among whites—of Louis Farrakhan's imminent death. These rumors claimed that reality will soon reflect the way that we wish it will be.

In contrast, bogey rumors reflect how we fear the world might become. The rumor of the death of an adversary is a pipe dream, but the rumor of the death of our leader is a bogey rumor. Claims about Farrakhan's demise could fall in either category. Rumors about the termination of the Voting Rights Act that have circulated among African Americans are bogey rumors, as is the rumor that the military draft may be reinstituted because of the conflicts in eastern Europe.

The third category, most of the rumors that we address, are "wedge-driving rumors." Knapp, working during World War II, found that two-thirds of the rumors he examined were of this type.[21] Even if we recognize that he likely oversampled these kinds of rumors, many rumors do serve to divide groups. These rumors reflect the alleged ill will that the target group bears toward the group to which the teller and the audience belong, dramatizing boundaries, in our case among racial and ethnic groups, government officials, business managers, and gang members. The claim that Farrakhan's illness was caused by poisoning from white doctors, under government directives, would constitute a wedge-driving rumor.

Rumors can send dangerous messages. In times of stress, such as war or rebellion, governments or private agencies often establish rumor control centers to diffuse tensions and anxieties. In war the critical ability of the population is reduced, suggesting that otherwise incredible stories may be believed.

Rumors involve collective problem solving. When things do not go according to plan, we cope with this ambiguous or unexpected situation by creating an explanation. We often reach out to others, creating new chains of communication and searching for information. In addition to hope, fear, and anger, a powerful desire for stability leads to the search for any kind of information, even if it is unverified.

Demands for certainty are likely in situations characterized by collective emotion.[22] While emotions help explain how rumors originate, the same motivations also help spread the rumor. Once created, rumors spread if conditions are ripe: some rumors die once they are spoken, others serve as a societal focus, and still others pass into the realm of "known knowledge," becoming taken for granted.

Broadly speaking, three approaches have attempted to explain the motivations behind rumor: the functional approach, the transactional approach, and the conflict approach.[23] The first of these approaches argues that rumor serves a function for a social system by asserting collective values. Rumor provides an indirect sanction, avoiding direct confrontation and strengthening group boundaries. To share a rumor is to announce that one is part of a community.

The transactional approach emphasizes the strategic value of rumor for its narrator.[24] Recall the children's taunt "I know something you don't." A gifted primary school raconteur can enthrall an audience by uttering these words. If the child tantalizes the group with delicious news, she gains attention and approval and is able to manage the impressions that others have of her. Rumor projects individual interests through information control. "Rumormongers" can become the center of attention.

The conflict perspective emphasizes that rumor is used as a political strategy for collective ends. In Washington, rumor is often used explicitly by power brokers as a "trial balloon" to gauge public reaction. Those who wish to persuade others often use the well-known technique of discrediting an opposition group through rumor. In revolutions, ruling classes encourage rumors against indigenous revolutionary figures to split the working class; rumor as sabotage may originate from above or from below as a weapon of the weak.

THE DYNAMICS OF DIFFUSION

Hot news travels fast. As a rule of thumb, the greater the news value of an event, the more quickly the story spreads.[25] Factors such as the time of day, the self-involvement of the audience, and the mode of transmission all affect diffusion. Information, if sufficiently important, does not wait for formal channels of communication to operate. When John F. Kennedy was assassinated, the majority of the population learned about the shooting not from the news media but from another person.[26] Often the report of Kennedy's shooting was accompanied by dark rumors of who might have been behind the crime, their motive, and what might come next. In the age of the Internet, rumors spread with a click of the send icon. When it was rumored that the Voting Rights Act of 1964 was scheduled to be terminated, many African Americans received multiple messages on the same day.

Although important rumors may be spread without regard for audience, in general rumors follow lines of acquaintance. This helps to explain why some rumors that are widespread in the African-American community are almost wholly unknown among whites, and vice versa. Since friendship ties do not easily cross racial boundaries, information does not either, and these different networks permit racialized information pools. Shibutani once noted that "culture areas are coterminous with communication channels."[27] Where social ties exist, such as in small towns, rumor communication is likely to be rapid.[28] Along with social ties, personal or group interest determines the path of a rumor.[29] Rumors about political scandal are spread largely by those with a strong interest in politics, whereas rumors about the sexual activities of celebrities are spread by a separate group. In the case of rumors about racial matters, in some cases the prime narrators or audience may be those with strong racial grievances. Attitudes are magnified under conditions of social strain and ambiguity.[30]

PATTERNS OF DISTORTION

One of the central features of a rumor is that it often does not remain static. The details of rumor often shift, but occasionally even the core meaning of a story is transformed.[31] Early research on rumor transmission dealt explicitly with how the content of rumors alters as they spread. Anyone who has played the game of "telephone," in which participants sit in a circle, with one whispering a phrase or sentence to the next, can recall the amusing and astounding ways in which information can be transformed as it is transmitted. Although this game is not an adequate model for rumor change, relying as it does on actual mishearing, the shifts in rumor content are real and may, in the case of hostile rumors, have serious consequences.

As rumors spread, the original text can become distorted.[32] While the "rumor shell" may remain, the contents of that shell are altered. In his important study *Remembering*, the distinguished British social psychologist Sir Frederick Bartlett described how memory is systematically altered.[33] By asking subjects to recall a story, Bartlett discovered that people retrieve narratives by means of mental schemas. They do not "memorize" a story, repeating it through rote memory, but instead develop a general mental outline—the shell—which they expand in the course of telling. For instance, if you attempt to describe a mugging, you will not have codified each act as it transpired but will recall some of the scene, with its cast of characters. From this, you can re-create the events, assuming the likely acts of the participants, and in the process often relying on stereotypes. Bartlett suggested that memory gaps were filled in by a process he named *social constructiveness*; people determined what "made sense" in those blanks spots. Later research found that the details that are remembered, forgotten, or added are connected to one's attitudes, beliefs, emotions, social affiliations, and prejudices.

The single most important set of rumor experiments were conducted by the social psychologists Gordon Allport and Leo Postman, who attempted to simulate rumor transmission by the public performance of "serial recall."[34] One of their procedures involved projecting a slide of a dramatic scene that included many details. Seven subjects who had not seen the picture waited in an adjoining room. After the projector was turned off, a subject who had viewed the slide was asked to describe it to a subject who had not. A third subject then entered, and the second subject described the picture as fully as possible. A fourth subject was informed by the third, and so on.

Through this study, Allport and Postman described the processes of leveling, sharpening, and assimilation. One mechanism that explains the form of rumor is forgetting, or what these researchers term *leveling*. The number of details at first declines sharply and then gradually stabilizes. Narrators trying to remember a complex story are likely to eliminate those details that seemed extraneous when they first heard the story. The second process involves emphasizing a few details, a process of *sharpening*, or providing the "headline" of the rumor. In sharpening, subjects emphasize a limited number of details from the larger set and give them greater weight.

The third, and most significant, mechanism involves *assimilation*, or transforming information to strengthen its cultural logic. Factors such as habits, interests, beliefs, and emotions can influence how information is recalled, as was exemplified most dramatically in one of the pictures that Allport and Postman used in their experiments. In this image a poorly dressed white laborer, holding a straight-edge razor, appears to be arguing with a well-dressed black man. When white subjects were asked to describe the picture, in over half the experiments the razor "magically" shifted from the white man to the black man, who was often described as "brandishing it wildly" or as "threatening the white man."[35] Many white subjects apparently felt that this switch made sense, even if they did not intend to be bigoted. When Fine attempts this demonstration in class, the razor still jumps from white to black more often than not, although today white students are mortified when they discover their mistake, embarrassment that surely was cold comfort to African Americans hearing about the shifting razor. The black subjects tested by Allport and Postman did not reach this erroneous conclusion, although perhaps they would have distorted a picture involving a white police officer.

Some researchers criticize this study by reminding us that the experimental conditions do not adequately simulate natural rumor transmis-

Figure 1. Ambiguous subway scene from Allport and Postman rumor experiment

sion, and rumors surely are more stable than they appear in Allport and Postman's portrayal. Yet the mechanisms of eliminating, emphasizing, and altering details are critical to understanding the dynamics of the rumor process.

THE DEMISE OF RUMOR

Just as rumor begins, so it eventually disappears when interest declines, all members of the audience hear the rumor, and the actions of forces of social control intervene. If rumor is news, once its newsworthy quality evaporates, so will its spread. Further, once it reaches its target audience, saturating the community, curiosity wanes unless new information is provided. Boredom limits the motivation for spreading rumor as the "exchange value" for narration declines. Many rumors evaporate as rapidly as they arise, particularly when public interest is drawn to other topics. The life of the typical rumor is brief.

Some rumors belong to a "rumor complex," that is, the topic involves an ever-expanding set of rumors. If rumors represent the attempt to solve a puzzle, multiple rumors represent alternative solutions. Fine studied rumors about Pop Rocks candies, fizzing candies that supposedly exploded when consumed.[36] These novel treats were a source of great interest to children, who speculated on how the candies were manufactured and subsequently spread the story of a child who had died from eating these "dangerous" sweets. In the absence of official information, many versions of the rumor were spread: that the candies were treated with acid, that they exploded in the child's throat, or that they ruptured the child's stomach. Other rumors claimed that the candies were taken off the market because of the death. These multiple reports kept the story alive, as preadolescents continually compared their information. Likewise, the stories about Tommy Hilfiger's "racial slur"—a story that is discussed in more detail in chapter 3—constituted a rumor complex. Did he claim that it was blacks that he did not wish to wear his clothing, was he pleased that he could pay Asian workers ("gooks") sweatshop wages, or did he enjoy having Asian Americans pay inflated prices?

Rumors also mutate as the situation changes. In a dynamic situation such as a civil disturbance, rumors respond to reactions of crowds and authorities. Some rumors light the spark for violence. Others explain the reaction of the police, and still others address how the community has responded or will respond.[37] As the puzzle changes, so do rumors that help us cope.

When rumors are linked to the possibility of public disturbance or significant corporate losses, groups often attempt to limit their spread. During civil unrest, war, or natural disaster, government agencies may establish rumor control centers, which have had mixed success in preventing rumors from multiplying wildly. Since we cannot know what might have happened in the absence of such agencies, their effectiveness remains open to doubt. However, no evidence suggests that they do harm, so the real question is whether they are worth the cost. These agencies attempt to provide "authoritative information" in times of public strain; when this information is credible, the false rumor is extinguished. Rumor control centers were popular during World War II and during the civil disturbances of the late 1960s. In contemporary America, which faces little civil unrest, rumor control is largely ignored. However, radio and television call-in shows and Internet chat groups may fulfill this role.

The "death" of a rumor does not mean that it will disappear permanently. Some rumors, labeled *diving rumors*, reappear after having entered the collective memory of the community. The rumor disappears for a while, but the shell remains available to be filled with new details. For the past several decades such a rumor has bedeviled suburban police departments. According to this rumor, a mother and her daughter are at a large shopping center, and the child announces that she has to use the rest room. The mother waits outside with her packages. After a long time, the child emerges, drugged, wearing different clothing and a crew cut, and accompanied by a stranger. The mother recognizes her daughter and scares off the other woman. When she reports the crime to the police, they inform her that the girl would have been sold to a prostitution ring. This story is the Orléans rumor described earlier, with new details for an American audience. Every few years the story reappears in a different region with new details, but the rumor shell remains constant. Even though the story vanishes after the police and the press debunk it, it is only hibernating, to emerge again when the circumstances are right. To a public swamped with news of genuine crimes involving missing children, the story makes such good sense that it could hardly be false, even though it is.[38]

ACCOUNTING FOR NARRATORS

To share a story is to vouch for its plausibility. As a consequence, narrators often find themselves married to what they say. A narrator who is considered trustworthy discovers that this trust rubs off on his or her truth claims. The position of a speaker contributes to how information is judged. Some individuals, by virtue of their location in a social network, are expected to have legitimate access to "facts," and so on these matters they are presumed to speak authoritatively. Reliability of information is judged, in part, by how it is acquired. These speakers are judged by audiences as having access to reliable sources. By virtue of their position—having access to those with authenticated knowledge—their statements are given weight. It is not that rumor narrators are particularly reliable—indeed, there is some evidence that early rumor tellers may be marginal figures[39]—but the perception of audiences contributes to how their information will be treated.

The concept of *plausibility* is critical to an evaluation of whether a statement is "factual." All truth claims are *potentially* problematic, if one pushes the point. Even eyewitness testimony is suspect. Court cases provide the defining instance of this problem, suggesting that opposing attorneys can undercut what people claim they witnessed. Eyewitnesses may be caught in a knowing fabrication, they may misunderstand or misinterpret what they sensed, or tricks of memories may make the report doubtful. In terms of informal information, audiences regularly assign motives to the speaker that potentially challenge his or her credibility. Three elements contribute to how we evaluate a source: *remove*, *realm*, and *motive*.

REMOVE

Most audiences give weight to the evaluation of truth claims from individuals who are defined as being in a position to know, as being "close" to the events, or as having trustworthy sources. We assume that government spokespersons are close to politicians—especially when they make statements of "fact" as opposed to suggesting motivation. We can question the president's press secretary's description of *why* the president acted, whereas it would be considered odd to question *whether* he acted. The press secretary has the authority to know the president's schedule because of his or her placement in an information network. We treat this information as "fact." In contrast, motivation can easily be hidden, making the leader "look good."

Audiences judge whether a speaker is likely to have acquired information from trustworthy sources and whether the information is plausible by virtue of the *process* by which it was obtained. When we claim to have heard information from a talk show on radio or television, a discussion group on the Internet, or a friend of a friend, often a salient part of truth claims, we are attempting to bolster our trustworthiness, given our remove from the reported "fact." Because of the social divide that separates blacks and whites in America, the remove of narrators may be particularly great when one is making claims about racial others.

REALM

The collective definition of what constitutes plausible information depends on our evaluation of realms of knowledge. Some realms are considered legitimate, while others are dismissed as deviant and are not taken seriously. For instance, in many American communities, "extranormal" perceptions (clairvoyance, extrasensory perception, and so forth) are suspect. Psychics routinely provide truth claims about the interpretation of the world, alleging that the positions of the stars and planets are a sign (or cause) of other events. Some accept these claims, others find them possible, and a few act upon them, but large numbers see this as entertainment, not fact. Deviant "scientists" populate the world with claims about yetis, UFOs, force fields, and chemical effects to which others give no credence. Skeptics do not even evaluate the "evidence" because the knowledge realm is outside what they consider plausible. Religious miracles are for some, though not all, markers of a claim outside a legitimate realm. Cultures give different status to realms of knowledge, affecting which information is seen as plausible.[40] With regard to racial rumors, most white Americans discount as implausible vast conspiratorial genocidal plots; African Americans are far more likely to think these claims are plausible.

MOTIVE

Motive is the worm in the apple of belief. Does the narrator have reason to shade information, to dissimulate? The assumed motivation of a speaker influences how audiences interpret a text. The philosopher J. L. Austin writes of the "illocutionary force" of an utterance, referring to what the speaker is attempting to do in making the claim.[41] What kind of statement is it by virtue of the likely motivation? Speakers attempt to channel the assumptions of their audiences by presenting "motive talk," providing their own views of their acts.[42]

Our judgments of a speaker's motivation relate to *interest* and *reputation*. In general, we are predisposed to accept the claims of others unless there are compelling reasons not to. We are likely to ask if the speaker has something to gain or hide and whether he or she has provided poor information in the past. Politicians, lovers, and parents know that they must interpret with care the claims of those who attempt to persuade them. In some cases, such as in many rumors, the speaker is not heavily invested in persuading us; the rumor may be told from a desire to entertain or to discover the views of others. Doubt is possible without questioning a speaker's honor.

The importance of *reputation* is well known to spokespersons, swains, and children, who after presenting information that is deemed false find that their later "sincere" claims are questioned ("the boy who cried wolf"). Each text influences the response to texts that follow, affecting credibility.

In racial rumors, reputation can be tricky and can vary in different communities. Many whites immediately dismiss information disseminated by someone they perceive as a militant, such as the Reverend Al Sharpton, whereas some African Americans will just as easily accept anything he says. In certain white communities, Pat Buchanan plays something of the same role. Some white listeners (and few African Americans) accept Buchanan's claims as gospel truth. Of course, it is worth remembering that substantial numbers of blacks disdain Sharpton's excessive rhetoric, just as many whites are unmoved by Buchanan's bombast.

THE CONTEXT OF CREDIBILITY

In practice, information is not always closely tied to its source, as the circumstances and settings of communication affect interpretation. As noted, we evaluate the narrator while also evaluating what is narrated. Yet on some occasions demands for information swamp the character of a narrator.

When information spread after the assassination of President Kennedy, few questioned the identity of the source, particularly when media confirmation quickly followed. These sources were *empty nodes* in a social system—that is, they could have been filled by anyone. In fact, much information was spread by strangers on that fateful day. Obtaining information was critically important, and it was assumed that others had no motivation to express anything other than the truth as they knew it.

Similar patterns of diffusion occur after sudden and cataclysmic disasters. On these occasions people disseminate information that may later be discovered to be inaccurate. Information is accepted as plausible because of the consensus of others and because one assumes that no one has motivation for "lying." Yet precisely for this reason, a set of secondary truth claims can be seen as plausible. One's critical ability has vanished. In such a situation the striving for information outweighs the evaluation of the narrator.

Shibutani emphasizes this feature of rumor when he suggests, "In disasters one of the first things that men seek, after saving themselves, is news. Sometimes they become so desperate for such information that they get careless about its source."[43] The care that one takes depends on the situation, particularly in terms of the *immediacy* and *importance* of the information. Accounts that are either immediate or unimportant are least likely to be questioned. Rumors of riots have great immediacy and importance, presuming a demand for action, whereas many contemporary legends tend to have the opposite characteristics: little immediacy and little importance, and they often are narrated in circumstances of good fellowship. Both texts are accepted on their face value. Those truth claims that are important but do not require immediate action are those that audiences should check—for example, claims that some product has long-term health risks.

The physical location of talk also affects its evaluation. Some contexts promote *action* or *sociability* and also build credibility. We define credibility at a cocktail party differently than at a scholarly seminar. One can "get away" with broader truth claims at the former before being called to account. Perhaps the need for sociability is so strong that questioning one's source might be judged as rude. In contrast, the narrower and seemingly more proven claims at a seminar might be accepted as definitely "true" with less criticism because we assume the seriousness of the speaker. Occasions that provoke *motivated narration* by those with interests in the acceptance of the truth claim, such as political rallies, lead to suspicion by those outside the movement. Printed claims are also judged on their context. For instance, audiences give different weight to claims made in different arenas, such as in an advice column, in an op-ed analysis, or as front-page news.

The style of presentation also affects a rumor's reception. While style has numerous dimensions, an important one concerns the speaker's desire to establish some distance from the text. Here the speakers do not demand total belief; they may even suggest that they doubt the truth of their own claim. Much informal talk carries a dollop of irony. Conversational markers, such as tone, gesture, and paraverbal cues, suggest how material should be treated. Some statements claim the force of fact, others disdain this goal, and still others do not seem to care how they are seen. Many narrators of rumor are not much concerned about the truth of their account; they maintain role distance, sparking discussion about the texts' validity and allowing audiences to select their own level of belief.[44]

THE DYNAMICS OF AUDIENCE

The proof of the pudding is in the eating, but the eating can be judged only by the eater. Sadly, students of rumor have often neglected the role of the audience. Audiences can be divided into present audiences and implied ones. Writers compose their words for an *assumed* audience. Those on television, film, video, tape, radio, or the Internet likewise find themselves talking to "empty" others, assuming how their audiences are likely to respond. With the increasing popularity of the Internet, computer chat rooms, and electronic mail, anonymous talk has exploded and continues to expand. Those talking on the telephone or those who are visually impaired face a similar problem, although these narrators can depend on spoken or paraverbal responses. The more feedback provided, the more the account can be shaped to make it suitable for an audience.

Audiences also differ in their emotions and attitudes, partially as a function of when and where the narration occurs and partially as a result of the characteristics of the audience and its relation to the speaker. Some audiences are prone to be critical, whereas others are accepting or "gullible." Although critical ability is linked to the topic, it also characterizes the audience. A community that is cynical and prone to conflict may be more accepting of texts that encourage suspicion than groups that are more dependent on consensus. Thus, some racial audiences, heavily laden with the burdens of an acrimonious history, may be more prone to accept rumors than audiences that believe in the likelihood of ethnic goodwill.

Audiences also desire to make talk flow to make their interaction pleasant.[45] Good talkers need good audiences, and to some degree, good audiences *generate* good talkers. Being a good listener usually does not mean that one is respectfully silent while an authority talks—the model of a lecture. In contrast, rumors depend on collaboration and requests for confirmation.[46] Often rumors are more like questions than answers. A good audience, in such cases, is an actively involved, questioning, participating audience, contributing to the achievement of the speaker's goals, whether or not the listeners accept those goals. This does not mean that audience members will believe a rumor as truth, but they will recognize that it *is* a rumor. Rumors depend not on a suspension of disbelief but on a belief in the *primacy of talk*. In this, what goes on in the head is of less significance than what goes on between bodies and mouths.

RUMOR AND THE FOLKLORE DIAMOND

In the introduction to his book *Manufacturing Tales*, Fine presented a model explaining the dynamics rumor and contemporary legend that he labeled the *folklore diamond*.[47] His goal was to provide a framework in which all approaches to the study of rumor and legend could be integrated. This model explains the development of rumor and contemporary legend as dependent on the relations among four sets of concepts: social structure, personal imperatives, performance dynamics, and narrative content. Simply put, the understanding of rumor is linked to the impact of the society, the characteristics of the speaker, the conditions under which the rumor is transmitted, and the content of the rumor. A full understanding depends on examining all four factors. Social structural forces (the societal, institutional, or contextual context) provide the foundation on which personal imperatives (the personality and psychic state of the narrator) and performance dynamics (the immediate setting or behavioral context in which the narrative occurs— the performance) operate, which then combine to shape the narrative content (or rumor text). The folklore diamond, focusing on explaining the content of the rumor or legend, links the social structure to the content of the rumor, through the mediation of the speaker and the situation (including the characteristics and reactions of the audience).

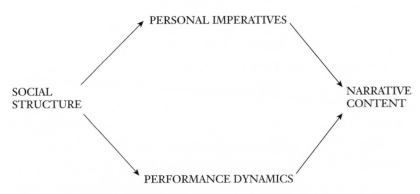

Figure 2. Folklore diamond

Our analysis relies on the folklore diamond to link structure, narrator, performance, and the content of racial rumors. It should be self-evident that the content of racial rumors reflects and transforms the structure of society. The relative and absolute positions of blacks and whites—economic, social, cultural, and political—affect how rumors develop. Structural discrimination and poverty affect the stories that are told and those that are found credible. To be credible a rumor must fit with the social structure as it is perceived by audiences. The social structure provides the base reality that rumors represent in either direct or distorted form.

Further, when one is dealing with contemporary rumors that address issues of race, one cannot deny that the personal imperatives of narrators—their beliefs and attitudes, conscious and hidden—matter profoundly. Speakers communicate messages that they believe are relevant, important, or entertaining. In this, they first rely on their own judgments. A person with racist or bigoted beliefs is prone to spread a different set of claims than someone who is more tolerant. Those who are unaware of their own prejudices, too, find certain information compelling and pass that along, even if they cannot judge why they made the choices they did. Further, the emotional conditions under which speakers spread rumors influence messages: angry, frightened, or confused people are more prone to spread stories that confident, secure, or compassionate people reject—not necessarily because they have decided to censor themselves, but because the rumor no longer seems plausible.

The conditions under which rumors are spread—the performance dynamics—are centrally important. A doleful fact of American life is the reality that blacks and whites often are part of communication channels that do not overlap. The rarity of candid cross-racial talk means that speakers—even well-meaning ones—do not learn that racial others may consider a rumor highly implausible. Sadly, even if they did learn, that information might only solidify the image of the other race. Stereotypical talk often is seen as normal and entertaining. With a supportive audience, the speaker finds the plausibility of his or her beliefs reinforced. Since the goal of communication is to promote identification and create satisfaction, it is evident how, as a function of the performance and the responses to it, stereotypes are reinforced.

These features channel the content of rumor, even if they do not entirely determine it. In an alternative, imaginary universe with different social structures, more accepting racial ideologies, people with broader backgrounds, and more open and diverse settings for talk, the content of rumor would differ. We would still communicate unofficial, unverified information, but it would lack the same racial power. Questioning would be more likely both within and between groups.

Having described the major approaches that have been taken to studying rumor, we turn our attention to the effects of categories of rumor and related beliefs in American race relations. Our argument in this chapter is that racial rumors, while distinctive in their content, are similar to other rumors in their structure and their dynamics, and that past research, even if not explicitly about racial matters, can help us understand narratives that are. Rumor can both solve problems and create problems. Ultimately, both the solving and the creation of problems derive from our attempts to make sense of a world that we feel we cannot control, and often one that we feel we understand only partially.

THREE

Mercantile Rumor in Black and White

Crown automotive air fresheners—plastic deodorizers, shaped like a king's crown and placed in front of the car's rear windows—serve as an indicator of the driver's gang allegiance. In New Haven, Connecticut, middle-class white residents claim that the presence of the air freshener indicates an affiliation with the notorious Latin Kings street gang.

Crown automotive air fresheners are produced by a corporation owned by white supremacists with close links to the Ku Klux Klan. The company's owners once unashamedly thanked African Americans for purchasing their products in an appearance on the *Jerry Springer Show*.

As rumors about Crown air fresheners indicate, Americans find their lives dominated by the constant presence of consumerism and concerns about the dangers of frivolous purchases. Whether we wake up listening to a mainstream, all-news station or a jammin' black format station, we will not have been alert very long before being inundated by an avalanche of commercial messages. Throughout the day we are bombarded by messages attempting to convince us that a given product or service will improve our lives and shape our identity. If we use the Internet in our work, we are subjected to banner advertisements and direct e-mail pitches. We live with corporations, and in some regards they become our family. But many consumers consider themselves members of decidedly dysfunctional corporate families.

Historians trace the origins of a market-dominated American culture to the decades prior to the turn of the twentieth century. The transformation of consumer goods from luxuries to necessities began with the emergence of mail-order catalogs and department stores crammed with merchandise for those with available discretionary income. Lenient credit policies enabled a larger segment of the population to increase its purchasing power. In time, store-bought goods became infinitely more status enhancing than homemade ones, and self-sufficiency became a badge of failure rather than an emblem of success. To buy is to be.

Not all Americans entered the world of consumerism at the same historical moment. Late nineteenth-century advertisers targeted their messages to appeal to those with money and to those who wanted the lifestyle depicted as belonging to the moneyed classes. It was easier to entice urbanites than to attract rural dwellers, and the constraints of city living prohibited the self-sufficiency still practiced in agricultural enclaves. Although mail-order catalogs endeavored to make all manner of merchandise available to people distant from upscale urban department stores, rural Americans still had a greater capacity to remove themselves from the reach of zealous merchants.

For the most part, African Americans remained outside the commercial marketplace longer than most of their white counterparts. Particularly for those in the peonage-style work arrangements common in the South during the late nineteenth and early twentieth centuries, access to cash was rare. Often these former slaves were forced to limit their shopping to stores selected or run by the owner of the land they worked.

The efforts of businesses to encourage consumers to demand an increasing list of commodities were not lost on black Americans. Nineteenth-century African-American leaders Ida B. Wells and Booker T. Washington rarely agreed on anything, but both lamented the tendency of some rural blacks to use hard-earned money to purchase luxury items through "on time" arrangements, the beginnings of a process linking African Americans to the commercial market.

In spite of the relentless campaigns urging them to purchase goods, white and black Americans have not surrendered to the commercial empire without some resistance and ambivalence. Consumers possess few resources with which to fight the seductive appeals crafted by advertisers other than personal decisions to refrain from purchasing products and spreading rumors about the nature of the companies and the quality of the goods. As a consequence, rumors and contemporary legends have assumed a prominent place in the anticorporate arsenal and serve, however unconsciously, as a form of resistance, a weapon of the weak.[1] These rumors serve as *truth claims,* which allege that consumers properly mistrust those products that they are ambivalent about purchasing.

In this chapter we offer several case studies of corporate rumor or legend cycles that have enjoyed substantial popularity during the past decade. Although both blacks and whites spread stories about corporations, these accounts are not identical. Black rumors play on the belief in racial animus by elites. Whites take the whiteness of corporate ownership for granted, and their stories address concerns that are not directly connected to race, even though they reflect similar underlying suspicions as the texts from African Americans. For whites race is assumed, while for blacks it is usually explicit. But both groups find rumors and legends appealing tools with which to question corporate integrity.

FAST-FOOD FANTASIES

In our hearts we believe that the mothers of America remain responsible for preparing the family meal. As a reality, we have been persuaded that dual-career families or single-parent households require prepared food, yet the older cultural images are hard to erase. Advertising agencies work diligently to persuade us that we can enjoy all the benefits of mass-prepared foods with none of the psychic costs, but their arguments are only partially effective. Fast-food restaurants are particularly at risk from what we call *Grandma's revenge*. Those who betray the family dinner pay the price.

While hamburgers, tacos, and pizza are sometimes served at dinner, no fast food is more linked to important family gatherings than fried chicken. To many, the mother who purchases fried chicken rather than preparing it herself has betrayed the hearth and home. In fact, mass-produced fried chicken seems to provoke more consumer uncertainty and anxiety than any other food product. Virtually every fast-food chicken enterprise has had to confront a string of nasty rumors.

The best known and most hardy of these chicken rumors is known as "The Kentucky Fried Rat."[2] As a high school student in the early 1970s, long before she knew the discipline of folklore existed, Turner heard and believed this story. The topic in her social studies class that day was consumer economics, and the teacher, Mr. Peters, was explaining to the students that federal regulations assumed that food processing plants could never be completely pristine environments. After the teacher stated that microscopic amounts of vermin and dirt were expected and tolerated in processed foods, an African-American student captivated the class with a story of what had happened to friends of her family. On the road late at night, they stopped at Kentucky Fried Chicken for a bucket of chicken. Eager to reach their destination, they opted to eat in the car, and each passenger grabbed a piece of chicken. A woman in the backseat asked the driver to turn on the interior light because she thought she must have gotten a piece of chicken that did not have all the feathers removed. After the light was turned on, they discovered that the passenger was holding a hairy, fried rat. A talented storyteller, Turner's classmate emphasized the last three words. She then repeated, "She had bitten into a Kentucky Fried rat!" The rest of the class, including the teacher, was completely "grossed out."

Nine years later Turner, by then a fledgling folklorist in graduate school, was assigned an article written by Fine on "The Kentucky Fried Rat." She then realized that she was one of countless consumers who had accepted the story as gospel truth. Interestingly, Fine's wife was at that time working for a large property-casualty insurance company, and she had been assured by a coworker that her company had once paid out on just such a claim. Race was not a significant variable in Fine's field study; most of his informants were white, and they believed the story. Turner's own experience confirms that blacks and whites alike find the story plausible. Her black classmate was comfortable sharing the narrative in a largely white class presided over by a white teacher. The story of the Kentucky Fried rat has few racial overtones. Over the years it has remained remarkably hardy, a perennial contemporary legend.

Fine's folklore diamond can be applied to Turner's potent memory. The first step is to examine the personal imperatives and the performance dynamics. Turner's classmate, whom we will call Diane, was a high-achieving, popular student, respected by her peers and teachers. That day's lecture on the regulation of processed food disturbed the class greatly. On the one hand, the teacher seemed to enjoy shattering the students' illusions about the purity of processed foods, but he also wanted to convince them that no real harm would come from consuming microscopic pieces of rat hair. An experienced and respected teacher, he no doubt wanted to avoid receiving any phone calls from parents chastising him for scaring the students out of eating that evening. This social situation allowed Diane an opportunity to reinforce his message and demonstrate her knowledge and sophistication to her classmates and teacher. Diane used his commentary to shape the narrative content of the legend. She uttered the words "fried rat" with great emphasis. Mr. Peters had described minuscule pieces of rat hair and evoked shudders from the class; Diane said "fried rat," and the class (including Mr. Peters) groaned.

Of course, the basis of the tale and the conditions of the telling were a function of a particular social structure. We live in a corporate environment in which fast-food restaurants compete for customers by providing quick food at relatively cheap prices. The belief that a corporation might, in fact, engage in such behavior is believable for many given the structure of the economic order and the way in which people respond to it.

As noted previously, Turner never questioned this legend's veracity. After all, she knew Diane and her teacher. She knew of Kentucky Fried Chicken only through its advertisements because no franchises were located near her school. Her mother, older sisters, aunts, or female members of their church congregations prepared the chicken she ate. Served at a table or on a picnic, the chicken was meant to be eaten after thanks had been offered to God, not in the dark backseat of a moving car, and she liked it that way. Diane's story urged her to avoid fast-food fried chicken and the hasty eating habits that it can enable. Thus it reinforced an already established view of the world.

Through coincidence, Turner's first extended research on a contemporary legend cycle highlighted the alleged misdeeds of another, seemingly similar, fast-food fried chicken franchise. When teaching a class on black literature in Boston, Turner recounted "The Kentucky Fried Rat" cycle and asked how many of the students had heard it. Many students, both black and white had; one young African-American male also shared a story he had heard from a coworker about Church's Fried Chicken. In his story, the contamination was a mysterious ingredient that was manufactured for the Ku Klux Klan, the alleged owners of the company, and intended to sterilize black males. The student affirmed the truth of his story by claiming that an exposé on the company had been broadcast on a television newsmagazine. Many black students in the class were familiar with the rumor. No whites were.

In her subsequent fieldwork, Turner asked potential informants if they had ever heard anything peculiar about a fast-food fried chicken franchise. White informants usually responded with a version of "The Kentucky Fried Rat." Some black informants also recited the rat story, some told the Church's story, and some shared both.

Soon Turner was collecting other examples of "pernicious poultry." In the early 1990s a story alleged that Al Copeland, the founder and CEO of Popeyes Famous Fried Chicken, had made a substantial campaign contribution to the senate campaign of David Duke, former KKK grand dragon, in Louisiana. This belief was compelling because Popeyes had assumed complete control over the beleaguered and financially troubled Church's corporation just a few months before this rumor surfaced. Rumor often follows the money trail.

Related stories developed around "secret" recipes used to prepare fried chicken. Each company takes pride in the recipes it uses to prepare its distinctive chicken. Some informants claimed that they had heard that Colonel Sanders, founder of Kentucky Fried Chicken, had stolen his special recipe from a black domestic. Other informants maintained that George Church stole his recipe from an African-American cook. Still others claimed that Al Copeland, owner of Popeyes, had stolen a recipe from a black domestic worker. We refer to these stories as the "Imitation of Life" cycle after a popular movie based on the Fannie Hurst novel in which a white businesswoman profits from her cook's prized pancake recipe.[3]

As Fine has noted, rumors about fast-food establishments can be divided into categories based on whether the corporation is malicious, deceptive, or careless. These fried chicken rumor cycles fall into all three categories.[4]

In most versions of "The Kentucky Fried Rat," the contamination is an accidental, onetime event. The corporation was not deliberately deceptive, but it was careless or sloppy. The unfortunate customer who eats the rat is a random victim. The rat has been fried because the owner of a particular franchise has allowed his store to become infested with rodents. Some informants do report that malicious young employees intentionally fried that rat to fulfill a dare or as a practical joke. This version targets employees and the uncaring corporation that employs, but does not supervise, them. No one claims that the corporation is intentionally serving rats to its customers, but only that it does not care as much as home cooks do. In many versions of "The Kentucky Fried Rat," the innocent customer who ingests the rat must have his or her stomach pumped. In a few versions the eater goes mad and must be institutionalized. But in all cases the contamination is limited to a particular time and place, often with the unfortunate store singled out.

To analyze these stories, we asked who had heard them and found them credible. For whom did the stories make "cultural sense"? Both whites and blacks were familiar with and claimed to believe the legend of the Kentucky Fried rat. The stories about Church's, Popeyes, and the "Imitation of Life" cycle circulate almost exclusively within African-American populations. They make sense within the black community, but whites usually find the claims ridiculous.

Most informants repeat "The Kentucky Fried Rat" in the form of a contemporary legend. It is often transmitted as a narrative with a beginning, middle, and end. The incident took place in the recent past. In many versions, the story ends with a comment suggesting that the corporation provided the victim with a generous financial settlement. The company has been punished, and the victim has received a significant financial compensation. If they do not quite have a happy ending, such stories suggest that justice was done, and the perceived threat to community was—at least temporarily—healed. One version collected in Michigan reports as follows:

> There was this lady and she went to Kentucky Fried Chicken and
> she went in there and she came out in the dark and it was raining,

and she sat in her car eating a bucket of chicken and one of the
pieces tasted funny. And she turned on the light in the car and saw
a rat. She took it back in there and sued them.

In this legend, the one best known to whites, the hapless consumer
(or the family in those versions in which the customer dies) obtains some
measure of relief; it recognizes that whites have the power to influence
the social structure. Of course, the story is told that this was a one-time-
only contamination, perhaps linking the contamination to poorly
trained, low-paid, alienated employees.

The stories that are widely known within the African-American
community have a different texture. The Church's/KKK/sterilization
cycle foregrounds intentional conspiracy and contamination. The owners of the corporation add the mysterious ingredient to destroy the
fertility of black males. Most versions of this cycle are more like rumor
than legend: brief accounts with few supporting details. The contamination is presented as an ongoing threat. Whereas a customer of
Kentucky Fried Chicken is unlikely to receive a fried rat, unwanted
sterilization still threatens all black males at Church's. In these rumors,
the corporation is perceived as having successfully masked its evil intentions.

Today a new rumor cycle has targeted Kentucky Fried Chicken. As
fast-food-savvy Americans know, the company changed its corporate
moniker to the more simple KFC in the 1990s. Most people assumed
the company wished to downplay the fact that its chicken is fried, an
undesirable process in this health-conscious environment. However,
this rumor suggests that the name change was inspired because KFC no
longer uses real chicken; instead, it uses "genetically manipulated or-
ganisms," kept alive through tubes inserted into their bodies to pump
blood and nutrients, without beaks, feathers, and feet, all in the name
of greater efficiency and lower production costs. As the following Internet version indicates, the rumor alleges that, based on a study at the
University of New Hampshire, the government forced the company to

alter its name and menu. The rumor demands that consumers protest this disgusting "fact."

> KFC has been a part of our American traditions for many years. Many people, day in and day out, eat at KFC religiously. Do they really know what they are eating? During a recent study of KFC done at the University of New Hampshire, researchers found some very upsetting facts. First of all, has anybody noticed that just recently, the company has changed their name? Kentucky Fried Chicken has become KFC. Does anybody know why? We thought the real reason was because of the "FRIED" food issue. It's not. The reason why they call it KFC is because they can not use the word chicken anymore. Why? KFC does not use real chickens. They actually use genetically manipulated organisms. These so called "chickens" are kept alive by tubes inserted into their bodies to pump blood and nutrients throughout their structure. They have no beaks, no feathers, and no feet. Their bone structure is dramatically shrunk to get more meat out of them. This is great for KFC because they do not have to pay so much for their production costs. There is no more plucking of the feathers or the removal of the beaks and feet. The government has told them to change all of their menus so they do not say chicken anywhere. If you look closely you will notice this. Listen to their commercials, I guarantee you will not see or hear the word chicken. I find this matter to be very disturbing. I hope people will start to realize this and let other people know. Please forward this message to as many people as you can. Together we make KFC start using real chicken again.

This text implies that the franchise has hatched this plot to save money by deceptively serving its customers faux chicken. Although some earlier versions can be traced, the texts began to circulate widely in late 1999, with a period of intense proliferation in January 2000. Almost as quickly as e-mails circulated to warn friends of the fake fried chicken practice, the company began an aggressive cyber-rebuttal policy. However, KFC had to hope that consumers would seek out and believe the company's Web site or one of the news stories that covered and debunked the rumor.

It is not surprising that contemporary legend cycles reveal consumer uncertainty over high-tech food. New modes of merchandising and preparing foods typically evoke customer reticence. Recent reports about advances in genetically altered foods are increasingly commonplace. Much to the dismay of many scientists and food industry leaders who clearly underestimated the symbolic loyalties people have toward their food, the public did not always react positively and enthusiastically to technological developments. Throughout the world, individuals and organizations criticized and protested the use of "impure" food products. Many companies were forced to abandon or postpone plans to market food products containing some genetically modified substances.

Clearly, the public's penchant for purity in poultry once again emerged. The Internet text that accuses KFC of culinary deception gives consumers a specific story with which to articulate their ambivalence about scientific intrusions into public and private kitchens. With their exotic experiments, scientists have taken something as familiar and fundamental as food and rendered it abstract and impersonal. This narrative names both the site of experimentation and a specific and cherished food: fried chicken. It offers a financial rationale for the company's conduct. Finally, by referring to the commercials and the name change, it empowers the listener to become a detective and uncover the company's duplicity. With one story, consumers can articulate a host of important issues. Whites and blacks report the same allegation, although Turner's fieldwork suggests that many black informants perceived a particular antiblack animus on the part of KFC.

What is it about fast-food fried chicken that stimulates both black and white consumers to speculate about its safety whenever it is prepared outside of the home? Fried chicken is personally prepared food that has been taken over by corporate capitalism. In his 1980 study of "The Kentucky Fried Rat" cycle, Fine elaborates on the ambivalent attitudes many consumers have toward the growth of the fast-food industry, as restaurant meals weaken the bonds of hearth and home. While nutritionists have never considered fried foods nutritionally adequate, the attacks on oil and fat have recently swelled, increasing consumer ambivalence about fried chicken. Like other foods prepared in boiling oil, fried chicken holds a prominent place on the taboo list of most nutritionists. Yet, while fried chicken may be a forbidden food, it is also a time-honored staple, with deep roots in American cuisine.[5] Many informants can name a relative or friend whose fried chicken recipe is tasty and special. In many communities, both white and black, chicken is often served in conjunction with church-sponsored events or for Sunday dinner. Even into the twentieth century, rural families often raised their own chickens, long after they started buying other meats at the grocery store. At Turner's twentieth high school reunion, white and black classmates reminisced about the terrific fried chicken prepared by Turner's Aunt Doll and sold at high school fund-raisers and basketball games. Fried chicken is, in the words of Claude Lévi-Strauss, "good to think" for whites and blacks alike; it provides a means of understanding American culture.

For black Americans additional associations are evident. For them, the nostalgia evoked by a family's fried chicken recipe is balanced by the media's former insistence on perpetuating negative stereotypes of blacks as unscrupulous chicken thieves and rapacious consumers of fried chicken. If we consider the major meat groups in America to be chicken, pork, and beef, chicken is generally the least expensive. Chickens are easier to raise on poor "dirt farms," making them an inexpensive source of high-quality protein. Throughout history, African Americans had more access to chickens than to other meat sources. Further, if one intended to steal an animal for its meat, a chicken would certainly be most readily available. Both during and after slavery, blacks had limited access to food. In order to feed their families, African Americans often stole chickens.

The image of the African American as a shameless chicken thief is sharpened by depictions of unkempt blacks devouring fried chicken, a portrayal that permeates American popular culture. In *Birth of a Nation* (1915), D. W. Griffith's classic depiction of the Reconstruction era, blacks elected to the state legislature sit in the chambers, eating chicken and casually tossing the bones across the aisles. African Americans are understandably disturbed by the persistent coupling of them with sloppy foods eaten by hand (fried chicken, ribs, corn on the cob, watermelon).

In fact, fried chicken is as American as apple pie. "The Kentucky Fried Rat" cycle reinforces age and class biases aimed at fast-food workers who have been given the responsibility that mothers previously had. As in accounts of irresponsible and malicious baby-sitters and nannies, American mothers have given up the responsibility for their families to "strangers." Great care must be taken in granting that responsibility.

The Church's and Popeyes stories that are transmitted by blacks have a different focus. These rumors emphasize the moral culpability of the corporation. The allegedly racist corporation not only is profiting from members of the black community but also is attempting to poison them. Perhaps the poisons that lead to sterility can be symbolically equated to cholesterol: both can lead to the death of the race. This threat is just as robust as is routine prejudice. Claims that allege that special recipes were "stolen" from black cooks without compensation further speak to the racial rapacity of white-dominated corporations: Why do these black cooks not start their own franchises? Once again, we find that the content of rumors mirrors the social structure.

Yet the persistence of the fast-food poultry texts also demonstrates some shared American food values. Blacks and whites may mistrust fast-food fried chicken franchises for different reasons, but we all harbor strong convictions about our chicken.

DANGERS OF THE MARKET

Fast-food contamination is not the only consumer fear; supermarket food cannot be trusted either. We may read the list of ingredients on the side of containers, but what do these words mean? Can we trust what we are told? Buying food products can be as dangerous as purchasing prepared foods. In some cases, as with fast-food stories, company owners are malicious, and in some cases the products themselves are contaminated—either on one occasion or routinely. Over the years, products as diverse as Coca-Cola, Tropical Fantasy cola, Bubble-Yum bubble gum, Nerds candy, Mountain Dew, and Uncle's Ben's instant rice have been targets of rumors. In addition, there are routine claims that beer and cigarette manufacturers are not what they seem. In some cases, particularly within the African-American community, rumors deal with racial hatred. In others, in those stories spread within the white community, the dangers are not racial but are grounded in fears of political extremism and religious fanaticism.

What do these target products have in common? We find that most are seen as attractively illegitimate by consumers. These are products that consumers feel ambivalent about, often linked to sugar, caffeine, tobacco, alcohol, or heavily processed versions of food that one should "properly" be preparing from scratch. These products are metaphorically killing us; the rumors that have emerged address similar themes, helping to tame unacceptable beliefs.

To examine this process and its linkage to rumors about race, we describe a set of Topsy/Eva rumors about Snapple beverages that developed in the early 1990s. For many people, iced tea is a refreshing beverage on a sweltering afternoon. Until recently, iced tea could only be prepared by chilling hot tea or adding water to a prepared mix. But as consumer interest in carbonated beverages diminished and preference for "natural" foods escalated, consumer interest in gourmet iced tea increased. The Snapple Beverage Corporation was one of the first to capitalize on—or perhaps to inspire—this new development.

By the spring of 1993, an Eva text had begun circulating about Snapple iced tea. The owners of the company, according to many white informants, were donating significant portions of their profits to Operation Rescue, considered by many as the most confrontational and radical of the pro-life organizations in the United States. Most of those who spread this rumor were pro-choice themselves and wanted to warn other pro-choice sympathizers that the makers of the beverage were funneling their profits to virulent antiabortion efforts. These rumors fit a pattern in that by buying products from distant and barely known corporations, consumers often wonder how their profits are used.

At approximately the same time, a Topsy version of the rumor emerged. Similar to the Church's cycle, the claim alleged that the owners of Snapple were members of the KKK. Like the owners of Church's, they, too, had added an ingredient to the recipe that sterilized black men. Many informants "proved" the allegation by pointing to the product's label, which boasts an encircled "K" and an old-fashioned sailing ship. The "K," according to believers, is a "hidden" message to indicate that the corporation is affiliated with the Ku Klux Klan. The ship is said to be a drawing of a slave ship.

In September 1993 the owners of the Snapple Beverage Corporation decided that these rumors were harming their profits and, perhaps more significantly, were personally offensive to the executives. Most corporations and the consultants who advise them are reluctant to issue public statements denouncing the rumors and legends that afflict them, believing that such denials may spread the rumors further. Reasoning that those consumers who have not heard a rumor may give it credence after hearing a denial, corporate leaders have been reluctant to take such a direct approach to rumor control. In contrast, Snapple issued press releases and purchased advertising space in local newspapers. Signed by the corporation's three highest executives, the advertisement was in the form of an open letter to customers. The letter was explicit and direct, claiming, "We are not involved in any way whatsoever with the KKK, Operation Rescue or any other type of pressure group or organization, period." The letter explained that the "K" on the label indicates that the product is kosher, and the scene on the label portrays the Boston Tea Party. In subsequent interviews the corporation's CEO, Leonard Marsh, maintained, "We are three Jewish boys from New York accused of supporting the Ku Klux Klan, something I despise. . . . I support people going against the Klan." Whether the fact that these corporate leaders were Jews made the rumors in the African-American community more or less credible is an open question given the fragile relations between contemporary blacks and Jews. Eventually the rumors faded.

Corporations that utilize unorthodox or targeted advertising strategies are sometimes beset by rumors. Church's, for example, did very little advertising, an unusual policy for a fast-food enterprise. At the time of the rumors about its iced tea, Snapple was buying large blocks of advertising time on both Howard Stern's and Rush Limbaugh's controversial but popular syndicated radio shows. Many informants considered the Limbaugh association particularly damning. Known for his zealous support of conservative causes, Limbaugh is likely to appeal to those segments of the population most inclined to sympathize with antiabortion activists and beliefs that some perceive as hostile to black achievement. That is, if a corporation had these ideological motivations, it might choose to advertise on the Limbaugh show to reach fellow believers. Spokespersons for Snapple vigorously denied any ideological connections between the company and the hosts of the radio shows. Snapple's management claimed that the primary reason for advertising on Limbaugh's show was the program's widespread popularity; the company simply wished to reach the largest possible radio audience. Limbaugh, however, as is his style, made the advertisements for Snapple personal and spoke fondly and familiarly about the Snapple owners. Surely it was a small leap to assume that Limbaugh was making a political as well as a commercial endorsement.

The fact that Operation Rescue is identified as the beneficiary of Snapple's profits is noteworthy. One well-educated informant claimed to have believed the rumor when she first heard it from a fellow participant in an aerobics class. Although she did not know the classmate well, she knew they had much in common. Both white and female, they were professional women in their thirties. The classmate's iteration of the rumor further connected them through their pro-choice politics. On the other hand, Snapple, a fairly new company, was pushing the informant to buy a new product that had previously been unnecessary. Despite being knowledgeable about the nuances of rumor, she had no doubts about the veracity of this text and readily believed that there was evidence linking the company with the militant pro-life movement. To this woman, Operation Rescue represents the antiliberal backlash at its worst. Members of the organization have assaulted and harassed pregnant women, their escorts, and doctors willing to provide abortions. For many pro-choice whites, Operation Rescue stands in somewhat the same relation to polite discourse as does the Klan for blacks.

Snapple, like many other products besieged by a Topsy/Eva rumor cycle, evokes complex responses on the part of consumers. Most of the informants with whom we spoke were fond of the beverage, yet they often referred to its hefty price. In many markets and cafeterias, Snapple costs nearly twice as much as popular carbonated beverages. To the owners of the corporation, the public's immediate love affair with Snapple was a financial boon. However, products that enjoy overnight success, appearing "from nowhere," often trigger consumer concern. How did the product become so popular so quickly? Something suspicious must be happening. These misgivings, coupled with health concerns about the product (because tea and coffee, which contain caffeine, were seen as potentially dangerous), led to harsh rumors. Eventually Snapple was sold to Quaker Foods, which found that the luster had worn off the product, leading to large corporate losses, but simultaneously the decline of the rumor. In time Snapple was sold again, but it has not regained its previous cultural prominence.

IT'S THE CLOTHES

What we put in our body helps to define what we are, but "foodways" fears by no means exhaust mercantile rumors. What we put on our body shapes our identity as well: our clothing is a central marker in permitting others to know how we think of ourselves and where we stand in the social order. It is said you can tell a person by the clothes that he or she wears. Clothing choices reflect our view of social propriety. While most consumers aggressively seek clothes with low prices, they prefer to purchase expensive clothes at bargain prices rather than cheap clothes at cheap prices.

Blacks learn early in life that they are apt to be judged by the quality of the clothes on their backs. As studies of the everyday experience of discrimination point out, for blacks to wear casual clothing leaves them open to the assumption that they are engaged in improper behavior.[6] While even a suit or a stylish dress does not entirely protect blacks from affronts, it serves to indicate legitimacy. Given the importance of clothing as a form of impression management, it is significant that in the early 1990s a series of narratives emerged about the sinister intentions and attitudes of clothing manufacturers.

FROM LIZ TO TOMMY

Few fashion designers have enjoyed the quick success and widespread popularity earned by Tommy Hilfiger and Liz Claiborne. And few companies have felt beset by rumors as much as these two fashion giants. By examining the similarities and differences between the circulation of the cycles that have developed about them, we can understand the impact of rumor in the 1990s.

In 1992, just as Turner was finishing writing *I Heard It through the Grapevine*, we both began to field inquiries about the Liz Claiborne company. In the Eva cycle, the well-known fashion designer Liz Claiborne is said to support satanic cults. This cycle was best known to white consumers, who often bolstered the text by citing an appearance by Claiborne on the *Phil Donahue Show*. Claiborne thus joins the corporate executives of Procter and Gamble and McDonald's as Satanists who "out" themselves on television. In a Topsy rumor, African-American consumers allege that Claiborne uses her profits to support the Ku Klux Klan. These informants defend their versions by claiming that the admission was made on the *Oprah Winfrey Show*. We find that rumors spread by whites are justified by reference to an event on a talk show hosted by whites (*Phil Donahue, Sally Jesse Raphael, 60 Minutes,* or *20/20*). In contrast, rumors in the African-American community often claim evidence from an appearance on the black-hosted *Oprah Winfrey* or *Montel Williams* show. "Proof" is linked to the racial context of the television program.

A common motif in many African-American narratives alleges that Winfrey asked Liz Claiborne why her garments made for the bottom half of the body—skirts, shorts, and trousers—were cut so small. Claiborne responded that she did not like to see African-American women wear her clothes. Knowing that many black women have large derrieres, she had the clothes cut small so they would be unlikely to fit the typical African-American female consumer. Oprah purportedly ordered Claiborne off the stage and went to a commercial. When the program resumed, she had discarded her own Liz Claiborne ensemble and finished the program in her bathrobe.

For several years, non-African-American informants who "knew" the legend cited Claiborne as a devil worshiper and authenticated the texts with references to the *Phil Donahue Show*. African-American informants who "knew" labeled Claiborne a white supremacist and cited the *Oprah Winfrey Show*. Most of these versions contained the additional motif about the shape and cut of the clothes.

The texts range from a brief, rumorlike format to longer narratives. This may be a result of the fact that African-American filmmaker Spike Lee perpetuated a version of the Claiborne/white supremacist incident both in print interviews and in lectures. In an interview for *Esquire* magazine in October 1992, Lee maintained the following:

> Last week, Oprah Winfrey had Liz Claiborne on the show. I guess
> she wears Liz Claiborne's clothes all the time. Claiborne got on
> and said she didn't make her clothes for black people to wear. Oprah
> stopped the show and told her to get her ass off the set. How you
> gonna get on Oprah's show and say you don't make clothes for
> black women? It definitely happened. Get the tape. Every black

woman in America needs to go to her closet, throw that shit out and never buy another stitch of clothes from Liz Claiborne.[7]

In contrast to Lee's confidence, we find no evidence linking the fashion designer to either a devil-worshiping cult or the Ku Klux Klan. However, a profile of Claiborne and her multi-million-dollar fashion empire does offer clues about the reasons the Topsy/Eva cycle emerged.

The existence of the Topsy/Eva cycle suggests that African-American and white consumers are ambivalent about clothes designed by the Liz Claiborne Company and about the company itself. To appreciate the appeal of this cycle, we need to "read" both the clothes and the corporation.

Turner once asked an African-American student who believed the rumor if she could remember where she first heard it. The student recalled being in a mall with a friend doing back-to-school shopping. She coveted a white cotton linen blouse from the Liz Claiborne line. It was "fine," she attested, but, because it was priced at over fifty dollars, it was more than she should spend on a simple white blouse. When her girlfriend saw her admiring the blouse, she grabbed it from her and told her that Liz Claiborne hated to see black people in her clothes. According to the friend, Claiborne purposefully designed the pants and trousers of her line small so that black women with large derrieres would have trouble wearing them and would choose another brand. The friend claimed to have heard the story on *Oprah*.

In 1997, clothing impresario Tommy Hilfiger was forced to confront a similar set of claims. Just when his clothes were getting the most floor space in department stores, African-American informants indicated that they had heard that Hilfiger had made public statements denigrating blacks. In most versions, Hilfiger had referred to blacks as niggers on *Oprah Winfrey*. In some versions, Hilfiger, like Claiborne, said he did not like the way blacks looked in his clothes. Some informants claimed that Hilfiger lumped blacks and Asians, or "gooks," in his assessment. The following text, collected in March 1997 from a male Filipino, unites both cycles: "Tommy Hilfiger allegedly said he never intended blacks/ Asians to buy/wear his products to the point where the groups make a large proportion of the sales. And if he had known, he wouldn't have made the clothing."

Subsequent texts stressed the high cost of the clothes. One young African-American man was returning to college after financial problems had forced him to interrupt his education. He had heard the Hilfiger text, believed it, and said it was a good thing he had heard it because he could not afford the clothing anyway. One Internet exchange on the rumor posted in May 1998 included the following:

1. All people that think he is racist are the people that are racist. It is the people that can't afford the merchandise that are mad.

2. tommy rulz!! tommy rulz!! tommy rulz!! r u all sayin that cuz u cant afford 2 buy them??? ha ha ha!!

The following, more extensive, remarks are compelling:

3. Even though there still lies a controversy of whether Tommy made some racist remarks somewhere along the line, confirmations have been made by both shows that Tommy supposedly spoke on. These shows confirmed that Tommy was never a guest. Around here in Philly, everyone wears Tommy something or other. Whether it's a Tommy coat to Tommy shoes, people here like Tommy. Although it is a very high cost at certain department stores that aren't worth mentioning, some might argue whether it's worth it. Adults just say that you are advertising for someone and they should be paying you, I believe that's just not so. I speak from a high school teen's point of view. I cannot tell people what to wear, neither can they tell me. I am wearing a Tommy shirt right now. When we wear a article of Tommy clothing, we are expressing our like for phat clothes from phat designers. Not that we are advertising for a certain person. Although I must admit those original "flag" t-shirts were quite obnoxious looking although very popular.

4. I know that Tommy Hilfiger merchandise is a little steep in price

but to me it is worth it for the casual yet contemporary look that Tommy creates. I feel that Tommy also allows me to personalize myself. I am one of those people who does not like to be "trendy" and wear what everyone else wears. Since I am in high school I like to be a leader rather than a follower.

We recognize the teenage impulse that requires conformity in order to establish one's self-image as a nonconformist. These texts also reflect the struggle that results from succumbing to peer pressure to wear the hottest clothing while rationalizing the expense of this obligation.

Understanding the popularity of these texts requires us to examine the clothes designed by these companies. From a stylistic perspective, Claiborne's clothes are "classics." As several informants stressed, most of her clothes never go out of style. No doubt the white linen blouse that appealed to this informant remained fashionable for several seasons. In their colors, fabrics, and styling, the items in Claiborne's line ooze "Americanness." The line frequently features solid, primary-color clothes with a heavy sprinkling of red, white, and blue. Claiborne designers rely on natural fabrics such as high-quality denims, heavyweight khakis, and expertly woven linens. During the spring 1993 season, one prominent ensemble was a red, white, and blue jogging suit, complete with stars and stripes. In short, the Liz Claiborne line supplies the clothes often associated with the look of an elegantly dressed "girl next door"—a patriotic, American girl next door. The clothes' classic quality encourages suspicion among some.

Claiborne does not work in kente cloth, the woven Ghanaian fabric currently popular with many African Americans. In the past several years, many young black consumers have taken to wearing "Afrocentric" clothes. Brightly colored, African-inspired, and loose-fitting, these garments make a cultural as well as a fashion statement. Until the early 1990s, Afrocentric clothes had to be purchased in specialty shops, and one did not find advertisements for them in the major women's fashion magazines.

The two styles of clothes—Liz Claiborne classics and African-inspired garments—are cultural and social opposites and could represent a dilemma for young African-American women, as personal dynamics influence the content of the rumors. Perhaps the Claiborne/white supremacist cycle was furthered by the unstated tension between the mainstream American image in the Claiborne line and the seductive appeal of the Afrocentric clothing. The choice between a classically tailored Liz Claiborne white blouse bought in a department store and a larger green, black, and yellow shirt purchased in a boutique reflects a choice between selecting the mainstream or pursuing the goals articulated in the black community.

Once a protégé of Ralph Lauren, by the mid-1990s Tommy Hilfiger was coming into his own with a line of clothes that appealed to younger and hipper customers than Lauren's but, like his mentor's, were too expensive for all but those near the top of the economic ladder. Hilfiger's garments, like those with the Troop label in the mid-1980s, caught on with many rap recording artists and were favored by adolescents and young adults. Many of the shirts and jackets in the line were decorated with Hilfiger's name in large, bold letters. Like Liz Claiborne, Hilfiger made extensive use of primary colors, including lots of red, white, and blue combinations. American flags and flaglike trademarks often embellish Hilfiger designs.

The ages of our informants offer clues about the differences between the appeal of the Liz Claiborne and Tommy Hilfiger clothing lines. Although many college-aged women were enthralled by Liz Claiborne clothing, we rarely identified interest at the high school age. The Claiborne company intended its products to appeal to women who were inclined to distinguish themselves from their younger sisters or daughters. Hilfiger's intended consumer base is much larger. His clothing is available in children's sizes, and teenagers are consistent consumers.

CLAIBORNE AND HILFIGER AS CONSPICUOUS CAPITALISTS

When we first contacted them in the early 1990s, representatives speaking on behalf of the Liz Claiborne corporate office seemed nonplussed by these texts. Slow to respond to inquiries, they eventually denied the rumors we had heard and argued that Claiborne did not appear on any of the talk shows. Beyond that, they refused to share any information on the rumors. Significantly, they never mentioned that Liz Claiborne herself was no longer affiliated with her namesake company. She is an image—real, but in effect a Betty Crocker figure. Like many companies, Liz Claiborne takes the position that any public comment on the rumor cycles might increase their credibility. Similarly, the talk shows have been very closemouthed about the rumors. They fear that any public comment, even a denial, will only fuel the accusation in the mind of the public. After denying the rumors, a representative of the *Oprah Winfrey Show* would comment on only one question. Asked if the fashion designer had ever appeared on the talk show, she responded in the negative.

In the rumors, informants treat Liz Claiborne as a fashion designer, as opposed to the head of a multi-million-dollar corporation. Informants stress that "she" does not like to see black women in "her" clothes. Rarely do informants use "it" or "they" to refer to the company. They imagine that Claiborne herself oversees all aspects of production.

Claiborne has entered the pantheon of Ray Kroc from McDonald's, Adolph Coors from Coors Brewery, and Al Copeland of Popeyes Famous Fried Chicken. These men were the CEOs of their respective organizations when rumors or contemporary legends became associated with them and their products. During her company's early years, Claiborne was often photographed with her models. She wore short, thick, dark hair in a pixie style reminiscent of Audrey Hepburn's and wore red-rimmed glasses over her deeply tanned face. Her tan was enhanced by her preference for white tops and trousers. In many ways she epitomizes the jokes black women tell about white women who try so hard to be tan. The popularity of the Liz Claiborne rumors suggests that consumers may be more likely to construct legends about corporations whose reputations are linked to a visible, high-profile CEO. This we term the *Henry Ford effect*, after the prominent automobile manufacturer who became in so many ways a cultural icon and a source for beliefs and rumors about the Ford Motor Company.

In 1990 the *New York Times* and the *Wall Street Journal* reported that Claiborne and her husband were retiring from their enormously successful company. The couple cited pressures from their work with nonprofit foundations and their commitment to environmental causes as their reasons for retiring. Their company was in good financial shape, and the shares they owned at that time were worth more than $100 million. Fashion and financial analysts attribute the company's remarkable success to Claiborne's design talents and her husband's financial acumen. Consider the following profile of a "typical" Liz Claiborne customer. According to an article in *Business Week*, the company imagines her to be "about 35 years old and probably not a perfect size 8."[8] Claiborne herself said, "I always knew I wanted to design for the busy American woman. And she isn't going to spend $2,000 on a suit."[9] According to one of Claiborne's founding partners, Jerry Chazen, "We knew we wanted to clothe women in the workforce. We saw a niche where no pure player existed. What we didn't know was how many customers were out there." In 1990 Chazen claimed, "I always felt that Macy's consumer is our customer. If she's pleased with our product Macy's has to write an order."[10] Claiborne developed a reputation as a designer who understood what clothing the working women of middle America wanted and would purchase. The company's goal was to sell women "designer clothes that are aspirational yet are accessible."[11] When Claiborne made personal appearances, her "fans" greeted her like a rock star.[12]

Attempting to explain Claiborne's popularity, journalists for the *Wall Street Journal* described the "modest" price of her clothes. In 1989, these authors perceived a navy blazer with a $152 price tag as modest.[13] For consumers accustomed to purchasing $2,000 suits, this may be so, but by the standards of many Americans—both white and African-American—Liz Claiborne clothes are expensive. Virtually all our informants admired the clothes themselves, but for many they were beyond their price range. This frustration was consistent with a desire to attack the company.

By the time Tommy Hilfiger launched his clothing line, designers who aimed their sights at both wealthy and middle-class consumers were the norm, not the exception. Hilfiger had apprenticed with a master designer and entrepreneur, Ralph Lauren. Following the path cleared by Claiborne and many other designers of the 1980s, Tommy Hilfiger constructed a provocative public image. He transformed himself into a celebrity in a culture that treasures celebrity.[14] With his Beatles mop-top hairstyle and lean body, he even resembles Liz Claiborne! But just as the image of a designer can be used to enhance the appeal of a clothing line, it can detract as well.

American consumers have an ambivalent relationship with the corporations that populate our economy. We are a capitalist nation that believes in the "free market" and that enshrines many holidays as "shopping days." Our belief in caveat emptor—let the buyer beware—justifies these rumors. Customers have become aware, rightly or wrongly, of corporate sins. High-powered advertising campaigns, increasingly sophisticated merchandising strategies, and omnipresent opportunities to purchase nonessential products permeate our day-to-day lives, and that gives us identity as consumers. Even though consumers may know that they should be frugal, what we buy confirms our moral virtue. This explains our infatuation with prestige goods, especially clothing: not only Liz Claiborne and Tommy Hilfiger but also other apparel, such as Troop clothing, British Knights, or Nike, each of which is expensive, self-enhancing, and tied to a belief within the African-American community that links the corporation to racism.[15] Although we know that we have clothing budgets, department stores croon a siren song that is hard to resist.

Consumers project their anxieties onto the corporation, justifying their own desire and sharing these anxieties in their performances. The belief that Liz Claiborne does not want black women to wear her clothing is a potent justification for avoiding the type of conspicuous consumption that one cannot afford anyway. It further distinguishes between the classic, white culture and the alternative, Afrocentric cultures. To whites ambivalent about the price of the clothing, the claim that Claiborne's profits might support devil worship provides the rationale for leaving the clothes on the rack. Thus, the claim that Claiborne is a racist or a Satanist masks concern about price—a concern linked to a sense of personal failure.

Public ambivalence about these pitches is exacerbated when we are given a single striking persona to match with a corporation, or the Henry Ford effect. One individual appears to be profiting from every hamburger, piece of fried chicken, beer, and plain white blouse we purchase. Who is this controlling stranger? We have relatively little to show for the expenditures, particularly with discretionary items. These conspicuous, charismatic CEOs use our money to advance their personal agendas. Social scientists speak of the process of "parasocial interaction," which recognizes that people often develop strong emotional ties with prominent people they have not met. Some of us feel that we know Lee Iacocca, Donald Trump, or Liz Claiborne. As a result, we come to believe that we understand their motives, a fertile ground for the development of rumor. In labeling Liz Claiborne a racist or a Satanist, consumers are really condemning her for being a conspicuous capitalist promoting conspicuous consumption.

A related process operates with anonymous CEOs. In this case, it is precisely the unknown character of the corporate leader that fuels the anxiety. The blankness of the leader provides a slate on which any concern can be written. While these corporations are not as likely to be attacked by rumor, when they are—as Procter and Gamble can attest—it is the anonymity of the corporate leadership that can be used to justify our belief that malicious intent is involved.

The Claiborne company markets its clothing as a means by which women can make a statement about their taste and identity. In a society that is riven by divisions between blacks and whites, it is possible to believe that a designer would not wish her clothing to be impugned by being worn by customers whose patronage might convince a more profitable market that wearing the clothing demonstrates a lack of good taste and a smudged identity.

NEW THREADS

There are two significant differences in the dissemination of the Claiborne and Hilfiger texts. The first has to do with the purported "target" of the designer. Many of our informants reported the anti-Asian version of the Hilfiger text. Whereas the Claiborne text of the early 1990s was very much a white and black case, the Hilfiger text of the mid-1990s reflects a multicultural sensibility. Further, informant reports of the Claiborne case were much more predictable in terms of the Topsy/Eva form. Whites usually told the Satanist version, and blacks reported the racist one. However, the Hilfiger antiblack text was reported by informants of all races. The texts we collected did not accuse Hilfiger of affiliating with the Klan or other white supremacist organizations, as is the case with most of the other consumer cycles. Instead, he was derided for using ethnic slurs on television and for insulting consumers who embraced his clothing. Hilfiger claimed that the first versions he heard connected the texts to African-American churches: "People told me that preachers in black churches in the South were telling the young people not to buy my clothes because I didn't care about them. It bothered me at first but then I realized that I know the truth and my customers know the truth and this is something that will happen to any designer that gets an urban customer."[16] These and other stories point out that Hilfiger contributes to several charities and is supportive of high-profile hip-hop artists such as Snoop Doggy Dogg. Because of the speed with which Oprah Winfrey rebutted the story and Hilfiger's own denials, the rumor's life was truncated. Yet as we finalized this manuscript, we had no trouble finding students who were familiar with it and claimed to believe it. They had either not heard the denials or were unpersuaded by them.

The Hilfiger text emerged during a period when consumer awareness of the exploitation of the fashion industry was high. Several months before the Hilfiger rumor emerged, Kathie Lee Gifford, a high-profile talk show host and owner of a signature clothing line, faced devastating headlines when it was revealed that underage seamstresses were forced to work long hours in unsafe foreign sweatshops and that even U.S. factories were using illegal practices to produce her clothing. Much of the publicity focused on the irony that Gifford ostensibly lent her name to the clothing line because she planned to give a percentage of her profits to her favorite children's charity. The press had a field day with this angle. Nike also faced unfavorable publicity when it was revealed that workers in Vietnam were subjected to cruel work conditions, even when compared to the typically brutal conditions elsewhere in Asia. Many colleges today have student-run efforts to eliminate the use of exploited foreign labor in the production of any clothing containing the school's logo or name. More than ever, consumers learned about the fashion industry's dirty laundry.

In spite of the cycles, Tommy Hilfiger's popularity shows no signs of fading. It was announced during July 1998 that Hilfiger had followed the trend of so many other fashion designers by expanding from clothing to home furnishings. Media stories have focused on the advertising campaign that includes replicas of rooms in the White House. Public appearances by the designer in malls have drawn crowds reminiscent of those that greet rock stars—or Liz Claiborne. Just as Hilfiger himself spun off from the tutelage of a more senior designer, so, too, will some talented young man or woman come along in the next few years to replace him as the hot designer. If this new designer puts a high price tag on her or his clothes, if she or he incorporates classic or patriotic emblems, if the advertising strategy is flamboyant and successful, if popular musicians embrace the threads, and if consumers continue to hear news about poor working conditions for fashion industry employees, consumers will voice their concerns through rumors similar to those that circulated about Hilfiger.

Further, many white informants professed a desire to stay away from the clothing on the grounds that the designer had embraced racist philosophies. In contrast to many of the previous cycles, there is some evidence that informants are crossing racial boundaries. Perhaps minority groups are enjoying more solidarity than in the past, and some whites are more willing to declare the alleged white supremacist enemies of minority groups their enemies as well.

The other major difference between Hilfiger and the earlier texts emerges in the mode of circulation—what we label the performance dynamics. The Tommy Hilfiger cycle stands as probably the first major Internet fashion rumor. Indeed, many reporters erroneously assumed that the text originated on the Net, but in fact it was first circulated by word of mouth. However, there is no denying that the Internet promises to have a profound effect on the distribution of contemporary legends. Hilfiger texts proliferate in cyberspace. Very quickly, this came to the attention of mainstream journalists. In the pre-Internet era, many journalists avoided reporting on racially tinged consumer texts because black informants were cagey about sharing their views with whites. However, the Internet allowed white journalists to eavesdrop on conversations among blacks. Because journalists were filing reports on the story, both Tommy Hilfiger and Oprah Winfrey made public comments denying the accusation within weeks after the cycles first achieved currency in cyberspace. Just as the rumor itself circulated widely on the Internet, the rebuttals were aired there also. In the earlier fashion cycles, such as those associated with Liz Claiborne or Troop, texts lingered for many months or even years before company officials made public comments. And when denials were issued, those statements were not widely circulated. The Internet permits rumors to spread more rapidly but simultaneously to collapse quickly as a community of users helps reinforce the denials. Yet even those who hear the denials and claim to believe the clarifications often stay away from the clothing. Repeatedly we hear comments like "Better to be safe than sorry" or "There must be something to it." To disbelieve a rumor in one's mind does not mean that one's actions will follow.

PURCHASES 'R' US

By now a few themes are evident in the examination of the racial basis of mercantile legends. These legends—as Topsy/Eva narratives—reveal blacks condemning corporations for their racial maliciousness, while whites hold that the evil goals of the corporation are linked to political extremism or religious cultism, not racial concerns.

For black consumers, the Ku Klux Klan emerges in most corporate Topsy cycles as their consummate enemy. Given the white supremacist organization's long history of antiblack violence and its attempts to magnify their numbers through the mass media, it should not be surprising that the group triggers deep fears on the part of African Americans, despite beliefs among many whites that the organization is marginal and nearly moribund.[17] We cannot be certain where the Klan will appear next in popular belief, but we can be certain that it will rise again. The media play a significant role in the narrations of many informants, although the preferred media have changed. Today television talk shows are most frequently cited as proof. Discussions of satanic ritual abuse and white supremacist activity abound on all the talk shows; one could imagine that villainous corporate guests might appear as well. A few decades ago, informants verified their commentary by saying, "I know its true, I read it in the paper." With the growth and popularity of the television talk show, newspapers have faded as a means of confirmation. By the time of the rumor linking Procter and Gamble to Satanism in the late 1970s and early 1980s, many individuals claimed that the company's CEO announced that fact on *Phil Donahue* or *60 Minutes*.[18] During that rumor's heyday, Phil Donahue's program was the only major nationally televised talk show. CBS's *60 Minutes* has been a popular newsmagazine since the late 1960s. By the time that Turner began collecting the rumor about Church's Fried Chicken and the Klan in the mid-1980s, the *Oprah Winfrey Show* was frequently named, particularly by black viewers. In the Liz Claiborne cycles, white informants usually named Donahue, a white host, and African-American informants usually named Winfrey, emphasizing the linkage between race and audience.

By the mid-1990s these sources were beginning to change as the Internet became more prominent in the lives of many upscale Americans. The Internet has become America's rumor bazaar. Increasingly consumers do not need to claim that they heard a rumor from television talk shows; they can announce that "it was on the Internet." How this will affect the credibility of sources remains to be seen, since Internet information is increasingly considered suspect, but, as always, a compelling story outweighs its source.

Ultimately these rumors suggest the power of corporations and the relative impotence of consumers. It is striking that in many versions the alleged Klan member or cultist proudly announces his or her misdeeds to a "black" or "Christian" audience—and gets away with it. According to the rumors, Liz Claiborne can reveal her scorn for black women and continue to profit, even if they boycott the product. The CEO of Procter and Gamble supposedly can say that he is a Satanist and that there are not enough Christians left to make a difference, and he is proven right by the continuing strength of his company. Even if we speculate that these rumors suggest on some level that consumers are angry and suspicious, they also suggest consumers' lack of political or economic power.

In a world in which race matters, even seemingly race-neutral, rational, bureaucratic corporations have been tarred with having a hidden agenda. It may be healthy to mistrust those who control so much of our lives, but when that mistrust implies a personal fear from agents of terror, it is time to rethink the basis on which citizens hold such beliefs and accept rumors that claim to provide the evidence.

FOUR

The Enemy
in Washington

Despite the rhetoric condemning drug use, the American
government, through the Central Intelligence Agency, has
engaged in a systematic program to import drugs—cocaine and
heroin—into African-American communities. The government has decided that such a policy would serve to keep black
communities politically weak and would simultaneously
provide secret funds for funding aggression around the globe.

One day a young white girl comes home from her public
elementary school and asks her father, after informing him
that they have been studying inventors, "Why haven't white
people invented anything?"

According to these and other rumors and legends, federal, state, and
local governments often pursue ill-conceived agendas. Whether it be
the Central Intelligence Agency or a local water district, governmental
bureaucracies are up to no good. Blacks have told us that malicious
whites control the government, and whites believe that those in power
place the interests of other races ahead of them. Even when race is not
an issue, both blacks and whites fret about those who are supposed to
be their representatives and their public servants.

During the mid-1990s, major media stories included reports of government malfeasance, corruption, and conspiracy. Within hours of the crash of TWA Flight 800 into Long Island Sound in 1996, accounts of strange lights and ominous missiles appearing in the summer skies moments before the catastrophic explosion were being reported by ostensibly reliable eyewitnesses. By the end of the first week of the ultimately fruitless investigation, compelling narratives that claimed the government was covering up the real cause had proliferated. Respected politicians took these charges seriously. Representatives of the agencies charged with investigating the cause of the crash were barraged by probing questions and hostile accusations that implied that the inquiry was yet another government cover-up.

The navy, the Federal Aviation Administration, and FBI were not the only government agencies to stand accused. Following a series of explosive claims first reported in the *San Jose Mercury News*, representatives of the CIA were fielding belligerent questions about its alleged role in illegal drug trafficking. According to an intensive investigation by reporter Gary Webb, overly zealous individuals on the CIA payroll in the 1980s had funded their support for the Contra war with profits made from the sale of crack cocaine to a notorious black drug dealer known as Freeway Ricky Ross.

Other stories about governmental misbehavior—some old and some new—circulated during this turbulent period. Allegations persisted that the official explanations for the deaths of John F. Kennedy and Martin Luther King Jr. were false. Rumors suggested a government conspiracy in the bombings of the Oklahoma City Federal Building and the Olympic Park in Atlanta. Disturbing stories alleged that the death of former secretary of commerce Ron Brown was the result of an antiblack conspiracy or part of a cover-up related to the Whitewater scandal and not an unfortunate, unavoidable plane crash.

Those who report these rumors frequently identify "the government" or one particular agency as the evil perpetrator. Of course, the government and its agencies wield no concrete power per se but only act through individuals. The government's integrity is only as solid as its employees. Indeed, if there is one belief that unites blacks and whites, it is that the government in Washington is not to be trusted. Mistrust of government is long-standing and endemic, and sometimes it is deserved. While Americans remain "patriotic," this patriotism is often mixed with cynicism and a sense of betrayal.

One challenge in unraveling governmental rumors stems from the undeniable reality that some public servants, presidents and postal clerks included, have shamefully exploited the power of their positions. Each government employee caught abusing his or her position undermines the reputations of all public sector workers. Perceptions about the use or abuse of political power undergird most rumors and legends in which the government is named.

For rumor scholars, the size and complexity of the government make it nearly impossible to isolate accurate evidence. We cannot prove that Flight 800 was not felled by friendly fire. We cannot demonstrate that no agency or government employee was ever involved in the circulation of drugs in black communities. We cannot pinpoint anyone other than James Earl Ray as involved in the death of Martin Luther King Jr. What we can do is compare contemporary rumors with past ones, point to those patterns that emerge most frequently, and call attention to the kinds of governmental conduct that most antagonize citizens, generating mistrust, suspicion, and anger.

Even though blacks and whites agree on the corruption and maliciousness of government, it is striking that blacks often see government as favoring whites, and whites feel precisely the reverse.[1] One finds echoes of the Topsy/Eva effect. Many within the black community believe that the government of the United States is racist and, in extreme versions, genocidal. Perhaps surprisingly, African Americans also believe that government is remarkably competent, able to engage in genocidal plots and assassinations of domestic leaders *without getting caught*. If only it could do everything as well as it kills blacks and imports drugs. While the seriousness with which these views are held varies, many people find such claims plausible. The fears of most whites toward their government are not as dramatic—after all, the large majority of elected and appointed officials are white. Still, there is the tightly held belief that the government consists of bureaucrats and "liberal activists" who promote the interests of minorities, or at least do little to stop the welfare fraud and criminal behavior that are seen as endemic. Our goal in this chapter is to explore how these oddly matching yet incompatible beliefs have developed.

WELFARE AS WE KNOW IT

In the spring of 1997, the World Wide Web homepage for the Invisible Empire of the Ku Klux Klan implored its readers to "end the invisible agenda to destroy the white race." The implicit assumption behind this injunction suggests that the U.S. government is inclined to implement the agenda of the supposed enemies of the white race. Learning of racist rumors, many whites assume that such texts are restricted to the KKK and similar polemical white supremacist organizations. But while white supremacists articulate the most outrageous doctrines, less politically extreme whites often find ways to justify their belief in softer versions.

Some white citizens feel that the government has constructed a web of secrecy, prompted by diverse pressure groups, that treats "normal" citizens unfairly. This belief is exemplified through rumors that suggest that government officials, through misguided affirmative action policies and quotas, give blacks special treatment; rumors that suggest that blacks are cheating the welfare system and that government officials are unwilling to stop this fraud; and rumors about incompetent black governmental workers. The themes inherent in these rumors could hardly be more different than the rumors in the African-American community, yet some commonalties in hostility toward the government exist. One wonders whether the material that is collected from explicitly racialist organizations (such as the Ku Klux Klan) represents only their vision of America or whether it stands for the private beliefs of many others.

Further, one finds rumors and legends about federal agencies (for example, the post office) that are believed to be largely black, although the rumors themselves do not deal explicitly with race. In these cases the rumors, seemingly race-neutral, are a surrogate for racial talk.

AFFIRMATIVE ACTION

Although the Supreme Court's 1978 decision in *Regents of the University of California v. Bakke* began the erosion of affirmative action policies in the United States, the 1990s will probably be remembered as the decade in which affirmative action was most dramatically under attack. We are not the first observers to suggest that it was the emergence and eloquence of African-American anti–affirmative action writers and leaders that facilitated the dismantling of several significant affirmative action guidelines. Like *Hunger of Memory* (1981), by the Latino author Richard Rodriguez, the book *The Content of Our Character* (1990) uses author Shelby Steele's experiences to decimate affirmative action. Along with Stephen L. Carter's much more measured critique in *Reflections of an Affirmative Action Baby* (1991), these largely autobiographical books and the prominent attention they received in the popular press emboldened affirmative action foes, who saw that one could criticize affirmative action without necessarily being portrayed as racist. Yet another black spokesperson, University of California regent Ward Connerly, led the efforts to rescind affirmative action policies in the California university system and then proceeded to lead the charge in dismantling the state's affirmative action policies.

In conjunction with the attention garnered by these individuals, as well as the reverse discrimination suits files by whites who perceived themselves as victims of affirmative action, the pros and cons of affirmative action were routinely debated. Many white Americans feel that they have been wronged by this system. For each African American who receives a job or a space at a college because of affirmative action, there are dozens, perhaps hundreds, of whites who can claim that they were the one who was denied that very spot. Who knows if Allen Bakke would have gotten that last acceptance had every black applicant vanished. A single decision may cause many to feel resentment. Further, hiring, selection, and promotion choices depend on confidentiality, leading to the assumption of preferential treatment. Anything that seems even slightly unusual will raise the ire of those disposed to feel aggrieved.

As a result of this anger and a proliferation of personal experience narratives, affirmative action became a central voter concern by the mid-1980s, redounding to the benefit of the Republicans. Previously positive words such as "fairness," "equity," and "justice" became seen as code words for "antiwhite."[2] By 1984, one of ten males felt that they had lost a promotion because of affirmative action,[3] and between 1979 and 1983, the U.S. Equal Employment Opportunity Commission received more than fifteen hundred complaints from white males.[4] More than 40 percent of whites felt that the chances were very likely or somewhat likely that they or someone in their family would suffer reverse discrimination in school admissions or hiring and promotions.[5]

Critics of affirmative action claim not only that these favored individuals are unqualified (ignoring qualifications, such as seniority or parental connections, that do not relate narrowly to ability) but also that the blame resides with the decisions of a hostile government. When the dramatic reelection television commercial for Senator Jesse Helms of North Carolina against his black Democratic opponent, Mayor Harvey Gantt of Charlotte, showed a white hand crushing a rejection letter as a voice-over said, "You needed that job, and you were the best qualified. But they had to give it to a minority because of a racial quota. Is that really fair?" it ostensibly was bashing the "liberals" who had instituted the policy. In a *Newsweek* poll, only 25 percent of the white respondents (and 62 percent of the blacks) answered yes to the following question: "Should there be special consideration for [blacks] to increase their opportunities for getting into college and getting jobs or promotions?"[6] California voters passed an initiative dismantling their state's affirmative action policies in 1996, which suggested the potential for nationwide moves.

Richard Herrnstein and Charles Murray, in *The Bell Curve*, their controversial assessment of the causes and effects of intelligence, present claims of veteran police officers who allege that because of affirmative action there are "people in the [police] academy who could not read or write." A former instructor saw "people diagnosed as borderline retarded graduate from the police academy."[7] A report published in the *Los Angeles Times* claimed, "When Robert Boggs was ordered to fill 10 [State of California Health Department] clerk-typist positions with minorities and told not to worry about whether they could type, he refused and was shuffled off, after a 15-year state career, to a do-nothing job."[8] While we cannot know if these bizarre tales have a factual basis, the way that they are presented is sufficient to classify them as "rumors"—fitting into a cultural logic and involving opposition to affirmative action policies not based on merit. As one white administrator noted, "I know personally of a situation where a person, a white male, you know, WASP person, scored very high on a standardized test and there was a minority who scored very low, barely passing. . . . And because she was a minority she received a job."[9] Many whites have similar stories that make concrete the charge that blacks receive special treatment.

One cannot know from these accounts what the speakers knew and how much weight to give them, but the fact that the stories are presented as true and cannot be disputed gives them a power that a mere opinion could not have. Statements such as these are truth claims that seem entirely plausible to white audiences. These policy concerns—often not easily discussed in polite society—are bolstered by the support that apparently "true" instances give them: rumor bolsters attitudes. The case of the incompetent black is matched with sad tales about the white who lost a job, college acceptance, or promotion because of race. The theoretical is made real through a narrative, whether or not that narrative is factual.

SCHOOL COLORS

As the preceding examples illustrate, rumors about racial matters in the educational system are quite commonplace. Two rumors of the 1990s reflect conspicuous dissatisfaction with the impact of multiculturalism on the public school curriculum. Most versions specify Washington, D.C., as their locale, although other cities that boast large black populations have their own versions. In the first, liberal parents in Washington, D.C., decide—like Jimmy and Rosalyn Carter—to send their child to the predominantly black local public school. Late in the school year the child asks, "Daddy, we've been studying inventors and famous people in school. Why haven't white people invented anything or become famous?" The parents immediately withdraw the child from school and either select an elite private school or move to the suburbs.[10] In almost all versions of this text, the family is specifically identified as liberal, thus implying a sympathy with efforts to incorporate black history into public school curricula. By enrolling their child in a public school likely to have a largely African-American student body, the parents reveal themselves to be tolerant and liberal, and they suffer the consequences in the biased and ideological education of their child.

Racial concerns emerge in private school settings as well. Following the election of Bill Clinton and the much ballyhooed decision he and his wife made to send their daughter, Chelsea, to a tony private Washington school, a rumor circulated that claimed Chelsea's English class was assigned to write an essay with the title "Why I'm Ashamed to Be White." Again, the educational establishment is "revealed" to be biased against whites.

WELFARE CHEATS

Much to the consternation of his more liberal supporters, President Clinton signed a bill in 1996 that mandated sweeping changes in the welfare system and delegated much decision-making authority to the states. Although the states now have widespread power and authority over the distribution of social services support, welfare is still the arena in which whites are most likely to see blacks as "consumers" of governmental services. For many whites, welfare funding is seen as an income transfer from "us" to "them." Some even see the growth in governmental welfare programs as the true legacy of the civil rights movement.

Many whites are unable to understand why blacks cannot get off welfare, why they make it a "way of life." Never mind that this is not an accurate view. Media portrayals of welfare recipients frequently highlight abusers of the system. Individuals who turn to the system when other avenues fail are not newsworthy. Most welfare goes to whites, and most recipients, regardless of race, use welfare as a short-term solution to devastating financial problems.

Some whites and blacks think that welfare constitutes "free money." Who wouldn't like to receive income without having to engage in tedious labor. After all, this is the appeal of lotteries. Stemming from this notion is the belief that people choose welfare and that they consider themselves lucky. A lifetime of welfare is equivalent to winning at Lotto. Many people accept the stereotype of the lazy welfare recipient. To bolster this belief it is argued that some cheats have gotten rich off welfare or that some wealthy individuals receive welfare checks. The key image in many of these stories is a cheat who drives a late-model Cadillac, suggesting—even in those texts in which race is not mentioned— that the perpetrator is an African American. These beliefs connect to the image of African Americans as dishonest and lazy, as well as enjoying ostentatious luxury to which they are not entitled.

From these accusations it is assumed that some black women deliberately choose to have children to increase their welfare payments and remain on the dole. In fact, welfare recipients have lower birth rates than nonrecipients in the same age brackets. These are the women that President Ronald Reagan referred to as "welfare queens."

If one believes that numerous welfare cheats exist, as these rumors suggest, it is not surprising that many working Americans are unenthusiastic about government aid. Welfare is an easy topic for demagogues and for politicians who wish to appeal to a middle-class constituency. It assumes that recipients are fundamentally dissimilar from the rest of the population. The dishonest recipient simultaneously "proves" that welfare is not really necessary and that recipients are not "us."

Similar themes are evident in attitudes toward the overuse of emergency medical services, which penalizes "honest" citizens. According to a woman who is quoted in Studs Terkel's book *Race:* "I was in the hospital emergency room one Sunday. They were going in there with sniffles that I would have . . . gone to a regular doctor. . . . These were not babies. These were thirty-, thirty-five-year-old men and women, who could have taken an aspirin."[11] Although the speaker claims at first that "it has nothing to do with race," she admits that these incidents are "where some of the racist feelings come into it."

The distaste for welfare recipients goes beyond attacking their greed, often focusing on their stupidity. As folklorist Jan Harold Brunvand describes in his collection of contemporary legends, *Curses! Broiled Again!*, many stories portray those who apply for welfare as fools. Lists of "hilarious" language slips circulate through Xerox and Internet lore. As one welfare recipient is reported as writing, "I am very annoyed to find that you brand my son illiterate. This is a dirty lie, as I was married a week before he was born."[12] Although these texts do not specifically mention race, it is easy to imagine that the welfare client—ignorant and immoral—might readily be seen as black.

This point becomes more salient by the claim that the government distributes money to those who merely request it. From this perspective, the government is in the business of finding welfare recipients, a belief that is bolstered by the public service advertising to ensure that citizens are aware of those benefits to which they have a legal right. One example of this theme, not strictly speaking a rumor, is the parody "Government Poverty Application" that Alan Dundes and Carl Pagter, students of

Xerox lore, discovered circulating in a Social Security Office in Glendale, California, as early as 1966:

GOVERNMENT POVERTY APPLICATION

The "Shorts" Form No. 1039A

Dear Citizen:

This form is being provided for your use if you have reason to feel that you can qualify for a Government Poverty Grant. May we ask that you carefully study the important questions on this sheet and answer them to the best of your ability. If it can be determined that you qualify as a "Povert," then a Government representative will call on you to determine how much money you need.

1. Do you eat as well as your neighbors? Yes ( ) No ( )

2. Do you know of other people who have more than you? Yes ( ) No ( )

3. Do you need more money to spend? Yes ( ) No ( )

4. Do you find it tough to pay your bills? Yes ( ) No ( )

5. Do you know of any reason why you should not qualify for a poverty grant? Yes ( ) No ( )

Please sign (or place your "X") in space below.

Name _____

(only one per applicant)

In order to assist you with the above questions and to help you qualify for a poverty grant, we submit the following suggestions:

The answer to question #1 should be "No";

The answer to question #2 should be "Yes";

The answer to question #3 should be "Yes";

The answer to question #4 should be "Yes";

The answer to question #5 should be "No."

BONUS OFFER: Do you know of three friends whom you think can qualify for a poverty grant? If so, please send their names and when these people qualify, we will send you another $1,000 POVERTY BONUS.

POVERTY MEANS PROSPERITY

Mail your application to the Bureau of Public Health Education and Welfare (PHEW)! BE SOMEBODY! BE A POVERT![13]

The government conspires with its clients ("poverts") to defraud the honest taxpayer. Since both welfare officers and welfare recipients are believed to be African-American, the racial dimensions of such beliefs are evident. Expanding the pool of recipients represents a bonus for each, and a blow to the hardworking (white) taxpayer. The us-them boundary separating honest citizens from their government is underlined.

BUREAUCRATIC INCOMPETENCE

Bureaucrats, incompetent clerical workers, and those who do not care enough to do their jobs properly are today's bogeymen. There is nothing inherently racist in this frustration. Yet often, among whites, the animus toward government is linked—implicitly, with a smile and a wink—to the hiring of African Americans in the government workforce. "Everyone knows" that the reason the federal government is so ineffective is because Washington has become a black-majority city and because in the aftermath of the civil rights movement, many African Americans were hired for jobs for which they are unqualified and in which they have little interest. This is made dramatically evident in a widely known riddle-joke:

Q. What is the largest shoe store in the world?
A. The post office. They have a hundred thousand black loafers.

Some readers (perhaps even African Americans) may have heard this joke—or told it—without the adjective "black." The joke can work as humor when it is "race-neutral," yet there is a common stereotype, based on reality, that the U.S. Postal Service has hired large numbers of African Americans. In Los Angeles, 63 percent of postal workers are black, whereas blacks represent only 9.6 percent of the labor force. In Chicago, blacks, who make up only 18.2 percent of the labor pool, constitute nearly 79.7 percent of postal workers.[14] As a consequence, the Postal Service is perceived as a minority institution. The cruel joke rests upon a cultural logic. Even when race is not mentioned, the claims of postal incompetence are grounded in white images of black ability and motivation.

Many African Americans perceive the role they have played in the postal service differently. For most of this century, the U.S. Postal Service provided blacks with job opportunities unavailable to them in other branches of government. Prior to the 1960s, many blacks with college educations discovered that although other doors were closed to them, they could easily pass the civil service tests required to work at the post office. Thus, while some whites may perceive the post office as the setting for incompetent black workers, many blacks view it as an institution that benefited from decades of service performed by overqualified but grateful citizens.

Rumors and legends about incompetent bureaucrats involve those themes that also characterize black Americans in the white mind. Obviously, one must examine the particular text, looking for what folklorists speak of as "isomorphism"—that is, the substitutions that can be used and still have the text make sense. Are blacks and whites interchangeable in a text about government waste and bureaucracy? Consider the belief that a government bureaucrat composed an enormous set of regulations on a trivial matter. As one version had it: "The Lord's Prayer has 56 words, Lincoln's Gettysburg Address has 266 words, the Ten Commandments, 297; the Declaration of Independence, 300. . . . In contrast a recent U.S. government order setting the price of cabbages had 26,911 words."[15] This false claim was traced back to the 1940s.[16] Yet one could hardly imagine that the story was told with an African-American bureaucrat as the author of the memo. Writing long, pompous memos does not fit the cultural logic of racism.

More plausible in light of racial politics are charges that claim that bags of mail have been lost or hidden for decades, that it takes months for a first-class letter to travel across town, or that magazines or checks are snatched by greedy postal workers. Government employees are a diverse group, even though all may be smeared in some stories, yet certain rumors are based so directly on stereotypical images that it is difficult to miss what they say about race.

BLACK TALK

Although government is supposed to protect its citizens, many African Americans find that government actions have done the opposite. Agencies such as the FBI, the CIA, the Centers for Disease Control (CDC), and the armed forces have been perceived as engaging in conspiracies to harm or even kill African Americans. The "government" or "administration" is often said to be in hostile hands. These rumors include the belief that the FBI, in collaboration with the CDC, committed the Atlanta child murders of the late 1970s; the idea that the federal government wanted the HIV virus to spread in order to decimate third world populations or African Americans, or even that the virus was created to achieve these ends; and the belief that the federal government directly imports drugs, including crack and heroin, into minority neighborhoods to keep these communities powerless. How can change ever be possible when the powers that be conspire against it? As political scientist Andrew Hacker notes in his book *Two Nations: Black and White, Separate, Hostile, Unequal:*

> At times, the conclusion seems all but self-evident that white America
> has no desire for your presence or any need for your people. This
> is not to say that white officials are plotting the genocide of black
> America. You understand as well as anyone that politics and history
> seldom operate that way. Still, you cannot rid yourself of some
> lingering mistrust.[17]

For many whites, such fears are nonsense, concrete demonstrations that the "paranoia" of African Americans prevents them from participating in a "rational" political dialogue. Yet the history of race relations in the United States suggests that such beliefs are historically grounded. Governmental support for the institution of slavery is the most dramatic episode, but even later government action supported the Jim Crow legal system of the South, the brutality of city police, and, of course, the social control function of the lynching mob. "Official policy" supported racial violence, and many African Americans accepted what media scholar John Fiske labels "blackstream knowledge"—knowledge that rejects the conventional claims of "their" government.[18]

Perhaps the single most significant episode of an ostensibly "benign" government that gave credence to these beliefs was the Tuskegee syphilis experiment, documented by James H. Jones in his powerful book *Bad Blood: The Tuskegee Syphilis Experiment* (1981). In 1932 the Public Health Service (the forerunner of the Centers for Disease Control) initiated a study of young African-American men who had contracted syphilis. Using the hospital at the Tuskegee Institute as their base, white doctors affiliated with the Public Health Service invited hundreds of black men from the surrounding rural area to undergo a free medical examination. After identifying 399 syphilitic men (who were told that they had "bad blood"), as well as 201 syphilis-free men who served as a control group, the doctors enticed the men to participate in their study by offering them regular physicals, transportation to and from the clinics, hot meals, treatment for minor ailments, and a guaranteed burial stipend. At first there was no effective treatment for syphilis (although the men could have been warned about the dangers of spreading the disease), but even after treatment was developed, the experiment continued to track the progress of the disease without making this treatment available to the subjects. The government did not run comparable studies of syphilis on white subjects.[19]

In *I Heard It through the Grapevine,* Turner recounts contemporary rumors and legends about the government from the late 1980s and early 1990s, including rumors about the assassination of black leaders Martin Luther King and Malcolm X by government agencies. Genuinely "new" rumors that bear no resemblance to any previously known texts rarely emerge, but in some rumor cycles, concerns about individuals or issues that were not relevant previously have captured the public's attention. These texts measure shifts in perceptions of political power.

THE CDC AND THE ATLANTA CHILD MURDERS

At about the time that the African-American public was learning of the gruesome Tuskegee syphilis experiment, a series of tragedies occurred in Atlanta, Georgia, that shook all Americans, but that particularly unsettled African Americans. Over a period of a few years, some two dozen young black children in and around Atlanta were brutally murdered. Every black parent in Atlanta—and no doubt elsewhere—worried about the safety of their children.

How could such a horrible set of murders occur? Who would do such a thing? Why were only black children targeted? Why were law enforcement agencies unable to protect children? The "facts" of the case, as publicly revealed, led reasonable people to believe that the killer was a person (or an organization) who hated black children, felt that they would not be missed, and believed that he or she would not be caught.

Many found the location of the murders more than coincidental. Because Atlanta was a center of Klan activity in the 1950s (the Klan held massive cross burnings on Stone Mountain, outside the city), it seemed plausible that the Klan was involved, and some rumors suggested that claim.[20] President Carter asked the FBI to investigate the possibility that there could have been a white supremacist conspiracy, telling *Ebony* magazine: "The possibility exists that there is a conspiracy. . . . The FBI is concentrating on that with the utmost diligence and is making regular reports to me. It's hard for me to form an opinion without having actual evidence to base it on. . . . But, yes, the possibility exists that there is a conspiracy."[21] Surely President Carter must have known something. The subsequent transfer of power from the Carter administration to

Ronald Reagan may have been seen as providing a climate in which conspiracy theories would not be given high priority. Finally, in April 1981, William Webster, director of the FBI, announced that twenty-three of the murders had been "substantially solved," based on circumstantial fiber evidence, a claim that the local Atlanta investigators were reluctant to accept. A young black man was arrested, tried, and convicted.

Some African Americans, noting that the FBI found no conspiracy, linked the Klan to the FBI, as in the rumors about Martin Luther King's murder, also committed in the South. Many informants attributed the spread of the rumor that the FBI was involved to Dick Gregory, the social activist and comedian. Whether or not Gregory was the source of this rumor is less important than the fact that to many informants the rumor "rang true"; it followed the cultural logic described previously, providing plausible answers to the unresolved issues of the case. The FBI's criticizing local law enforcement personnel (many of whom were black), accusing the victims' own families, and pushing for the arrest of a black suspect on little evidence suggested to many that the bureau was following a pattern established under J. Edgar Hoover. Even the vigorous claims of innocence of the FBI rang hollow, given the bureau's history. After all, who but well-trained FBI agents could murder all those children, leaving few clues and effectively covering their tracks?

But Atlanta had another claim to fame that made government involvement in the murders particularly meaningful: it was the headquarters of the Centers for Disease Control, the renamed Public Health Service, the agency responsible for the Tuskegee experiment and an agency working with the FBI in attempting to solve the child murders. A significant proportion of the rumors attempted to link the murders to medical experimentation, often naming the CDC, sometimes in conjunction with the Klan or the FBI. Many rumors linked the murders to the need for interferon, sometimes collected by removing the child's pancreas and in other versions removed from the victim's genitals by a syringe.

The murders occurred at the time that interferon was being publicized as a possible cure for certain cancers. Even though the CDC claimed that it was not involved with interferon research, its prominence as an internationally respected scientific organization bolstered such a connection. This, coupled with its inability to aid in solving the murders and its troubled history with African Americans—in particular African-American males—made such a claim plausible. According to the rumors, black males were guinea pigs once again. The fact that interferon is naturally produced by the human body suggested the possibility of "harvesting" this lucrative cure-all from those whose worth seemed less than the value of the chemicals in their bodies.

This claim, too, was attributed to Dick Gregory, as well as to the prominent black author James Baldwin. In his book *The Evidence of Things Not Seen*, Baldwin identifies Gregory as *his* source. Baldwin states with deliberate ambiguity:

> [Gregory] suggested . . . that the key to the Terror was in the nature
> of a scientific experiment. I am being deliberately vague, but the
> nature of the experiment was based on the possibility that the tip
> of the Black male sexual organ contained a substance that might be
> used to cure cancer. . . . I tend to doubt Dick's suggestion because—
> apart from the fact that I want to doubt it—it seems such an
> untidy way of carrying on a scientific experiment. But, then, one
> is forced to realize that a scientific experiment *must* be untidy: that
> is why it is called an experiment.[22]

Clearly Baldwin finds this belief sufficiently plausible that he chooses to include it in his book.

The interferon explanation provides a credible answer to the question of why a government conspiracy would undertake these homicides at that time. If the FBI was involved, there must have been some important goal, not merely general racist attitudes. No one believes that the American government routinely engages in genocidal policies. For some it was the unique biological makeup of black children that was crucial—-

in Baldwin's version the (uncircumcised) tips of their penises.[23] As one informant recounted, "I heard it was the CIA or the government who was killing the children for experimenting with their bodies, blood, etcetera. It's been said that only black children's biology was the source of human flesh needed for these experiments." Even if there were nothing special about the biology of black males, they are still seen as "disposable," useful to serve the needs of the majority white population.

REPARATIONS: THE SEEMINGLY BENEVOLENT STATE

Similar to those corporate rumors that promise medical technology in exchange for product labels, some rumors about governmental action appear on their surface to support a benign view of the state. The government can destroy, but, because of its power, it can also provide. In the case of African Americans, a recent rumor cycle suggests—incorrectly—that the U.S. government had approved reparations for African Americans for their ancestors' years of slavery. This connects with the rumors in the slave community in the months immediately after the Civil War that the government would provide them with property taken from white plantation owners.[24] After all, the government had just fought a bloody and divisive war against their enslavers; why would the victorious side not punish its enemies? Most wars result in the land of the losers being distributed among the victors. In many versions of this rumor, this disbursement of land was set for January 1, 1866, the third anniversary of Abraham Lincoln's Emancipation Proclamation.

For many blacks the news that the government had finally acceded to their demands for reparations surely seemed to be good news, even though it also must have appeared rather surprising, given the hostility of many white legislators to the idea. Oppressed peoples may trust in the beneficence of the ruler, believing that desirable policies adopted by the ruler were not carried out because of the unfaithfulness of underlings—what historians label "naive monarchism."

Although that belief proved false, more than a century later, in the fall of 1994, a belief spread among some southern California blacks that they could take an income tax deduction of $43,209 (note the precise dollar figure) for reparations for their ancestors' enslavement and subsequent discrimination. This was a modern equivalent of "forty acres and a mule." The Internal Revenue Service was reported as receiving (and rejecting) twenty thousand reparation deductions.[25] The belief was so potent that in the summer of 1997, President Clinton assured voters that his comments about an apology for slavery would not be coupled with the granting of reparations.

Significantly, folklorist Jan Brunvand reported that a similar rumor had spread in the 1980s during the pro-military Reagan-Bush years.[26] This text claims that Congress had passed a bill granting World War II veterans a dividend of sixty-five cents per $10,000 of their veteran's insurance for each month of their active duty. The catch was that the dividend could not be paid unless requested. The Veterans Administration labeled the report as a hoax, but it clearly paralleled the story about black reparations. These rumors reflect underlying beliefs about the government's awareness of past injustices. In order to believe that the government was willing to distribute funds to veterans or to the descendants of slaves, one must believe that the government knew that these groups had been insufficiently compensated. Frustration with the extraordinary quantities of paperwork that accompany even the simplest transactions with the government materializes in these beliefs. While providing compensation, the government takes advantage of its ability to obfuscate. It acknowledges wrongdoing but then uses its ability to complicate applications in an attempt to minimize the number of people who are willing to go through the requisite procedures.

The reparations rumor cycle must be addressed in light of the fact that Congress passed a property redistribution act in 1866 that was vetoed by President Andrew Johnson. Since then, calls for compensation for slavery have been made by many African-American leaders, including Dr. Martin Luther King Jr., Whitney Young, Jesse Jackson, and Louis Farrakhan.[27] The federal government has compensated the families of Japanese Americans interned during World War II and some Native Americans whose land was improperly taken. Each of these acts sets a precedent.

THE PLAN

The death of Secretary of Commerce Ron Brown, an African American, on April 3, 1996, fueled numerous rumors alleging that the plane crash that killed him in Croatia was not an accident. Even before his funeral, African-American informants speculated that the charismatic Brown was the latest victim of "the Plan." For those who subscribe to it, the Plan refers to a secret governmental mandate to eliminate African Americans from positions of power. Older informants often name Adam Clayton Powell Jr., congressman from Harlem, as one of the first victims of the Plan. Because of misuse of government travel funds, Powell was expelled from Congress by his colleagues. Although evidence of wrongdoing was compelling, Powell's loyal constituents in New York and legions of supporters elsewhere argued that his transgressions were no worse than those of other elected representatives. Other politicians had sinned in worse ways but had not been expelled. Because Powell was black, unstinting in his efforts to eliminate racial discrimination, and willing to use his congressional platform to support demands from the streets and pulpits of African-American communities in the 1960s, his behavior was scrutinized; when it came up short, he was removed from office. Pleased by their success in ousting the flamboyant black politician, white elites decided to discredit as many black leaders as possible, or so the Plan suggested.

Informants too young to remember the Powell incident of the mid-1960s often refer to the troubling case of Marion Barry, mayor of Washington, D.C., in the 1990s. Barry's majority black electorate endorsed him almost as enthusiastically and unconditionally as had Powell's. Many of Barry's constituents dismissed his well-known sins, but federal law enforcement officials were less tolerant of having a crack-smoking womanizer running the nation's capital. Through a well-publicized sting operation, the FBI garnered sufficient videotaped evidence for Barry to be convicted on drug charges. Enough of Barry's Washington constituents were so appalled by how he was manipulated by the law enforcement community that they returned him to his mayoral duties in the first election after his release from prison.

Like many prominent African Americans, Ron Brown claimed numerous firsts in his list of accomplishments. As chair of the Democratic National Committee, he was the first black leader to head a major party's national committee. Although he was not the first African American to be appointed to a presidential cabinet, he was one of the few blacks picked during Bill Clinton's first term to escape harsh and debilitating criticism from conservative opponents. Although at the time of his death he was under investigation for financial misconduct, his original nomination was not as contentious as those of other black Clinton insiders such as Lani Guinier, Jocelyn Elders, Henry Foster, and Alexis Herman. Those who find the Brown rumors credible often refer to the hostility faced by these other African Americans who were nominated for high office.

Rumors questioning the official investigation of Brown's death also materialized in circles dominated by whites. According to these accounts, quite popular on the Internet and on talk radio, Brown, like White House lawyer and Clinton crony Vincent Foster, was killed by diabolical liberals determined to protect the unscrupulous president and his wife from unfavorable revelations about their personal investments and campaign financing strategies.

For both blacks and whites, the circumstances surrounding Ron Brown's death were ripe for rumormongering. Many Americans find it difficult to accept that inclement weather and/or mechanical troubles can cause an American-made aircraft to crash. Because Brown's accident occurred in Croatia, dangerous terrain to most Americans, rumor believers find it plausible that saboteurs could have undermined the airplane's structural integrity while successfully maintaining the guise of an accident. The fact that Brown, like many Clinton associates, was being investigated for improper financial conduct also contributes to the evidence. Many journalists and media pundits expected that Brown would keep his high-powered position in spite of the pending inquiry. Believers reason that since insufficient evidence would be found to disgrace Brown, another route to destroy a powerful African-American man was needed.

For African Americans, Ron Brown's position as secretary of commerce was a significant achievement for a black man. Brown's international trips in the company of major corporate leaders were well publicized, and he was credited with success in his dealings with powerful multinational corporations. Here was an African-American man entrusted with major economic responsibilities likely to impact the direction of the nation's financial policies, not just the domains of education or welfare.

Finally, Clinton's own behavior following the funeral services for Brown puzzled and dismayed African Americans. Walking away from the ceremonies, Clinton was "caught" on camera laughing and chuckling. Realizing the inappropriateness of his jovial posture, Clinton conspicuously altered his demeanor so as to appear more bereaved.

For these reasons the April 3, 1996, incident invited speculation. In addition, the puzzling and still-inexplicable approach taken to investigate the crash added fuel to the fire; indeed, many individuals who normally might not have questioned the tragic accident were inclined to do so because the investigation was so haphazard. The fact that many details of the crash as first reported had to be corrected was also worrisome to many. For example, the initial news reports laid much of the blame for the crash on the weather. As Christopher Ruddy, the journalist who has done the most extensive research on this incident, notes, *Newsweek* reported that it was "the worst storm in ten years." *Time* reported that "the worst storm in a decade was raging." Even Hillary Clinton wrote in her weekly column that the plane crashed "in a violent rainstorm."[28]

However, word soon emerged that the weather really was not as inclement as these first reports indicated.

According to the writer for *Flying* magazine charged with scrutinizing the aeronautical aspects of the crash,

> The weather at Dubrovnik at the time of the accident was 400
> broken [more than 50 percent cloudy], 2,000 overcast with five miles
> visibility in light rain. The surface wind was 120 degrees at 12 knots—
> right down the runway. Upper winds were probably stronger and
> more southerly. Soundings were not available for Dubrovnik,
> but Brindisi, Italy, about 185 nm to the south, reported 160 at 25
> knots at 3,000 feet and 170 at 24 knots at 5,000 feet.[29]

These are not considered particularly hazardous flying or landing conditions, and most of us who travel somewhat regularly on commercial aircraft have probably experienced much worse. The fact that *Time*, *Newsweek*, and the First Lady all employed hyperbolic language in their descriptions of the weather contributed to the plausibility of a cover-up.

Two additional deaths following the accident further contributed to the distrust of the official story. One flight attendant survived the crash. According to witnesses, Air Force Technical Sergeant Shelley Kelly's injuries were not life-threatening when she was loaded into a helicopter and transported to the hospital. She died en route. Three days later Niko Junic, the airport maintenance chief, died by supposedly self-inflicted gunshot wounds. A failed romance allegedly drove him to commit suicide before he could be interviewed about the accident.

If African Americans immediately assumed that the accident was staged even when few details had been released, the official response assumed accidental reasons for the crash, even prior to learning of details. Before investigators arrived on the scene, the White House had dismissed the possibility of a hostile attack. As one informant pointed out, Croatia and the Balkans had long been in the news as the site of armed conflict. The conviction that the plane crash could not have been connected to the Bosnian conflict seemed untenable. Assuming that the crash of a U.S. Air Force plane is an accident is also contrary to protocol, which normally dictates a two-tier investigation. For this flight, only the second tier was performed. The first tier, known as the safety board, is conducted in secret. Its goal is to determine the cause of the crash, and it is nonpunitive, meaning that parties who may have made a mistake that caused a crash are more likely to acknowledge their error. Following the safety board, the accident/legal investigation determines where the legal blame for a crash can be assigned. According to an air force spokesman, the safety board was skipped because of its secret component and the apparent fear that this component would only fuel mistrust.

Most conspiracy theories point to the mysterious disappearance of crucial evidence. In the crash of Ron Brown's plane, the missing evidence is X rays of the late secretary's corpse that might confirm or deny allegations by air force pathologists that a hole of the shape usually associated with bullet injuries was noted in the very top of Brown's head. Apparently fifteen X rays that were taken of Brown's head disappeared from the official file. This "discovery" was made by the photographer who took the photos in the first place, who recalls pointing out to staff in the pathologists' quarters that Brown's head showed evidence of a gunshot wound and what is called a lead snowstorm. Those who subscribe to the theory that Brown was murdered combine the fact of the missing X rays with the fact that no autopsy was performed on his corpse.

We could devote this entire chapter to the Ron Brown incident. Both those who believe and those who disbelieve the conspiracy theory have amassed a body of compelling evidence. Was Ron Brown murdered? We cannot say. For our purposes, we want to highlight two points. First, the speed with which the rumors spread before actual evidence emerged indicated that this episode was ripe for speculation. Second, some conspiratorial claims are correct, and others are not. Perhaps definitive evidence will someday confirm in which category the Ron Brown story falls, but we doubt it.

COMMUNITY DESTRUCTION

Many of those who accept racial conspiracy rumors claim that the ultimate goal of the conspirators is to prevent blacks from gaining access to the corridors of power. One way this can be accomplished is by inhibiting political, social, cultural, and economic mobility. Probably no rumors are more widely known among African Americans than those that link the proliferation of illegal drugs in predominantly black neighborhoods with policies of governmental hostility or, in more moderate versions, calculated indifference. Illegal drug use continues to plague African-American families, and many blacks maintain that it could be alleviated if the government truly wanted to curtail it. (Whites typically see drug use as a matter of individual will and self-control.)

By the late 1980s, Turner began to hear rumors from her African-American informants that the United States government was heavily involved in importing drugs into their communities. Perhaps no other racial rumor was as widely known. According to a *New York Times*/CBS News poll of New York residents, one-quarter of the black sample agreed with the statement that "the Government deliberately makes sure that drugs are easily available in poor black neighborhoods in order to harm black people." Perhaps more striking was the 35 percent who claimed that it "might possibly be true." Only one-third of the sample claimed that it was "almost certainly not true."[30]

Versions of this rumor collected recently are worth exploring for several reasons. The fact that so many informants continue to find these allegations plausible, despite continued denial by a Democratic administration that emphasizes its racial compassion, is compelling. Also, highly contested information about governmental involvement in the circulation of illegal drugs has recently garnered a great deal of media attention.

At least since the 1960s, when heroin addiction escalated precipitously in many black neighborhoods, some African Americans have attributed the omnipresence of the narcotic to governmental efforts to halt black progress. Heroin's popularity has escalated and declined cyclically in the past forty years, but in spite of a wealth of information about the negative effects of drug use, new and more potent strains of dangerous drugs continue to seduce young people. In looking for a cause for the human destruction generated by drugs, many speculate that the same government forces that were once officially empowered to restrict black freedom now forge chemical shackles.

Many versions of these rumors circulate. Listed here is a range of responses to the instruction "Briefly describe any theories you may have heard linking drug abuse among blacks to a white conspiracy or plot." We also asked the follow-up question "Do you subscribe to any of the conspiracy theories or know anyone who does?" The following selections were collected at the end of 1996 and the beginning of 1997.

Text No. 1. Female African American in her early twenties:
The U.S. government "allows" drugs to come in and floods the black community with drugs in order to keep them subdued, and from organizing. . . . I partially subscribe, in that there does not seem to be a lot of action (in my experience) to stop the use of drugs in the black community; it is only a problem in the white community.

Text No. 2. Middle-class African-American woman in her midforties:
[I] have read media articles and viewed media clips indicating there was a conspiracy perpetrated by the FBI and other government agencies and individuals to dump drugs in the black community. For long-term dependency creating long-term dollars for the white man who, of course, owned the means by which these drugs made their trek to this country and ultimately to black communities. . . . I tend to believe there is some validity to the theory because in order for the drugs to make it to black communities there would have to be government cooperation and big business, with white-controlled money.

Text No. 3. African-American female in her early twenties:
I heard that during the Bush administration that American planes

shipped cocaine and heroin into the United States and George Bush knew it. . . . No because it didn't seem plausible to me, but the person who told me said his uncle said it was true.

Text No. 4. Twenty-year-old African-American male:

I've been told by my father that all of the politicians and government officials who advertise and promote drug education programs to eliminate drug use are hypocrites because they know the government and other big industries ship the chemical products down to Central America, where the basic elements of the drug [are] grown, to have it processed there to be transferred back to the U.S. in hidden cargo. The drugs are purposely introduced to predominantly black neighborhoods across the nation, e.g., crack in '82. The conspiracy was to eliminate or prevent blacks from prospering. . . . Yes, I do. My father, his friends [believe] because of past conspiracies revealed—Tuskegee experiment and annihilation of Black Panthers.

Text No. 5. White forty-nine-year-old female:

[I heard] that the CIA in an attempt to raise money for support of illegal movement with the Contras in Latin America is selling crack cocaine in major urban U.S. cities to blacks. Therefore this conspiracy will do away with blacks and raise money at the same time. Further, the placement of this information on the Internet got it out to the public and could not be covered up. . . . It does not surprise [me] if this information is correct given my disregard for the CIA.

These five texts, selected from a collection of over a hundred, reflect most central themes. Virtually all African-American informants had heard and could repeat a rumor. As the fifth version indicates, whites are also familiar with the text.

Referring only to a "white conspiracy or plot," the original query lacks any link to a specific source of the conspiracy. Three of these five informants mention the government specifically, and the fifth pinpoints the first Bush administration. In addition to Bush, other informants interviewed attributed the animosity to former President Reagan and also to President Clinton. One informant specified J. Edgar Hoover as being responsible for the introduction of crack cocaine in the early 1980s. In earlier research on this query, numerous informants laid the blame on the former FBI director. Since Hoover died years before the crack epidemic, we can surmise just how much power his image exerts over some African Americans.

The nation's two premier law enforcement agencies are specifically mentioned frequently. As the second text indicates, many informants specify a particular law enforcement agency and indicate that additional entities might also be involved. The CIA is mentioned twice as often as any other agency. Occasionally informants mention the army or just "whites" as being the instigators of the conspiracy.

Although many informants identify "drugs" as the unwanted contraband, cocaine and heroin are the substances to which they refer. Indigenous to South America and Asia, respectively, the raw material must be imported illegally into the United States. Once hooked on these drugs, many individuals resort to criminal activity to support their habit. Attending school or working for a living is sacrificed by those trapped in the drug culture.

Informants ascribe two fundamental motivations to the government officials who pave the way for drug dealers. As the first text suggests, many informants believe that the goal of the conspiracy is to inhibit black accomplishments. By encouraging addiction, the government discourages political, social, and economic progress. The reference to organizing in the first text suggests that the government is particularly eager to inhibit black political activism. To substantiate this accusation, many informants cite the extreme and illegal lengths to which the FBI went to squash the Black Panther Party. Shortly before these versions were collected, the Mario Van Peebles film *Panther* was released, and many informants reported being persuaded by the film's reference to an FBI decision to link its anti-Panther plan with one to promote drug use. Making money is the second motive. To some, selling drugs to blacks enriches ruthless white entrepreneurs. Other informants maintain that inner-city drug sales finance political policies that are supported by conservatives.

Informants offer various reasons for believing these rumors. Although most blacks have heard of the rumors, many, such as the third informant, dismiss their validity. Other informants who find the claims credible justify their belief with references to documented examples of governmental callousness toward black well-being. The fourth informant refers both to the FBI's campaign to destroy the Black Panthers and to the Tuskegee experiment as evidence that the government is willing to harm blacks. Other informants argue that African Americans lack the tools for large-scale drug importation, noting that they are unlikely to control the airplanes and ships necessary for transporting drugs. Drug users are merely pawns in this scheme. Individuals such as the first informant believe that if law enforcement agencies truly wanted to eliminate the drugs, they could. Many African Americans agree with her contention that drug interdiction efforts are more common in white-dominated communities.

These examples were collected after the publication of the "Dark Alliance" series in the *San Jose Mercury News*, beginning in August 1996. In these articles Gary Webb, a respected investigative journalist, chronicled a connection between the initial appearance of crack cocaine in the South Central area of Los Angeles and individuals with strong ties to the CIA's efforts to sabotage the socialist government of Nicaragua. Webb's sensational story and the newspaper's decision to make the installments available on its Web site created a maelstrom in the print and broadcast media, as well as complaints from the agencies accused in the story. African-American elected leaders, the most vocal of whom was Congresswoman Maxine Waters, who represents the South Central neighborhood of Los Angeles into which the crack cocaine was supposedly funneled, demanded a thorough investigation.

The story remained prominent during the fall and winter. The Dark Alliance Web site received an unprecedented number of "hits," and other media outlets were forced to report the accusations. Waters's South Central constituents and African Americans throughout the nation were unimpressed by official denials. Many were doubtful that an internal investigation would ever uncover any serious wrongdoing.

In May 1997, the editor of the *San Jose Mercury News* issued a statement in which he backed away from some of the claims made in the original series. Acknowledging his responsibility for the story's content, he reviewed claims that he believed were insufficiently substantiated. Many referred to this editorial as the newspaper's retraction or mea culpa. Gary Webb, author of the original series, vehemently disagreed with the decision to issue the editorial. He stands by his story as it was originally reported.

Webb's Dark Alliance series and the extensive press it received for almost a year introduced many white Americans to a different way of understanding black views on illegal drug traffic. Leaders such as Maxine Waters and celebrities such as the popular black talk radio host Joe Madison used Webb's series to justify their demands that the law enforcement and intelligence communities disclose their activities. For many African Americans, the series provided a plausible paper trail that verified information they already "knew."

Webb sticks by his report, and others who have examined parts of the record suggest that individuals with at least partial CIA support may have had some role in the movement of cocaine from South America to South Central Los Angeles.[31] Perhaps the government did not have an ongoing organized plot to supply drugs to gullible young African Americans to destroy their potential for moving out of the ghetto, but perhaps the government looked the other way.

Many African-American young adults have witnessed firsthand the destruction that crack cocaine has caused. Turner's third informant indicates that he heard this text from his father; like many other informants, he reports that he was persuaded that by smoking crack, he would succumb to the desires of an oppressive white government. This warning had the effect of preventing drug experimentation. The government serves, in effect, as an old-fashioned bogeyman in warning children away from deviance.

In discussing corporate rumors, many informants claim that a corporation's refusal to discredit a rumor increases their belief in the rumor's veracity. The same rationale emerges in texts about drug proliferation. Informants wonder why the CIA and other agencies would not want to do all in their power to discredit the rumors, if they had no factual basis. Even if the Dark Alliance series is inaccurate, law enforcement agencies and politicians can no longer claim that they are unaware of African-American concerns. It is unlikely that the government could ever prove to hard-core conspiracy theorists that it was not engaged in a plot to undermine the black community, but many informants would welcome a successful war on drugs.

For some the widespread existence of this belief—defined as a paranoid fantasy—represents the fundamental problem. Rather than examining how they can better themselves, many blacks see themselves as helpless. As one black man currently imprisoned for selling drugs reports, perhaps with some self-interest:

> What, then, is irrational about our fears? And if there is no proof
> that a conspiracy exists to destroy the black assertive-minded
> male, what proof is there to say none exists? Certainly it would be
> irresponsible to equate *all* of the social ills that face blacks as part
> of a gigantic conspiracy to destroy us. But it would be equally
> irresponsible to deny such a conspiracy does not exist. Motive,
> means, and opportunity are usually the elements that must be
> overcome to either prove that a crime either existed or was committed.
> These elements can be established in the case of a conspiracy to
> destroy "undesirables," specifically the black male. Drugs are but
> a small means in this madness. While we—blacks—may have
> the power to "just say no["] to this menace, we are powerless to say
> anything about the unseen . . . the unseen power structure behind
> it all.

African-American social critic Shelby Steele makes this point:

If you actually believe that the society in which you live is feeding AIDS and drugs to you, to eliminate you, you're not going to see your own possibilities in that society. . . . You're not going to make the effort to move into the American mainstream. It's a profoundly destructive belief.[32]

Destructive it may be, but it does serve to deflect blame from one's own community and to explain how these drugs enter the community.

CONCLUSION

The rumors described in this chapter paint a dispiriting picture. For a government to function properly and *morally*, it should be an honest broker among its citizens. Even when it is not fair, at least some measure of consensus should exist on the way in which it is unfair. Surely blacks and whites could agree on who benefited at whose expense, yet this is not how social psychological processes operate. Opposing groups can easily feel aggrieved. Both blacks and whites feel that their government—a democratic government—is not upholding basic principles of justice and equality.

Again, the model of the folklore diamond, as described in chapter 2, helps to explain the content of these governmental rumors. The social and political structure helps to provide the grounding for these beliefs. The reality of the way that blacks and whites confront the government connects to individual predispositions to believe and also to the dynamics of performance. The experiences of individuals with governmental institutions—such as the frequent interactions with the police among blacks or with bureaucrats, especially at the post office and the Internal Revenue Service for whites—set expectations among individuals. The common concerns of citizens lead rumors about government misdeeds to be particularly potent in appealing to audiences. These individual and social factors, in turn, affect what claims about the government will appear to be plausible and memorable.

While individual rumors are unique to a particular racial group, the rumors together represent a large-scale version of the Topsy/Eva cycle. Similar concerns with the equitable use and distribution of resources are found in both sets of texts. While whites do not have the same level of palpable fear—unless they are extremely paranoid, they do not believe that the government is plotting to use the bodies of their children for medical research—the anger and frustration among many beleaguered taxpayers is near the surface.

How can the government *seem* to be fair? The problem of racial bias often involves appearance and is not necessarily a problem of reality. Even if the government were nondiscriminatory, that would not necessarily eliminate rumors of bias. In fact, there may be actual racial bias, which may benefit one group in one arena, and another group in a different arena. There is not even agreement on what constitutes racial bias: whites believe that racial targets are morally wrong, while blacks feel that, without such targets, government will inevitably be unfair. A color-blind government, while perhaps desirable in theory, is impossible in the world in which we live.

Blacks and whites must confront the proper role of government in distributing resources and must consider the controls necessary to prevent governmental malfeasance. To the extent that a general climate of trust can be established, the suspicion of the racial biases of government can be alleviated. The question that hangs over racial dialogue is the communitarian one: How can we assure that our government is truly ours? Often the chasm between government and citizen is as deep as that found on the racial divide.

FIVE

The Wages of Sin
Stories of Sex and Immorality

A couple decides to spend their honeymoon on a tropical
Caribbean island. Shortly after they arrive, their hotel room is
ransacked, and all of their belongings are stolen except their
toothbrushes and a camera. Of course, the resort replaces
their belongings, and the rest of the vacation passes pleasantly.
On their return, they have the film developed, and to their
dismay they discover a photo of the toothbrushes sticking out
of the buttocks of one of the local criminals as he moons
the camera.

The HIV virus is not a natural disease but was developed by
the United States government at its biological weapons
laboratory at Fort Detrick, Maryland, to use against undesirables
such as gays and blacks, who the government knew would
spread the disease through sexual promiscuity and drug use.
Further, the medicine AZT doesn't retard the HIV virus
but makes the virus more virulent.

Rumors focus on those topics that people find most compelling. Along
with money and crime, sex is high on that list. Immorality, whether
sexual or otherwise, is close behind. In this chapter, we examine those
narratives that deal with how blacks and whites talk and think about

sexuality and morality. Given that sexual excess and moral turpitude have traditionally been parts of the stereotype that whites apply to blacks, many, though not all, of the stories in this chapter are spread by whites. The toothbrush story is a dramatic example of the depths to which whites believe that black criminals will sink. Blacks, of course, have their own beliefs, but many focus on the fear that the white power structure is out to destroy them, rather than that individual whites intend to abuse them.

These beliefs that stress immoral behavior and genocidal intent are particularly distressing in that, if one examines official statistics, these should be banner days for African Americans. While these rumors are being spread, African Americans are increasingly found in positions of power and influence—in the military, in politics, in education, in the media, in the arts, and even, to a more limited degree, but significantly, in the economy. The black middle class is now approaching the white middle class in income. While there remains the "intractable" problem of the "underclass," "the truly needy"—notably unwed mothers and unemployed black males—some have argued that this is primarily a function of class and not race.

Many white Americans believe, sincerely, that they have transcended overt discrimination. They cheer at breakthroughs for black Americans, particularly when they do not see them as having any direct bearing on their own life chances. Bill Cosby, Colin Powell, Michael Jordan, and Oprah Winfrey are identified as American heroes. Doesn't this suggest that the old stereotypes are dead?

Whenever ethnic and racial groups are seen as socially and culturally distinctive, they acquire stereotypes in the eyes of majority groups; assumptions, large and small, are made about their characteristics.[1] It has been argued that racial and ethnic stereotypes fundamentally fall in two categories: those that picture the target group as clever, tricky, mean, and stingy (stereotypes of Jews, Gypsies, Scots, and Koreans fall into this category) and those that picture the group as stupid, violent, drunken, and lustful (stereotypes of Italians, Irish, Hispanics, and rednecks).[2] While some ethnic stereotypes involve a mix of these core themes, and others draw upon different elements (Germans, Arabs, the French), these two images predominate. These stereotypes are found directly in insulting talk, they are found humorously in "ethnic joking," and they appear in the cultural logic that helps determine what we believe about the "actual" behaviors of individual members of other racial and ethnic groups, notably in conditions of "tolerance."

The classic, racist view of African Americans within the white community is a dramatic example of the second type of stereotyping. Blacks are imagined to be stupid, violent, drunken, and lustful—a view that adheres particularly to black men. The media publicity over the antics of biter Mike Tyson and choker Latrell Sprewell sometimes seems to swamp the quiet dignity of their colleagues Evander Holyfield and Michael Jordan. In the words of sociologists Joe Feagin and Hernan Vera,

> The cognitive notions and stereotypes of contemporary racism,
> which include myths of *the dirty black man*, the dangerous black man,
> the lazy black person, the black woman's fondness for welfare, and
> black inferiority and incompetence, make as little empirical sense as
> the hostile fictions that underlay the Nazi Holocaust. . . . Racism
> is a fundamental part of U.S. culture and is spread throughout the
> social fabric. Because virtually all whites participate in the racist
> culture, most harbor some racist images or views.[3]

Feagin and Vera immediately dismiss these stereotypes and assign blame, despite the barriers that such blame places on an open dialogue.[4] The argument, grounded in the processes of unconscious psychodynamics, is that whites may be projecting their own deepest fears onto blacks, symbolically being imagined as "gorillas in their midst."[5]

A problem for many is that statistics seem to provide prima facie justification for some of these beliefs. One can point to a variety of statistics that seem to support these group stereotypes: homicide rates, figures on death from cirrhosis of the liver, welfare rates, rates of illegitimacy and abortion, failure rates at school, and low IQ scores. Yet statistics are numbers, collected for particular purposes, depending on the categorizing schemes of those in power, and they often are used in ways for which they were never intended. IQ scores, for instance, are designed not to categorize groups but to evaluate individuals, based on the values and beliefs of educational gatekeepers. Further, even if they are valid as measures, numbers by themselves do not explain cause. The discouraging reality is that widely held stereotypes derive from a world in which the stereotypes seem justified, even though this justification may misstate the causes of these phenomena, ignoring the results of other, more powerful societal forces such as discrimination or the hostile beliefs of others.

RUMORS AND "FAMILY VALUES"

Perhaps the stereotypes that have proven hardest to address, secret and transformed as they often are, involve fantasies connected to African-American sexuality, often linked to rumors about rape. As Joel Kovel notes, "Sex fantasies erupted whenever the power relations were threatened. In the colonies, the slightest rumor of a slave revolt was accompanied by wild stories of blacks wreaking their ultimate revenge in the wholesale rape of white women." Kovel goes on to explain that similar fears continue to arise whenever blacks protest grievances.[6]

As a consequence of these images, a string of nasty rumors (and jokes) target black Americans as lacking the moral values—the family values—of white Americans. These values include moderating sensual satisfactions (sex, drugs, gluttony, rules of defecation and urination) and generally postponing pleasures in the name of other virtues. Blacks, it is said, do not choose to delay gratifications. From this perspective, the problem of the underclass is caused by the "culture of poverty." Sociologist William J. Wilson argued in his book *The Truly Disadvantaged* that one part of the problems of the inner city derives from the fact that stable and relatively affluent black families have taken the opportunity to move to more pleasant environments, leaving a moral vacuum in their old neighborhoods.[7] While others argue that the separation between black social classes is not as great as Wilson suggests, because visits and other connections are common, still the absence of a diverse class structure within the neighborhood may have consequences.[8] Of course, social structural features such as an absence of opportunities for steady employment and barriers to upward mobility are even more important. However, in the views of many whites who consider the depressing statistics, the problem is with those who choose to behave immorally. People do have free will, don't they?

These stereotypes come to be seen as central to interpreting racial character. Consider this "humorous" "Application Form for Mike McGee's Militia" spread in Milwaukee. McGee was a black Milwaukee alderman who had threatened violence against the city unless Milwaukee spent $100 million to improve economic conditions for blacks.

> Yo Mamma's name:
> Yo Daddy's name (if known):
> Yo auto: Cadillac. Lincoln. Financed. Stolen
> Yo marital status: Common law. Shacked up. Gay.
> Yo place of birth: Free clinic. Alley. Zoo. Colonel Sanders. Unknown.
> Yo prior experience: Govt worker. Evangelist. Dope dealer. Postmaster. Pimp.
> Note. No photo is necessary since yo all look alike anyway.[9]

This anonymous racist flyer, not strictly rumor, covers many of the bigoted themes of African-American immorality, suggesting that the categories in the survey characterize all African Americans. Presumably it is spread not because it is racist but because it is "funny." That is, it expresses—in exaggerated form—characteristics that the audience assumes are widely accepted. While tolerant whites would immediately disown this scurrilous document and would suggest that it spreads only in a few intolerant corners of society, images of African Americans as illegitimate, dishonest, involved in drugs or prostitution, working for the government, and interchangeable are widely known and find their expression in rumors and other forms of popular culture, suggesting that tolerance may only be a thin veneer. Yet even those who are most offended by the flyer's existence (and it is sometimes anonymously placed on the desks of black coworkers) will recognize its jocular tone.[10] Its embarrassed defenders may suggest that anyone who would become irate at such a document surely "can't take a joke."[11]

Not all rumors are ostensibly humorous, such as those that suggest blacks desire to rape white women. A series of rumors reported from the World War II period emphasized that blacks would take advantage of the absence of white soldiers to violate their women.[12] It was claimed that "every Negro man will have a white girl when the white boys go off to war." A black man was reported to have told a young white couple, "You'd better be necking now because after you go off to war we'll be doing the necking." Another black was allegedly overheard choosing the white woman he wanted when her boyfriend left for war. In some instances, whites exacted a terrible revenge:

> Well, a lady was sitting on the front porch rocking her baby. Along comes this nigger and says, "Your husband has been called to war, now who's going to love you while he's gone?" The lady says, "My baby will love me." "No," says the nigger, "I'se going to love you while your husband's gone." So the lady says, "Just wait until I put the baby to bed." And when she comes back, she has a big durn shotgun in her hands and kills the nigger on the spot.[13]

Today this rumor would not be acceptable because of its offensive imagery, but the themes still survive.

Attitudes toward gender are occasionally linked to these stories. Sometimes it is asserted that the white woman is not raped or harassed but is a willing participant, although the virility of the black man is crucial. One rumor depicts a pre-wedding bachelorette party:

A young Italian-American couple is about to be married. A few days prior to the wedding date, the girlfriends of the bride-to-be throw her a bachelorette party. They hire a black male stripper. Everyone gets quite inebriated and the girlfriends egg on the bride-to-be to join the stripper in the bedroom for "one last fling." The wedding takes place, and then the honeymoon, and shortly thereafter, the newly-weds discover that they are expecting a baby. A natural childbirth is planned, with the husband assisting. But when a brown-skinned, nappy-haired infant emerges, the husband flees from the delivery room and isn't heard from again for months. Eventually he returns and the marriage is annulled.[14]

This rumor manages to demean both the immoral black stripper and the lascivious bride—the "Bad Bachelorette."[15] This story has been collected from around the United States and serves interests of both racial and gender politics. It connects to concerns of white men with the "violations" of their women. By contending that these events actually occurred, one justifies one's fantasies.

The danger from black semen is matched by a fear of black germs. Certain whites still believe that blacks have "cooties" or invisible germs that can be spread by touch. Some white salesclerks try not to touch black hands for fear of contamination, although they would heatedly deny this accusation.[16]

Open (and excessive) sexuality is only one of the sins of which blacks are accused (and for which they are envied), yet sex is not the only bodily satisfaction. In 1976 President Gerald Ford's secretary of agriculture Earl Butz was forced to resign for offering the following "joke" depicting the desires of black Americans: "I'll tell you what coloreds want. It's three things: first, a tight pussy; second, loose shoes; third, a warm place to shit. That's all!" Butz summarized in vulgar language the claim that African Americans are consumed by physical pleasure. Of course, pleasurable intimacy, comfortable clothing, and appropriate housing are goals for many, but they have been transformed into immorality. A particularly graphic rumor was spread in Cleveland in the early 1960s:

A woman went shopping in downtown Cleveland, properly attired
in dress, hat, and gloves. Although she was somewhat hesitant to go
alone into the downtown area, because the black population had
become more obvious and more aggressive of late, she felt that her
proper attire would somehow armor her against insult. Arriving
downtown, she went to the May Company, an aging but still elegant
department store. She entered the ornate self-service elevator. Just
as the doors began to shut, two large black men got on. Instead
of facing the front of the car, they faced her and approached, forcing
her to move to the back corner of the car. Slowly and deliberately
they both unzipped their pants, and urinated all over her![17]

That this story could even be told as a true happening suggests
the depth of immorality of which whites considered blacks capable.
Even if this story represented a rare event, it served to warn women that
shopping downtown was the equivalent of visiting a dangerous and
exotic land, a realm filled with dangerous primitives who behaved
like animals. The story represents a dramatic depiction of an "urban
jungle."

Yet it is not only cities where such dangers lurk; immoral black men
may be found anywhere. The well-known "toothbrush" story, referred
to earlier, is such an example:

A day after arriving in the Bahamas, a honeymooning young couple
discovered that their hotel room had been ransacked and that
everything had been taken except their camera and their toothbrushes,
which were left hanging in the bathroom. Hotel insurance covered
their losses and they still had credit cards which they'd carried
with them out of the hotel. . . . they decided to complete their
vacation and make the best of it. They reported the crime to the
police and filed their insurance claim. Then they bought some new
clothes and other needed items, which was literally everything
except toothbrushes and a camera. Their honeymoon turned out
to be wonderful after all, until they got home and developed the film
from their camera. Then they got the shock of their lives. In

one picture . . . the toothbrushes had been photographed stuck into the rectum of one of the thieves who was mooning the camera.[18]

There are, of course, many variants of this story, not all occurring in the Caribbean, but often the thieves are labeled as hotel employees, Rastafarians, island natives, or gang members. Like many legends told among whites, the race of the figures need not be explicitly mentioned. The message of the danger from immoral racial and cultural others is readily apparent.

O. J. AND RUMORS OF SEXUAL MORALITY

News stories often represent a basis from which rumors of immorality develop. Criminal accusations and subsequent trials present morality plays that various groups manipulate and elaborate in light of the structure of credibility. Prominent trials ("trials of the century") make cultural sense. Because one is dealing with explanations for things that "actually" happened, one cannot dismiss them out of hand, but they are often selected from a set of competing reportable events because they enable one to address central social issues. By elaborating on news accounts, dry fact can be invested with emotion. These stories are seen as something that "enquiring minds want to know."

The American fascination with the O. J. Simpson murder trial in 1994–95 is drenched in beliefs about racial morality. From the standpoint of white Americans (as filtered through black eyes), even an admired and nonthreatening personality such as O. J. Simpson is fundamentally no different than our mundane stereotypes of black males: an abuser, a drinker, a killer, a person without moral grounding. Assumptions arose quickly about Simpson's guilt, his motivation, and his moral character, long before evidence was placed before a jury. In the words of media critic John Fiske, O. J. Simpson was "Hortonized," referring to the use that supporters of the 1988 Bush campaign made of furloughed criminal Willie Horton to discredit Massachusetts governor Michael Dukakis. The police mug shots used by *Time* were made more dramatic by the newsmagazine's decision to darken Simpson's skin.[19]

Assumptions about Ronald Goldman defending Nicole Simpson, after courteously returning her eyeglasses, fed the belief of the "good white man protecting the pure white woman against the racial-sexual threat of the Black man out of control."[20] Some of this material found its way into the mass media, while other information was constructed from what seemed reasonable. White fears of interracial sex—especially between a black man and a white woman—must be disguised: the criminal charges against O. J. provided the opportunity for interracial sex to be discussed indirectly.

Not surprisingly, these images of a demonized O. J. were largely absent in the African-American community. Polls conducted throughout the criminal trial demonstrated that many African Americans believed Simpson was innocent, suggesting just how wide the divide between the races is, and suggesting that the subtext of the trial was about the proper relations between black men and white women. For many African Americans the charges represented the white power structure's attempt to get back at this uppity Negro. Blacks claimed that they were only judging the facts, and that their belief in O. J.'s innocence was not based on racial sympathy. Black informants noted a double standard at work in the white public's rush to judgment, apparently eschewing the well-worn "innocent until proven guilty" edict.

One explanation was that the murder was committed by the Mafia or white extremists as retribution for Simpson's relationships with white women, and that O. J. was subsequently framed as a punishment for his sexual transgressions.[21] The police frame-up was similarly a result of racist cops targeting a black man who did not know his place. The same evidence that the white community could construct as representing O. J.'s culpability might also represent a gigantic police conspiracy against an innocent man. Yet there is a need to go beyond this: to find the guilty parties. Mark Gerson, a Jersey City high school teacher, reports the range of explanations among his inner-city students:

> One student suggested that Ron Goldman killed Nicole before
> killing himself and then throwing away the knife. Another believes
> the dog did it. Shenia suggested that Al Cowlings, Simpson's best
> buddy, did it. Bryant believes the killer is O. J.'s son. Philip blames
> "that fag dude who wants to marry O. J."; that would be Kato
> Kaelin, Simpson's houseguest. . . . Jon, a bright student, had his
> own scenario: O. J. was shaving and cut himself. Kato took the
> blood from the shaving cut, brought it to the crime scene and
> dumped it.[22]

If one lives in a world in which the police can do whatever they wish, manufacturing and manipulating evidence at will, and in a world in which black men, no matter how prominent, are always at risk, such scenarios about the Simpson case are plausible, if not likely. The multitude of facts that are widely available can be used in any number of explanations. Most African-American informants were easily able to identify individuals in their own families who were unfairly targeted by law enforcement officers or self-appointed vigilantes.

THE EPIDEMIC OF AIDS RUMORS

Dramatic rumors develop around topics that are simultaneously important and ambiguous, and for which the critical ability of the audience is low. In such situations, people are all too willing to believe whatever they hear. Perhaps no subject better illustrates the way that a salient issue can be transformed into a set of rumors than AIDS. Indeed, in retrospect one could easily have predicted that the AIDS epidemic—deadly and unlike other diseases—would produce a wealth of claims. How can we interpret an invariably fatal malady that in its early years had such narrow targets: the "four H's" (homosexuals, hemophiliacs, heroin addicts, and Haitians)? While scientists and the general public better understand the syndrome after two decades, the disease's origin and control are ripe for speculation. Initially hidden by the mass media and exploding during a conservative Republican administration that, at first, seemed unconcerned, and after a decade characterized by a perceived moral decline, AIDS seemed to be part of a morality play. With scientists uncertain for the first several years about what kind of disease they were confronting and how easily it might spread, the ambiguity provided a breeding ground for rumor. As sociologist Tamotsu Shibutani notes, "Spectacular events with possible consequences for millions result in a sudden increase in demand for news that cannot be satisfied even by the most efficient press service."[23]

The potential of the epidemic to justify all kinds of claims is dramatically evident in the beliefs of those who argue that a medical syndrome labeled AIDS does not exist and/or that the HIV virus plays no role in the development of full-blown AIDS. Few deny that vast numbers have died and that the primary modes of transmission are through sexual contact and drug use, but whether a single "disease" exists and how this disease originated are matters of considerable debate. While AIDS is a "gay disease," it is also a "black disease," in its origins, transmission routes, and patients. Black Liberation Radio claims that globally 80 percent of those with AIDS are black and, it notes, mostly not homosexuals or intravenous drug users.[24] Indeed, after the four H's, blacks were seen as the next vulnerable group—and an intractable one, a belief supported by such newspaper headlines as "AIDS More Prevalent among Black Military Recruits" or "Special Help Needed to Halt Black AIDS Cases."

For African Americans (and for many gays and lesbians), the argument that the HIV virus was manufactured by the government was disturbingly plausible. Many prominent African Americans, including Louis Farrakhan, Spike Lee, Grace Jones, and Bill Cosby, as well as doctors, lawyers, and professors, have expressed the belief that AIDS might have been deliberately created. In 1989 an aide to Eugene Sawyer, the black mayor of Chicago, was fired for claiming that Jewish doctors were injecting black babies with AIDS. Perhaps even more disturbing is the fact that some African Americans prominent in the fight against AIDS, such as Dr. Abdul Alim Muhammed, once the codirector of the AIDS transition team for Mayor Marion Barry of Washington, D.C., the most prominent black anti-AIDS figure in the nation's capital, and the recipient of a half-million dollars in federal grants, believes that AIDS is a "genocidal weapon." If black experts believe this, surely it is understandable why others agree.[25]

The AIDS conspiracy has been reported by guests and audiences on numerous talk shows, particularly those with black hosts, and black newspapers. The *New York Times*/CBS News poll of racial beliefs asked whether it was true that "the virus which causes AIDS was deliberately created in a laboratory in order to infect black people"; 10 percent of the black respondents agreed, and 19 percent felt it might possibly be true.[26] These figures compare to 1 percent and 4 percent among white respondents. A 1990 study by the Southern Christian Leadership Conference of African-American churchgoers found that one-third of the sample believed that AIDS was a form of genocide, and another one-third were unsure. More than one-third believed that HIV was produced in a germ-warfare lab, a view held by 40 percent of Washington, D.C., black college students.[27]

This story connects with the belief among gay men that the virus was part of U.S. biological warfare research that either accidentally escaped into the public or was used as a tool to target third world countries or the newly empowered gay community.[28] Although it is now part of the distant history of the disease, when AIDS seemed to affect Haitians disproportionately, the belief was that it was being used to reduce the number of Haitians immigrating into the United States illegally.[29] Haitian informants suggested that the American government's dislike for Haiti's president-for-life, Jean-Claude "Papa Doc" Duvalier, was critical in the decision to spread the disease. Africans (notably those in central African states such as Zaire and Uganda), for their part, felt that they were the targets of this biological weapon. One Jamaican-born college student combined the two rumors by reporting that "the AIDS virus was started in Africa and Haiti by the government." Linked in the minds of many informants were the categories of "nonwhites," "Africans," "Haitians," "third world peoples," "blacks," "minorities," and "oppressed people."

Whether one believes that the spread of the HIV virus was the aftermath of a biological weapons test (in central Africa or Haiti) that went terribly awry, or whether its intended goal was mass destruction and genocide, powerful fears are at work. The first explanation—a "moderate" view—appears more prevalent. According to one account: "The AIDS virus was created in a CIA laboratory. The CIA brought it to Africa to test on blacks, thinking they could watch it, but it got out of control. This is why doctors cannot come up with a vaccine that will work on it. [This proves the virus] has to be man-made." The second explanation is reflected in the statement of a young woman, part African American and part American Indian: "The story was told to me by an aunt. Apparently the CIA was testing to find a disease which would resist any cures known to man. They did this testing somewhere in Africa. The purpose of finding this incurable disease was to bring America back to the old days of the moral majority. Therefore, this disease was to be transmitted sexually among outcasts of society, namely, people of color and gay men." Those who scorn such explanations must wonder how numerous fellow citizens can live comfortably in a society dominated by such evil people.

Surely in the aftermath of any event is it reasonable to ask who benefits. The answer for many African Americans is that white America benefits by being rid of blacks and drug addicts. Perhaps AIDS is a form of population control or a response to a changing economy that now requires fewer manual laborers. One college student alleged: "During the Carter Administration there was a document that said by the year 2000, one hundred billion [*sic*] Africans had to be destroyed."[30]

For some people, AIDS represents an "ethnic weapon"—a biological weapon that would attack the genetic structure of certain racial and ethnic groups but not affect others. Others believe that germ warfare laboratories have attempted to create a melanin-sensitive gas that would bind to black skin and not to white. One article, published in an American military journal by Carl Larson, a Swedish geneticist, lends credence to the belief that experts are interested in weapons that might affect the enzymes of different populations in distinct ways—what have been labeled ethnic weapons.[31] Rutgers University faculty associate Leonard Cole reports that Pentagon researchers exposed dockworkers at a navy base in Norfolk, Virginia, to an "organism meant to simulate a fungus disease that might affect blacks more than whites."[32] While there is no evidence that the research yielded practical results, and while some American researchers claim to be aghast at the prospect of ethnic weapons, an observer could conclude that the government might be secretly studying such weapons, *if only to cope with their use by an enemy force*. What would we think of our military establishment if it was not working on strategies to defend against such potential weapons?

The possibility of ethnic differences in response to disease fits folk beliefs. From this standpoint, it is striking that in the early years of the epidemic some believed that Asians were immune to the HIV virus, and that intercourse with Asian-American women might even provide immunity—a rumor that disappeared in the wake of the spread of AIDS in India and Thailand.

In the view of some, AIDS represents a subtle and sophisticated form of ethnic cleansing. Indeed, the rumors are so strong that AIDS represents a deliberate strategy of the American government that the Central Intelligence Agency was moved to respond:

> We believe that rumors linking the CIA with the development or the spreading of the AIDS virus, especially in Africa, may be the result of what we would call "disinformation" efforts of hostile intelligence services to damage the United States. The CIA has had absolutely nothing to do with either the development or the spreading of AIDS or any other virus. The CIA is not carrying out experiments in this regard and you may document this by

corresponding with either the House or Senate Select Committees on Intelligence, which monitor Agency operations. The CIA has undertaken to try to understand the effects of the AIDS virus around the world, since it is clear that the spreading of such a disease could constitute a threat to US national security.[33]

By contending that the CIA story can be *confirmed* by other, sympathetic governmental committees, the CIA is assuming the absence of suspicion. Evidence that military agencies *have* experimented by spreading (harmless) viruses in American cities vitiates much of the power of the explanation, along with the fact that the CIA admits that it is studying the virus for its role in national security. Thus, a person who is inclined to accept conspiracy theories would likely be unpersuaded by this rebuttal.

A report from 1988 is even more explicit about the possibility of the spread of rumor by the enemies of America, noting that "the largest Soviet disinformation campaign of recent years had made the totally false claim that the AIDS virus was created in a U.S. military facility in Fort Detrick, Maryland."[34] The rumor is attacked by means of its external source, but this does not undermine its credibility within our own society.

These rumors, like others discussed throughout this book, are historically and culturally rooted. Keith Brown reports, after his brother's death from AIDS: "Because of who's being devastated the most, and growing up in the U.S. and knowing the history of slavery and racism in this country, you can't be black and not feel that AIDS is some kind of plot to hit undesirable minorities." Yet, he adds, needing to defend himself against charges of paranoia, "I hope I don't sound too radical, because I'm not. I don't want to believe that AIDS is some kind of Government plot. . . . But I guess I do believe it."[35]

Brown's belief is based both on who benefits and on the historical understandings by which many black Americans judge what is plausible, which generates a powerful mistrust toward a quasi-Nazi government and simultaneously provokes embarrassment about reporting these paranoid beliefs in "tolerant" settings. The reality of the Tuskegee syphilis experiment makes otherwise bizarre claims seem reasonable. Past conspiracies give rise to the credibility of current ones. Tuskegee is the parable by which blacks assess plausibility of public health interventions. As Stephen Thomas, a professor at Emory University, notes: "It has transcended being a historical event and turned into an *urban legend,* a personification of medical abuses and racism" (emphasis added).[36] One reaps what one sows. A related set of beliefs developed at the end of the nineteenth century as blacks migrated in large numbers from the familiar South to the unfamiliar North. In these rumors, the enemies were white men in white coats who allegedly were on the lookout for human specimens to use in scientific experiments.[37] According to these texts, medical schools needed bodies and corpses on which to conduct tests. Enterprising young medical students filled this need by ambushing unsuspecting blacks and taking them to their laboratories. Mark Riley, a radio talk show host in New York, claims, "As an African American who knows something about our history, I can't rule out conspiracy as regards AIDS or crack."[38]

One particularly chilling claim heard over Black Liberation Radio involves the black worker in a vaccine laboratory in California who transposed the labels on two parcels of what was ostensibly identical vaccine: one was designed for a white clinic, another for a clinic that served black clients. When the error was discovered, there was a mad scramble to retrieve and readdress the packages.[39] This account only underlines the considerable irony that a disease targeted at minorities and deviants now could threaten heterosexual, middle-class whites, although even here the precautions of safe sex are precisely those that conservative, religious leaders would favor in the absence of the virus. These telling details, odd but comprehensible, provide a plausible patina to explanations that others would find incredible.

Belief in the deliberate spread of the HIV virus is likely to cause the target group to feel powerless, and indeed, there is evidence that these beliefs keep African Americans from having their children vaccinated,[40] from receiving AIDS tests and early medical treatment, or from using condoms, practicing safe sex, or using clean needles. Dr. Barry Primm, an African-American member of President Reagan's Commission on AIDS, noted, "If I had as many people out there pushing the combat against AIDS as I have pushing the notion that it's a white man's plot, we would be winning the battle."[41] People dismiss their personal risk and blame it on the machinations of others, discounting the credibility of health care workers who attempt to protect minority communities. Indeed, the proposal to use condoms is attributed to government attempts to push minority population control or to the belief that lubricated condoms cause sterility. Some African Americans with HIV believe that the medication AZT actually speeds up their symptoms, and they refuse to take the drug.[42] This is particularly tragic for pregnant women, among whom research has found that taking AZT can reduce the baby's chance of being HIV-positive from 25 percent to 8 percent. One Atlanta study found that 80 percent of women who should have been taking AZT or other drugs were not doing so. Some suggest that even if a fully effective HIV virus could be discovered, many African Americans would not take it because of their fear of being "guinea pigs for some evil agenda."[43]

The fact that AIDS is transmitted by activities that are seen as immoral makes the rumors more salient. The disease depends on the activities of black and gay bodies. Black recognition that whites see them as promiscuous and as drug abusers makes it credible that white scientists might construct a "moral virus" that primarily attacks those who engage in those behaviors. The alleged immorality of blacks makes the targeting of an AIDS conspiracy seem so plausible.

The parallel fear among whites is that AIDS may enter the heterosexual white community through unprotected sex with blacks, who, some fear, attempt to infect white women deliberately. Such concerns speak to the same images of sexual immorality. AIDS in its earliest days was linked to "Haitians," an association that later was demonstrated to be misleading, and needle-sharing drug users, connecting the disease to blacks until blacks themselves were subsequently defined as an at-risk group. The scientific theory that the HIV virus emerged out of the African jungle, from the bites of African green monkeys, also linked the disease to African Americans. Blacks and gays were easily perceived as moral deviants—implicitly, if not explicitly. Essayist Susan Sontag prefaces her comments about AIDS origin beliefs by calling attention to the psychological centrality of the African association:

> Illustrating the classic script for plague, AIDS is thought to have started in the "dark continent," then spread to Haiti, then to the United States and then to Europe. . . . It is understood as a tropical disease: another infestation from the so-called Third World. . . . The subliminal connection made to notions about a primitive past and the many hypotheses from animals (a disease of the green monkey? African swine fever?) cannot help but activate a familiar set of stereotypes about animality, sexual license, and blacks.[44]

Or as writer Cindy Patton suggests: "AIDS is a class illness: people who share certain common characteristics are vulnerable to particular types of diseases (in this case sexual practice, poverty, immigrant status, and race are other qualities that define disease classes). Put another way, types of people get the diseases they deserve."[45]

Persistent beliefs about black sexual licentiousness have permeated Western culture since English explorers visited the west coast of Africa in the 1550s. More than four centuries later, many whites still assume that people of color overindulge their sexual desires. Since AIDS is in part a venereal disease and a disproportionate number of blacks are infected, these beliefs are reinforced. Further, the spread of the disease within the black community and the possibility of sexual transmission provide a tocsin against interracial sexual contact. Why threaten lynching, when a virus is as effective in curbing sexual appetites? After all, white sexual appetites are seen as more easily controlled than black ones.

Those few cases in which black prisoners who either were infected with the HIV virus or claimed to be infected attempted to bite guards or police provide a breeding ground in which it could be alleged that blacks were scheming to expand AIDS into the heterosexual white population. Headlines such as "Black Man's Teeth a Deadly Weapon, Jury Rules" makes concrete the dangers that blacks pose to the body politic. Just as AIDS conspiracy rumors reflect black fears of white malevolence, rumors about African-American revenge suggest that the reverse is equally true: this Topsy/Eva cycle is filtered through the glasses of immorality and sexual politics.

CONCLUSION

Sexuality and morality are characteristics by which we make attributions about our fellow citizens. The fact that blacks are often defined by whites as being immoral and promiscuous produces a set of fearsome rumors. Further, the fact that blacks recognize the existence of these stereotypical beliefs leads to counterrumors that allege that whites use these beliefs to harm blacks by playing upon their sexual habits. The theme of sterilization found in many of the mercantile rumors in chapter 3 also addresses sexual excess, as do those claims in chapter 4 about the government's attempts to use black male organs for medical research. In the tension between blacks and whites, sexuality represents the heart of darkness in which fears, prejudice, and paranoia can easily hide.

Sexual rumors are often hidden talk. The personal imperatives that contribute to the creation of rumor are often well hidden and fully denied. These fears of sexuality cannot easily be described or found in open settings. Yes, we talk about sexuality, but we are often careful about the circumstances in which these rumors are spread. More than most topics in the book, these rumors are concealed from public view. The divisions between black talk and white talk may be particularly dramatic in this instance. For that reason, the content of rumors may be especially surprising and troubling to those outside of the racial community of the rumor's audience. In addition to these rumors being pernicious, they are powerful and especially difficult to uproot.

SIX

On The Road Again
Rumors of Crime and Confrontation

The city of Salt Lake City, Utah, is bracing itself for attacks
by radical black activists, angered by stands of the Church
of Jesus Christ of Latter-day Saints, which they claim discrim-
inate against African Americans. The radicals, as well as
their white supporters, are hiding in canyons around the city,
waiting to attack. The city residents fear that the invaders
are planning to blow up reservoirs and poison other water
supplies, leaving residents to die of thirst.

As part of a gang initiation, new gang members will drive
around the city at dusk with their headlights off. Those citizens
who flash their lights as a kind-hearted warning will find
that gang members will shoot them, either on the spot or
after following them home.

While blacks are nervous about the intentions of predominantly white
institutions, whites fear blacks both as individuals and in social groups.
With regard to crime, most of the rumors are spread by whites, whereas
black concerns focus on how institutions single them out for injurious
attention.

Neither group lacks some justification for its fears. For instance, in
recent years, white Americans have learned of the code "DWB," which

black Americans have long recognized as "driving while black." Because of a practice known as racial profiling, African Americans are pulled over by police at a significantly higher rate than white motorists. For most, their only offense is the color of their skin. Even when no evidence of a crime exists, law enforcement officials stop, search, and sometimes assault black drivers. Blacks report that while nearly any thoroughfare might be the site of an unprovoked search, most searches occur either on the major interstate highways in states where drug trafficking is considered likely or in upscale, white neighborhoods. The police justify these searches on the grounds that statistics suggest that blacks are disproportionately more likely to engage in criminal activity. Blacks and civil liberties authorities are quick to point out that the presumption of innocence until proof of guilt protection extends to all Americans. To blacks, this practice reflects the offensive and "criminal" treatment to which they have been long subjected. In contrast, when whites speak of criminal activity, they are preoccupied with random violent crime.

In survey after survey, Americans in the 1990s identified violent crime as a paramount concern. In rural enclaves, suburban communities, and urban domains, Americans fear unseen, brutal enemies. Reliable statistics suggest, however, that many of our fears are misdirected and unwarranted. According to FBI statistics, rates of violent crime have declined, not escalated, during the 1990s, and they continue to do so in the new millennium. Although America is still a more dangerous place to live and work than is much of the Western world, we are safer than in previous decades. Moreover, as has long been the case, we are most likely to be attacked by someone close to us, as opposed to the rare homicidal stranger. Female murder victims, for example, are most likely to have been killed by their own fathers, husbands, or boyfriends. Children under the age of four are more likely to be killed by family members than by anyone else. Our workplaces can be dangerous if we get in the way of dissatisfied employees or off-balance coworkers. Students are most apt to be killed by classmates. One's most likely attacker is a person of one's own race.

Many Americans stubbornly refuse to acknowledge these uncomfortable truths. With only a few exceptions, news stories about violence committed by one's intimates are treated as unthinkable aberrations, and reports about stranger violence are conveyed as the norm. We fret about what scholars label "stranger danger." Every Halloween, warnings proliferate about razor blades in apples and other sabotaged treats. Worried parents take their children's goodies to hospitals for X-ray inspections. Yet, according to an exhaustive survey, the only documented instance of a child fatality caused by a toxic treat turned out to be an instance of a youngster being poisoned by his own stepfather for insurance.[1]

The problem is, of course, that heinous crimes do occur. Whether we live on a dirt road or in a plush urban penthouse, we are wise to lock our doors. Neighborhood watch programs increase the safety of communities once protected by the casual oversight of friends and family. In most parts of the country, women are well advised to avoid midnight strolls. And if they take solace in cyberspace relationships, they should not reveal their real names and addresses to unknown chatmates. Parents should warn children against getting into the car of or taking sweets from a stranger. Elderly citizens should opt for direct deposit. But for many, reasonable precautions are not enough. Terrified of becoming the next crime victim, some people become prisoners in their own homes. In some frightening cases, people harm friends and family members with weapons purchased for protection.

This problem is exacerbated by the media's preoccupation with sensational criminal activity.[2] Popular television series rehash ostensibly true crime stories. Newspapers and magazines regularly exploit any gruesome occurrence. Blockbuster movies routinely depict conflicts between pathological killers and the heroic, indestructible cops who pursue them. Genuine and reenacted stories make crime seem even more personal. Seeing an elderly woman brutally mugged makes other senior citizens feel vulnerable. Encounters with individuals who resemble the mugger/actor they have seen on television stimulate uncertainty and fear. Aware of the similarities between themselves and the victim, they conclude that they might be next. As one frustrated citizen noted, after denouncing racism, "Why shouldn't elderly white ladies be wary of their purses when the statistics bear out the fact of the objects of black street muggings—The weak and innocent. So don't accuse whites of stereotyping—better to stereotype and be safe."[3] Is this a comment filled with hate and fear, or one based on good, if sad, judgment?[4]

Former New Jersey senator, New York Knicks basketball star, and presidential hopeful Bill Bradley addressed a similar issue with somewhat more measured language:

> Today, many whites responding to a more violent reality . . . see young black men traveling in groups, cruising the city, looking for trouble and they are frightened. Many white Americans, unfairly or fairly, seem to be saying of some young black males, "You litter the street and deface the subway, and no one, black or white, says stop. . . . You rob a store, rape a jogger, shoot a tourist, and when they catch you, if they catch you, you cry racism. And nobody, white or black, says stop."[5]

It does not matter whether the image is literally true or whether it is an ironic counterpoint to centuries of oppression, but this belief affects the public behaviors of both blacks and whites. Anger affects fantasies, perceptions, and the stories that people relate. We focus on those things that match our emotional state.

Bradley's comments suggest that fear results when whites see blacks on *their* streets. In many cases, the randomness and innocence of white victims is emphasized, contrasting with the demonic nature of the alleged black attacker. These are stories of heinous attacks that have not been reported in the media. Yet often the stories are told as factual happenings, and the race of those involved is unstated but implicit in the telling.[6] This permits tellers and audiences to persuade themselves that they are not racist, and indeed, depending on one's definition, they may not be.

Our goal in this chapter, which focuses on tenacious rumors about crime, is not to deny the reality of violence in America. Rather, we examine what our willingness to accept uncritically the more resilient stories reveals about racial attitudes. Because of the media's extensive coverage of violence and the insecurity many Americans feel about their safety, numerous rumors and legends about crime circulate. We cannot cover them all, so we have opted to limit our comments to some of the more prominent texts that describe the supposed aggressor actively seeking victims or the reverse, in which an individual is victimized when he or she strays from home turf.

THEY ARE COMING TO GET US

The presumption that black men harbor violent criminal tendencies is not new. Throughout modern history this image has been manipulated to serve the needs of the dominant culture. The slave trade was often justified on the grounds that barbarous, heathen Africans had to be enslaved to save their progeny from certain damnation. As early as 1712, rumors of alleged attacks on white women by blacks were spread in New York City.[7] The shackles and chains that accompanied chattel slavery were similarly said to be necessary instruments for controlling the savage impulses of the slaves. Images of brutal blacks proliferated in the years following the Civil War. Northerners and Southerners alike feared the consequences of the blacks' newfound mobility and freedom. White supremacist groups such as the Ku Klux Klan justified their activities on the grounds that they were doing society a service by punishing licentious blacks. With its scenes of lawless, marauding black soldiers, unkempt, illiterate, chicken-eating black congressmen, and a bug-eyed, lascivious black rapist, D. W. Griffith's epic film *The Birth of a Nation* (1915) contains a range of antiblack images that have influenced American popular consciousness for the remainder of the twentieth century. Blacks were told to "stay in their place." Throughout American history, a mobile African American has been seen as threatening. Yet because of the civil rights movement, most codified restrictions against blacks were erased in the 1960s. African Americans were more free than ever before to move into any school, occupation, or neighborhood that they had the resources to enter.

FEARS OF INVASION

As dangerous as lone black men seem to whites, groups of black men are even more frightening. A fascinating case study of the ways in which rumors develop about African-American groups can be seen in an examination of several cycles that emerged during the early 1970s within Utah's Mormon community.[8] Although several free and enslaved blacks accompanied the Mormon leader Brigham Young when he led his pioneer followers into Utah in the nineteenth century, the denomination in the United States has attracted few African Americans. Like other white Americans, Mormons long believed that peoples of African descent were inferior. During the nineteenth century, conventional Christian doctrine held that blacks were being punished by God for the sins of their biblical ancestors. Many Mormons subscribed to the then popular notion that blacks were the unworthy descendants of Ham and thereby deserved subjugation. Well into the twentieth century, officials of the Church of Jesus Crist of the Latter-day Saints (LDS) employed this rationale. In 1949, church officials reiterated Brigham Young's words, saying, "Why are so many of the inhabitants of the earth cursed with a skin of blackness? It comes in consequence of their fathers rejecting of the power of the holy priesthood, then that curse will be removed from the seed of Cain, and they will come up and possess the priesthood, and receive all the blessings we are now entitled to."[9] In many respects, Mormon attitudes and policies about blacks kept pace with those of the society at large. In the 1960s, when civil rights issues were widespread, the church issued a position paper stating, "We would like it to be known that there is in this Church no doctrine, belief or practice that is intended to deny the enjoyment of full civil rights by any person regardless of race, color, or creed."[10]

Yet, the church did lag behind other denominations in one significant area. Until 1978, black Mormons were not allowed to serve as priests in the LDS Church. By the late 1970s this type of blatant, overt discrimination was the exception and not the rule in the rest of American society. This exclusion caused trouble both within the Mormon community and outside of it. Many Mormons were distraught by the church hierarchy's refusal to reverse its position on this issue. Just as many Americans can remember where they were when they heard about the assassination of John F. Kennedy, many Mormons can identify where they were on June 9, 1978, when the church finally declared blacks eligible for the priesthood. This discrimination also disturbed people outside of the church. During the civil rights movement, this prohibition received national media attention, and Mormon authorities found themselves defending what many outsiders maintained to be a manifestation of blatant Jim Crow–style discrimination.

Two distinct rumor cycles emerged as the church grappled with African-American demands for equality and access. The first focused on a planned invasion of Utah by blacks (and, sometimes, "hippies"). These texts alleged that the black radicals were conspiring with other counterculture organizations against Mormons. Some of the rumors pinpointed the most prominent radical leaders, while others focused on the rank-and-file membership. Eldridge Cleaver of the Black Panther Party, who was mentioned by name, was said to be hiding in Salt Lake City, waiting for his comrades to arrive in order to take over the city. In other versions of the rumor, blacks (and hippies) were said to be hiding out in the canyons surrounding Salt Lake City, waiting for the call to storm the metropolis. Places and events significant to Mormons were often specified in the rumors. Some texts warned Mormon drivers that Black Panthers intended to attack the cars of people driving to and from the General Conference, an important event in the LDS calendar. In other reports, anonymous Black Panthers were said to be sneaking guns and ammunition into the city. Some said the revolutionaries' ultimate plan was to take over the General Conference and the church office building in order to punish the church. In some versions, the Panthers' plan was to assassinate the Mormon leaders known as the General Authorities. Some informants claimed that riots led by professional assassination squads would move from neighborhood to neighborhood, eliminating Salt Lake's Mormon elite.

Several of the rumors that emerged clearly identified those aspects of Mormon life about which followers were likely to feel vulnerable. Access to water is a persistent concern for residents of Utah, an arid state given to prolonged droughts. One informant claimed that the Students for a Democratic Society (SDS), in conjunction with the Black Panther Party, planned to blow up the Mountain Dell Reservoir. Water that was not destroyed was to be poisoned. In some versions, young black children were to sell candy bars filled with broken glass to Mormon children. After crippling the population by destroying the water and contaminating children's candy, busloads of blacks would descend upon the city. According to one informant, the invaders were expected to attack the residents' food, water, and air supply.

A second rumor cycle focused on the fate that awaited Mormons beyond the borders of Utah. While Utah boasts an extremely large Mormon population, members of the LDS Church live throughout the United States and in all corners of the world. Most Mormon young people are required to complete a two-year mission during which they focus on converting others to their faith. For this purpose, they accept assignments throughout the world. Missionaries serving in those parts of the United States torn apart by racial strife were often identified as potential targets of violent blacks. Sometimes these threats were evident as soon as a Mormon left the Utah "safety zone." It was said that cars with Utah license plates were stopped and the occupants asked if they were Mormons. They were told that "Mormon-lovers" were unwelcome. Mormons in San Bernardino, California, another city densely populated by Mormons, heard that church members had been pulled from their cars and beaten by blacks.

Some informants described how Mormons attempted to thwart the

Panthers and their counterculture cohorts. In response to these wide-spread rumors, Utah residents formed Neighborhood Emergency Teams (NETs) to deter invasions. The extent of NET preparedness became fodder for rumors. Some informants claimed that the Salt Lake City police department had developed a riot control weapon out of old amphibious tanks. It was claimed that members of the world-renowned Mormon Tabernacle Choir were required to get passes as part of the church's security measures. When the invasion did not materialize, many Utahans who had subscribed to the belief maintained that their countermeasures deterred the assault. One informant claimed that their foes abandoned their plans when they realized they would never be able to defeat the army of missionaries the church would summon.

While the Black Panthers did call public attention to the church's bigoted position toward its African-American parishioners, the militant political organization devoted its energies toward American communities with larger black populations. Tackling the Church of Latter-day Saints, with its few black followers, was never a priority for the Panthers. Why, then, did these rumors enjoy such popularity in Utah?

Television stations in Utah, as elsewhere in the United States, showed images of somber, law-abiding civil rights activists, as well as more radically inclined, disobedient black protesters. These unfamiliar images prompted many people to attempt to reconcile their own attitudes about African-American equality with the demands being articulated. Hearing African Americans chant "Black is beautiful" and denounce segregation was uncomfortable. Some Utahans held onto the prejudices of their forebears. Asked how they felt about civil rights activity, several informants asserted that they believed that blacks did not deserve all the rights and privileges for which they were fighting. To such individuals, the rumors confirmed their attitudes, verification that their long-standing belief in white superiority was justified. By articulating and sharing these rumors, Mormons established collective solidarity. The rumors also allowed those who circulated them to personalize and localize remote happenings. The specter of black men and women marching with clenched fists in Oakland or Chicago is given meaning in Provo and Ogden.

Of course, not all Mormons expressed these beliefs. For them, the church's refusal to admit African Americans into the priesthood was a source of profound conflict with their spiritual beliefs. Hearing the demands of black activists contributed to their guilt and frustration. Putting themselves into the position of the black activists, they imagined that the Mormons would be an apt target.

By prohibiting blacks from assuming the priesthood, Mormons attempted to maintain a space that was off limits to blacks. With the news about African-American determination to seize previously restricted terrain, church members shared narratives to reconcile their local circumstances to national events. Ironically, the leadership of the LDS Church eliminated its last official racially biased policies in the late 1970s after the Black Panthers and similar activist organizations had been crippled by internal discord and external interference. Eventually the rumors faded. But this example illustrates the ways in which individuals and communities combine their beliefs about a racial minority and public information about that group into narratives that can be used to justify their apprehensions.

CRIME WAVES

Eventually organized black activists ceased to be front-page news; however, rumors and legends about black criminality continued to flourish, emphasizing the dangers of individual black men eager to invade white space. Given the unrelenting media attention devoted to the high black crime rate, the white public finds virtually all stories and claims about African-American criminals plausible. This is described dramatically in folklorist Eleanor Wachs's book, *Crime-Victim Stories*, which scrutinizes texts collected from city residents during the late 1970s and early 1980s. Wachs argues that urban dwellers are convinced that their community is characterized by interracial discord. Each crime committed by a black or Hispanic man represents that race to the victim and the victim's friends. The crimes support a cultural logic based on racial prejudice. One effect of a crime victim's stories, and the rumors based on them, is that they permit the narrator to express negative feelings by incorporating ethnic slurs or stereotypes into ostensibly "actual happenings." In these stories, as they are usually told, the race of the perpetrator is mentioned, and in some situations it may come to be a central point: "A black kid, you know, did this" or "Two blacks came up to me and put a knife in my side." Even when race is not explicitly mentioned, narrators of these tales realize that their audiences will know to whom they refer and often simply use the word "they" to stand for a fully understood racial characterization, as when one says, "They just want to harm you." Narrators sometimes reinforce prejudice by using racial slurs in their accounts, ensuring that their audience understands the "lessons" to be learned. Consider the following "true" story shared by one of Wachs's informants:

> My mother was mugged. . . . She was coming home from bingo.
> My mother, the bingo maven. Did not win that night. So she had a
> few dollars and her bingo chips . . . and all the crap she keeps. And
> P.S. this kid comes over. She said he was about sixteen years old.
> Nice black boy [sarcastic]. And as she was putting the key in the
> door, the front entrance, he pushed her and tried to grab her bag.
> My mother started screaming. He knocked her down. He grabbed
> her bingo bag. And she went running upstairs. . . . She never saw
> the kid again in the neighborhood. And she moved right after that.
> "That's it, I can't take it any more." She was really frightened. [11]

Along with these personal narratives, a set of unsubstantiated rumors addresses similar fears of violation by African Americans.

A dramatic example of a story dealing with urban crime involves a female victim turning the tables on a (presumably) black criminal, who fits the stereotype because of his violence and the gold chain worn around his neck:

> A woman riding a Manhattan subway feels her gold neck chain
> being snapped loose just as the train slows down at a station. Reacting
> automatically, she reaches over and snaps off the chain that's around
> her attacker's neck, and he runs out the door and up the stairs.
> Later, a jeweler tells her that the chain she grabbed was pure gold.
> Her own chain was an inexpensive fake.[12]

In this text both the woman and her attacker are in transit. She is brave
enough to utilize the public transportation system in the first place and
needs no Good Samaritan male to rescue her. Unafraid of her assailant,
she counterattacks.

Two of the most persistent crime legends are referred to by folklorists as "The Man in the Backseat" and "The Choking Doberman" and
are often associated with suburban or rural communities. Jan Harold
Brunvand, certainly the most prolific writer on such texts, titled his
second legend book after the latter. To legend scholars they are classics—texts in which citizens claim to know they are true because they
happened to the ever-present friend of a friend.

In many versions of "The Man in the Backseat," a service station
attendant "tricks" a woman into not driving from the station in order
to protect her from an assailant who has sneaked into the backseat of
her car:

> Becky stopped in the gas station and asked for $2 worth of gas.
> When the attendant finished putting in the gas, she handed him
> a $10 bill. He looked at it for a minute, then he said, "I'm sorry,
> but this bill isn't any good. You'd better come inside the station."
> Quite confused, she got out of the car and went inside the station
> with the attendant. When they got inside, he locked the door and
> went over to the telephone. "There's a Negro on the back
> floor of your car," said the attendant, and he called the police.[13]

In other versions, the woman is closely tailed by a trucker who sees
the shadow of a man about to pounce on the female driver. He keeps
flashing his lights to warn her.[14] According to a collection of versions

from folklorist Xenia Cord, nearly half specifically mentioned a black man; the others, not mentioning race, allowed the listener to project whatever race "made sense."[15] This rumor, suitably changed to make sense of its new locale, began appearing in white communities in and around Los Angeles in the aftermath of the 1992 uprising following the controversial verdicts in the trial of the Los Angeles police in the Rodney King beating. The story represents a model of black violence that recurs to fit the circumstances of the day.

In today's world, we eat, sleep, and occasionally even give birth in automobiles. Thus, the woman's car symbolizes a home. She is secure as long as she does not leave it. By exiting it even temporarily, she renders herself vulnerable. However, a valiant white male rescues the unfortunate damsel before the trespassing intruder can overpower her. In telling, retelling, and updating this narrative, believers assuage their anxieties with the message that quick-thinking males can still protect helpless women.

"The Choking Doberman" has the near victim arrive home only to discover her large dog gagging. One version from *Woman's World* magazine reads as follows:

> A weird thing happened to a woman at work. She got home one
> afternoon and her German shepherd was in convulsions. So she
> rushed the dog to the vet, then raced home to get ready for a date.
> As she got back in the door, her phone rang. It was the vet, telling
> her that two human fingers had been lodged in her dog's throat.
> The police arrived, and they all followed a bloody trail to her bedroom
> closet, where a young burglar huddled—moaning over his missing
> thumb and forefinger.[16]

In most versions, the dog is a Doberman pinscher. When this story is presented as true, it is often two or three *black* fingers that were found in the dog's throat.[17] Here the noble veterinarian has partnered with the brave pet and the local police to rescue the woman from the lurking criminal.

These rumors focus on white women as the near victims of an African-American criminal.[18] A lone white woman is moments away from being the victim of a crime, and in each case the crime is thwarted. In "The Stranger in the Backseat," a white male Good Samaritan comes to the rescue of the damsel in distress. In some versions it is the quick-thinking service station attendant, and in others it is the diligent truck driver who saves the day. In "The Choking Doberman," the veterinarian becomes the hero. Of course, the dog has also done its duty in protecting its mistress. The inept criminal has invaded the woman's territory and is punished for this intrusion. The fact that he has tried to assault her in her home or in the backseat of her car suggests black sexual violence. With the help of white male protectors, the woman is not violated by the black aggressor.

In contrast, the gold chain story has a distinct feminist undercurrent. The plucky heroine does not wait for a male fellow passenger to save her jewelry; she does it herself. She is more of a risk taker than her sisters in "The Choking Doberman" and "The Stranger in the Back-seat." After all, a metropolitan subway is a much more public venue than one's car or home. We are conditioned to believe that we will be safe in the latter, whereas we recognize danger in the former.

The fact that so many people share these stories suggests that they serve dual purposes. On the one hand, these are cautionary tales, warning whites of dangers lurking in the dark corners of their homes and cars. On the other hand, they suggest that whites will ultimately triumph over trespassing African Americans. A knife-wielding black man is no match for a Doberman pinscher or a clever gas station attendant.

Savvy politicians know how to capitalize on and manipulate the white public's fear of black crime. This was epitomized when the 1988 presidential campaign of Democratic hopeful Michael Dukakis was soundly thrashed by the controversial Willie Horton advertisement. A group supporting President Bush developed an ad that featured an unkempt, bearded black man who had committed sex crimes while on a weekend furlough from a Massachusetts prison. The dark-complexioned Horton became a tangible example of what many white Americans fear—the brutal black stranger released from a controlled environment. To be sure, Willie Horton was a real person who committed real crimes. The power of the image came partially from prejudice, and partially from an immediate social problem. Of course, women are more apt to be raped by an acquaintance, but this threat is simply too personal and frightening. It is more comfortable to direct one's fears outward.

The widespread tendency to link black mobility with criminal behavior has harmed the cause of integration, posing a barrier to African-American access to middle-class space. For instance, when civic leaders of the small, placid city of Dubuque, Iowa, attempted to integrate by attracting African-American residents, an uproar ensued, largely connected to fears of crime. One resident wrote to the local newspaper, the *Telegraph Herald*, that people had good reason to be fearful: "We want to keep our town just like it is, a great place to raise a family, not frightened enough to stay in at night and close our windows."[19] Such comments imply that African Americans motivated to settle in Dubuque would not crave a family-oriented community and crime-free environs. The same images and fears, bolstered by similar statistics, arise whenever integration threatens.

Although they would vehemently deny any racist inclinations, many whites still hope to keep blacks at arm's length. There are few municipalities in which the debates over public transportation routes have not been undergirded by racial considerations. In suburban Gwinnett County, outside of Atlanta, residents overwhelmingly defeated the extension of the MARTA subway system to the county in part because of fears that "criminals" would travel the subway to bring drugs and lawlessness to peaceful neighborhoods. Similarly, in the Portland, Oregon, metropolitan area, opposition to a light-rail link was tied to fears of black residential migration. The expansion of public transportation opens the possibility of a fearsome integration, and many white suburbanites would rather cope with inconvenience than with their fears.

GANG BANGERS

Black crime is fearful enough for whites, but the combination of African-American violence with collective action leads to profound dread. The word "gang" can evoke visceral reactions. Yet a historical analysis reveals that the concern over black gangs is a cyclical phenomenon that can be inflamed by a prominent journalistic report, a lurid television special, or the diatribe of an ambitious politician. Certainly from the 1940s on, beliefs in the destructive impulses of minority gangs have swept the white community. In Los Angeles in 1943, the unambiguously negative images of the Mexican-American "zoot-suiter" contributed to the "zoot-suit riots," in which naval personnel and other sympathetic whites attacked young Mexican-American men who were suspected of being in gangs and of attacking female relatives of servicemen. Following the Topsy/Eva pattern, beliefs spread in the Mexican-American community that it was the servicemen who were molesting and insulting Hispanic women. As the violence escalated, injuries were sustained on both sides. As sociologists Ralph Turner and Samuel Surace pointed out, the tension stemmed originally from the fact that young Mexican-American men were transformed into symbols of danger, and then a spark could lead to violence.[20]

Of course, the strongest effects of gang activity have always been felt on the gangs' home turf—in minority communities, yet this did not prevent whites from feeling that they would be the victims of this pent-up rage. Indeed, this core belief reflects a psychological insight: if one has oppressed a victim, one easily imagines that the victim desires revenge.

We know that public discussion measures not only the seriousness of a problem but also its symbolic resonance—the extent to which it captures public concerns, and the extent to which these concerns and the definition of the problem are created through the activity of "moral entrepreneurs" (i.e., those journalists, academics, or politicians who participate in "policy arenas").[21] This understanding of the development of public debate has been termed the *social constructionist* approach because it asks how social problems are constructed.[22] It does not suggest that there are no social problems; in fact, there are too many of them, but only some, at certain times, reach levels of significant public concern. Some become what sociologists term *moral panics*, in which much public attention is focused on alleged harms. Gang violence, with its fearsome imagery, is one of those concerns that flickers in and out of public attention.[23] At times, any congregation of (dark-skinned) young people in a public place constitutes a gang, whether or not they consider themselves to be part of an organization or engage in unlawful activity.

In most cities and neighborhoods, gang violence is quite rare. Even in the inner cities, streets are mostly peaceful, and most youths are not members of violent gangs. In fact, it is still the case, as youth researcher Lewis Yablonsky claimed nearly forty years ago, that the allegiance of youths to their gangs is loose.[24] The gang typically constitutes a "near-group." If some dramatic event is occurring, participation will be higher because people wish to be "where the action is," but most gang members are occasional at best. Yet this is not the public image of the gang.

In many recent rumors about gang activity, the brutal initiation motif is central. Gangs supposedly conduct initiations, a private right of passage, in a public and threatening fashion. In late 1993 a rumor spread through America—by fax, photocopied flyers, and e-mail, as well as through news accounts and face-to-face interaction—that a local gang had established an initiation ritual for new members. These recent technologies, affecting the situational dynamics of rumor diffusion, certainly speeded the process by which information became shared and perhaps gave it extra credibility, since hundreds of people received the same "personal" warning in a matter of moments.[25] In some versions, however, it was assumed—quite improbably, given gang rivalries—that this was a national initiation. This rumor, unlike many of the rumors discussed in this chapter, was spread in both white and black communities, although, as in the other cases, whites were more often seen as the victims.

One fairly typical flyer warning about this gang initiation described the "Lights Out" rumor:

BEWARE!!

There is a new "Gang Initiation"!!!!!

This new initiation of MURDER is brought about by Gang Members driving around at night with their car lights off. When you flash your car lights to signal them that their lights are out, the Gang members take it literally as "LIGHTS OUT," so they are to follow you to your destination and kill you!! That's their initiation.

Two families have already fallen victim to this initiation ritual.

BE AWARE AND INFORM YOUR FAMILY AND FRIENDS.

DON'T FLASH YOUR CAR LIGHTS FOR ANYONE.

THIS INFORMATION WAS PROVIDED BY THE CHICAGO POLICE DEPARTMENT.

THIS IS NOT A JOKE.

In some versions of this rumor, a date is mentioned for this initiation. Although some flyers state that the information was provided by Chicago police, in the earliest version of which we are aware, from August 1993, the Memphis police had to deny that they were faxing warnings about an upcoming gang initiation. According to Jan Harold Brunvand, the cycle peaked just about one month later during the third week in September 1993, when versions proliferated nationwide. Grady Harn of the Sacramento Police Department said that police departments across the nation were warned that the weekend of September 25–26, 1993, was "Blood" initiation. All "Bloods" were to drive around at night that weekend, shooting all individuals in the first car that did a courtesy flash to warn them that their lights are off. The message was "Be cautious if encountering any autos with lights off this weekend."

As a people we are improving in our ability to recognize a rumor or contemporary legend when we hear it, possibly as a result of Brunvand's popular series of books on "urban legends." Yet the danger from the gang initiation was so dramatic and the story seemed so plausible that many people felt it was "better to be safe than sorry." Law enforcement agencies claim that there was no evidence of such a planned initiation, which was fortunate because police had to spend much time that weekend comforting worried citizens. The only connection between an actual case and the rumor of which we have learned occurred in Stockton, California, the previous year. There two teenagers apparently opened fire on a car after its driver indicated that the lights on their car were off. These teenagers may not have been gang members. The image of the brutal initiation corresponded to concerns about drive-by shootings in which innocent bystanders were caught up in drug-related gang violence. In inner-city neighborhoods, residents learn to duck when a car drives by without its headlights on because they know a drive-by shooting may be in progress. By "purifying" the story of the accidental murder and eliminating the element of instrumental behavior in protecting one's drug turf, the "Lights Out" rumor transforms gang violence into pure evil.

Gangs, of course, do have initiations, but they typically involve members attacking the initiate to see if he can "take it." When a young man is invited to join the Hispanic gang Little Watts, in Los Angeles, he must go through an initiation called "Fifty Count." The new initiate stands in the middle of a circle of six gang members. A counter stands outside the circle and counts off. When he says "One," a member from the circle rushes the initiate, punching, kicking, and spitting. When that member is finished, the counter yells "Two," and another member attacks, and so on through the number fifty. If the members approve of the initiate's strength and poise, he is invited to join the gang. Similar rituals have been reported from African-American gangs in Chicago and New York. Sometimes, however, the initiation involves fighting with other gangs or participating in gang-related crime, such as burglaries. In all these cases, the violence either is directed within the gang or is directly instrumental in benefiting the gang. There are no instances of gangs demanding random violence as a condition of membership; gang members realize all too well that such an initiation would rapidly provoke a harsh reaction from the police and public.

"Lights Out" is the archetypal crime rumor cycle of the 1990s for several reasons. As with many other rumors and legends of this decade, new technologies contributed to its dissemination. Class issues begin to eclipse race in some tellings. "Gangs" were described by informants in multiracial terms. Asians, Latinos, blacks, and even white religious cult members were all identified as potential members of the offending group. In addition, middle-class Asians, Latinos, blacks, and whites all expressed belief in the text. Emerging thirty years after the climax of the civil rights movement, the text also signals a shift in attitudes about young men from the lower end of the socioeconomic scale. It may not be a coincidence that "Lights Out" emerged when many politicians were criticizing midnight basketball programs and other efforts to reach disaffected minority youth. In the early 1990s, social programs were in disfavor. "Lights Out" allowed believers to justify cutting support to the young underclass on the grounds that good works (flashing lights or a scholarship program) are rejected by recipients.

A string of related stories demonstrate convergence of the themes we have described. One story reflects the classic "stranger in the backseat" motif, described previously, but with the additional claim that the attack was part of an initiation ritual. This version, collected in northern California in 1993, has a twist at the end:

> A woman drove into a self-service gas station at night. She went
> inside and paid the cashier twenty dollars in order to fill her car with
> gas. When the meter reached the ten-dollar mark, it clicked off.
> She went back to remind the cashier that she had paid for twenty,
> not ten, dollars' worth of gas. The cashier then explained that
> he had seen someone sneak into the backseat of her car when she
> wasn't looking. He had phoned the police but wanted to make sure
> that she didn't drive off, so he made sure that she didn't get all
> the gas she paid for. When the police arrived, they found the stranger

in the backseat who confessed that he was participating in a gang initiation that required him to steal a car and rape a woman.

Other gang-related texts claim that as an initiation the gang member must rape a blond virgin, a cheerleader, or a sorority sister. One woman was apparently so concerned about these rumors that she transferred from the University of California at Berkeley to Smith College in bucolic Northampton, Massachusetts, after hearing that an Oakland gang required its initiates to go to Berkeley and rape a sorority girl. Unfortunately for her, the story had spread east, where it involved the Hartford Kings of Hartford, Connecticut, the most notorious gang in the area. These initiates were required to travel to Smith to rape sorority girls. In fact, the rumor of a gang invasion was so prevalent that one school in South Hadley, Massachusetts, closed temporarily. Salt Lake City was shaken by the false claim that a local cheerleader had been raped by a gang, and some school authorities warned cheerleaders not to wear their uniforms in public because "some gangster is going to pick up on [the rumor]."[26] These rape rumors have dramatic parallels with the rumors that once led to black lynchings throughout the South. Further, they exemplify the brutal double meaning of the phrase "gang rape."

Because these stories are presented as "true," and because they often do not explicitly specify the race of the gang members, the tellers and the audience can escape the stigma of racism that would be present if they had claimed that most young black men were sexual predators. The theme is transformed into an acceptable narrative.

In some instances, the castrated boy motif is transformed into a gang initiation story, as in this text collected by folklorist Richard Dorson and his collaborators from Gary, Indiana:

I heard a story . . . about a little white boy who had gone shopping with his mother in K-Mart and he had to urinate. So, for the first time the mother decided to let him go in by himself to use the men's washroom, rather than going into the women's with her.

He was in there an exceptionally long amount of time, and she got worried and asked some gentleman to step in and see what the problem was, if there was a problem. And they found the little boy laying in a pool of blood with his penis cut off. Subsequently they found three little black boys walking through the store with a bloody penis in their pocket. As it turned out, they had cut the little white boy's penis off as an orientation, a method of getting into a gang.[27]

Castration stories involve projection, related to deep themes, including the loss of male control;[28] they relate to more than the violent threat from gangs. The image of the emasculated white male is still powerful, as if we are being warned, in the words of folklorist Barre Toelken, to "watch out for those people, they're out to get us and they'll be likely to attack us in the most vulnerable places and the most objectionable ways."[29] Perhaps, as black listeners would surely note, it represents patterns of behavior toward blacks.

Folklorist Alan Dundes reminds us, in describing "projective inversion" in this mutilation by a black gang (in essence, a lynch mob), "The white males have metamorphosed their own fears of the stereotyped super-phallic Negro male into a form where their victim becomes the aggressor. The wish to castrate black males is projected to those males who are depicted as castrating a white boy. This makes it possible to blame the black victim for the crime the white would like to commit."[30] Indeed, as Dundes notes, castration was one of the tools used in the rural South to keep black men in their place. Although Dundes's psychoanalytic orientation may rely too heavily on unconscious psychodynamic processes, there is no doubt that the rumor brings to public dialogue central moral concerns and stereotyped images of black gang members.

In public sentiment, contemporary gang activity is directed outside of their world. Gang members are leaving the "hood" to spread terror as a means to demonstrate their toughness to their peers. To be sure, gangs have been responsible for numerous crimes during the past few years. Although crime is a legitimate concern, these rumors operate on the level of fantasy, not reality.

CONCLUSION

From social, economic, geographic, and cultural perspectives, we can measure great progress for African Americans since the heyday of the civil rights movement. Yet the rumors that have emerged about black crime, spread among many white citizens, suggest that acceptance has not been total. As we have emphasized, the rumors about crime detailed in this chapter do play off crime rates that remain too high. The rumors, while misguided, are not psychotic. Still, they reveal core elements of distrust that are not grounded in reality. It is unfair to suggest that most whites consciously accept the canards that all blacks are violent, dangerous, and immoral. A survey would find little support for such bald claims. However, although these themes are not consciously accepted, they clearly have not vanished. From generalizations of a race as a whole, they depict individual incidents—incidents that are often told with race being a part of the telling but tacitly understood by many as they visualize the crime. Just as rumors about the racial bias of corporations are largely spread among blacks, the rumors about crime are found among whites, although, as we have noted in connection with both the Hilfiger rumors and the gang initiation rumors, there is some evidence that this may be slowly changing.

We emphasize that the reality of crime statistics and economic inequality fuels the fears of individuals, permitting these rumors to serve various personal imperatives. In addition, a community's interest in ensuring safety and security creates numerous places in which the stories will be told. The emotional resonance of crime talk opens up the performance dynamics, with audiences demanding as much "information" as the narrator can supply. With the rise of the Internet, these stories can rapidly reach a large and rapt audience. The power of crime as discourse, coupled with the historical conditions of the relationships between blacks and whites, leads to the specific content of these rumors—the invasions, malicious attacks, and violent gang initiations—as suggested in the folklore diamond.

Crime rumors represent a set of core images that, acquired in childhood and reinforced through folk ideas of politics, are difficult to erase. For whites, while racially unpleasant images can be denied vigorously and sincerely, they sometimes appear when least expected. Their presence—the recognition that they are not totally erased and cannot be as long as statistics and authenticated incidents give them credence—makes a free and comfortable racial dialogue difficult.

SEVEN

Cries and Whispers
Race and False Accusations

On October 25, 1994, a surly black man wearing a dark ski mask stopped a compact car in a small South Carolina town, forcing the white woman out of the vehicle, kidnapping her two young children, and driving away. The woman appeared on national television to plead for the safe return of her toddlers. The woman was Susan Smith.

On November 28, 1987, a black teenager was found in a large garbage bag in a small town in upstate New York. When she was discovered, her face and body were smeared with dog feces, and the words "KKK" and "Nigger" were scrawled across her chest. She said she had been raped by four white men, including a police officer and a member of the district attorney's office. Supporters demanded the appointment of a special prosecutor to investigate the police and law enforcement agencies. The girl was Tawana Brawley.

As these two infamous examples attest, some of the saddest indicators of racial mistrust are the all-too-frequent and often well-publicized attempts of malefactors to escape blame by accusing a mysterious figure of a racial attack. In examining false racial accusations we turn briefly—

but not too far—from the consideration of rumors to examine those truth claims that operate much like rumor: the motivated lie. In the previous chapter we examined rumors about imaginary crime; in this closely related chapter we keep our attention on criminal acts, examining real crimes and powerful, but false, claims.

Like rumor, a false accusation gains its credibility from assumptions about how the world operates; indeed, for its audience, the false accusation has the same standing as a rumor. For its audience, a false accusation is, like a rumor, a truth claim. It is a public claim about the world that makes sense. That these false accusations should be so common and should mirror rumor themes so closely provides a depressing window on American race relations. We find a disturbing pattern in which members of one race can generate sympathy and potentially escape blame by claiming that a member of the other race has caused them or their loved ones grievous harm. Again we see, in the willingness to believe the worst of others, echoes of white racial bias and black paranoia. In this dynamic, false accusations are part of the same pattern of relations that this book addresses.

In one sense it does not matter much whether the accusations are true. For a time the relevant audiences treat these accusations as true and act upon them as true, reinforcing other, noxious beliefs. Yet, of course, in another sense, nothing could be more important than whether the stories are true or false. First, innocent citizens can have their reputations destroyed, spend money defending themselves, and possibly even have their lives threatened. This is dramatically exemplified in the case of lynchings, in which an accusation from a white citizen was tantamount to proof. White women could blame black men for a variety of real or imagined attacks and have their claims accepted without question. Black men were, for whites, totally believable perpetrators.

A troubling finding, whose full implications are unclear and perhaps indicate several problems, is that a study of 130 incidents of serious police brutality against citizens found that in 97 percent of these cases black or Latino citizens were the victims; white police officers were centrally involved in 93 percent of the cases. Yet officers were punished for brutality in only 13 percent of these incidents. Does this mean that many guilty officers were let off without punishment or that many innocent officers were falsely accused—or both?[1]

The spate of racial claims of black propensity to criminal activity derives from a deep historical tradition. The cultural logic on which these claims depend has remained vigorous. Because whites have easier access to the forces of social control, many of the claims insist that blacks have perpetrated dastardly crimes. Recently the accusations have begun to flow in the other direction. With the increasing power of the black community in urban areas and the importance of blacks as voters, claims such as that of Tawana Brawley are taken seriously. On college campuses, black students have claimed that they have been the victims of white racial harassment, only for it to be discovered later that their harassment was at their own hands. Most recently, the rash of black church burnings in the South have been accompanied by charges that the fires were the work of the Ku Klux Klan and other racist scoundrels. Although federal law officials emphasize, after an exhaustive study, that there was no large-scale racist conspiracy, some of the fires were racially motivated, and for some the denials of conspiracy ring false given the history of southern racial violence.

The prevalence of false charges increases the distrust of all claims in much the same way that false accusations of child sexual abuse in divorce cases cast a suspicious pall on all such allegations. These lies provide a blanket defense. Thus, when we are told that racial harassment is increasing on campuses and that in most instances no perpetrator has been caught, one can wonder whether the "victims" are themselves victims or perpetrators. Could ministers be setting their own churches on fire?

In his book *Race*, Studs Terkel tells a small, yet emblematic, story that crystallizes this concern:

The eleven-year-old black kid, with his comrade-in-mischief, a
twelve-year-old white boy, cracked the window of an elderly neighbor.

It was a small stone, sprung from a slingshot. When the woman confronted them, he was an indignant counsel for the defense. "You're accusing me just because I'm black." Why do I think he had heard this somewhere before?[2]

These charges multiply the harm of the original act because they serve to inflame and infect our hearts and souls.

In this chapter we describe four accounts of false accusations in detail: two in which whites were falsely accused, and two in which blacks were the target. There have been other cases, of course, but these well-publicized incidents have received the largest amount of publicity and entered public discourse.[3] Part of our argument is that these accusations gain their power because of the willingness of the mass media to publicize and amplify the claims. Particularly in the early days of the stories, the claims are typically taken at face value, exacerbating the tension and in the process gaining a larger audience. While one can sympathize with media that have no easy way of checking a story without considerable background work and that operate in a competitive market, we argue that a more critical judgment, greater decorum, and more public responsibility could diminish the circuslike atmosphere that sometimes prevails.

Whenever a crime "victim" (or a "witness") maliciously and dishonestly accuses someone as the perpetrator, we have a false accusation. No statistics exist to indicate how common these claims are. Criminologists have surprisingly, to our knowledge, not conducted research on "false accusations." We begin by examining two cases in which black women accused whites of attacking them verbally and physically; both Sabrina Collins and Tawana Brawley were taken seriously by officials and black leaders, but neither was able to demonstrate that her claims had any validity. In the next two cases, whites—Charles Stuart and Susan Smith—murdered relatives (respectively, a pregnant wife and two young children) and then accused blacks of committing the crime.

Although we can describe Susan Smith and Tawana Brawley as sisters in crime, in an important sense this is misleading. Blacks construct stories in which they are the victims; in contrast, for whites it is their family members who are victims. It is hard to know how to balance Tawana Brawley's claim of rape with Susan Smith's tale of kidnapping as stories. However, it is important to remember that aside from the false accusations, there were no crimes committed in the cases of allegations made by blacks, whereas the two cases involving whites were murders with actual bodies.[4] The two cases involving African Americans involved women who wanted attention and attempted to avoid blame; the two white cases involved individuals who did not want to suffer the consequences of their crimes.

SABRINA COLLINS

On Sunday, April 22, 1990, readers of the *New York Times* were shocked to learn of racial attacks on an Emory University freshman. According to the story:

> Repeated written and verbal racial attacks, varying from epithets scrawled around her dormitory room to death threats sent through the campus mail, have rendered an Emory University freshman almost mute. Sabrina Collins, a premed student on the dean's list and a varsity soccer player, has spoken little since her April 11 hospitalization, said William Fox, a vice president of the university and dean of campus life. . . . But if Ms. Collins has been silent, different factions at Emory have been vocal, variously deploring the incident and, in one case, saying it represented a festering issue of racism on campus. "To my knowledge, we have not experienced a harassment case against another person of any race like this in recent history," Mr. Fox said.[5]

This incident had a traumatic effect on the Emory community, an Atlanta university that prided itself on tolerance. Yet within a few weeks stories began to circulate that Ms. Collins was seen as a suspect, that she had poured bleach on her own clothing, mutilated her stuffed animals, and scrawled "Die, nigger, die" on the walls of her room in lipstick. Her white roommate's notebook had been stolen and later returned with the words "Nigger lover" scrawled on it.

By May 31, based on a handwriting analysis, fingerprints, and a pattern of misspellings, the incident was being described as a hoax, staged by Collins herself, perhaps to divert attention from accusations that she had cheated in a chemistry class. The monthlong campaign of racial harassment permitted her to blame her poor grades on stress. Even with the results from the Emory security force and the Georgia Bureau of Investigation, some black students continued to assert that Collins was a victim, pointing to certain ambiguities in the investigation and to her nearly catatonic behavior in a mental institution. Despite the false accusations, neither the state of Georgia nor Emory University chose to prosecute Collins, and Emory indicated that it would pay her medical bills.[6]

This incident is, by itself, fairly minor. Apparently no white student was seriously investigated, and perhaps only Collins's white roommate was seriously inconvenienced. Yet the earnest attention given to the charge reveals just how attuned institutions can be to the possibility of racism. Suddenly Emory University felt the need to discuss the racial climate on campus, previously a secondary issue. Perhaps this was a necessary debate, but surely one would have wished for a more productive context. Black students and their white allies went on the attack with claims of racism, and the administration adopted a defensive posture. Despite accusations of cheating, the university attempted to be supportive of this student, at least as much in its own interest as for reasons of compassion. The possibility of racism was sufficiently plausible in the university setting that the charges, however frivolous they turned out to be, had to be taken seriously. Students often perceive their campuses as hotbeds of racism, and while we would have to be foolish or naive to claim that there are no racist students in a large student body, universities are less subject to overt racial attacks than many other locations.[7]

TAWANA BRAWLEY

Sabrina Collins flickered across public memory for a few weeks and then disappeared into obscurity. The same cannot be said of Tawana Brawley. One of the most dramatic and disturbing incidents of false accusation concerns this African-American teenager, invariably described as a cheerleader, from Wappingers Falls, New York, a village of six thousand located fifty-five miles north of New York City. Ms. Brawley was discovered on November 28, 1987, in a large plastic garbage bag, in a grassy area near an apartment where she had previously lived. She had been missing for four days. She claimed (partly in her own statements and more explicitly through those of her advisers) that she had been raped and assaulted by four white men, including a police officer and a member of the district attorney's office. Her face and body were smeared with dog feces, her hair was matted, her jeans had been burned, and the words "KKK" and "Nigger" were scrawled across her chest. Subsequent investigations over the course of the next year painted a picture that was considerably different and that connected this young woman to a troubled home life and some unsavory companions.[8]

Shortly after Brawley was discovered, three black activists took up her cause and served as her advisers and spokespersons. In the process, these three—the Reverend Al Sharpton, and two militant attorneys, C. Vernon Mason and Alton Maddox Jr.—through effective use of the media shaped public knowledge of the case. These men had become famous in the African-American community in New York (and infamous for many whites) through their provocative but successful insistence on obtaining a special prosecutor in the Howard Beach case (in which a young black man was chased into highway traffic in a white Brooklyn neighborhood). They attempted a similar strategy here, claiming a massive cover-up and refusing to allow either Tawana Brawley or her mother to testify to a grand jury. They successfully forced New York governor Mario Cuomo to appoint Attorney General Robert Abrams as a special prosecutor, but relations between the activists and Abrams quickly soured into unpleasant, and some claimed anti-Semitic, attacks. Governor Cuomo was likened to Lester Maddox and Attorney General Abrams to Hitler; the Brawleys' refusal to testify was compared to the actions of Rosa Parks and Dr. Martin Luther King Jr.[9]

It now appears that Brawley, perhaps with the connivance of her mother, created the story of her attack to avoid the rage of her common-law stepfather, a man who was on parole after serving time for the shooting of his first wife.[10] Sadly, this small family drama, poorly conceived and executed, was picked up by black activists and later by the media, and it became blown out of proportion. One certainly imagines that in this case the goal was to deflect blame rather than to target a specific other person, although here, as in the case of Charles Stuart, actual people (notably an assistant district attorney) were placed under suspicion because of the seriousness of the charges. Some years later this man won a highly publicized libel suit against Brawley's advisers.

Because of the charges and countercharges in the Brawley incident, for a time many blacks and some whites saw the judicial system as having broken down, even though investigating without a complaining witness surely placed enormous constraints on the detectives. At first it was widely assumed that someone must have done something to Tawana Brawley. As *Newsday* commented in an article entitled "It's Time to Show Concern for Tawana Brawley," "With all the incriminating detail that only she has, the criminal justice system could then go swiftly to work so that the perpetrators are found and punished."[11] The *New York Times* investigated the case intensively because it was convinced that Brawley had been victimized, and perhaps not incidentally because it wanted to sell papers and demonstrate its commitment to the African-American community.[12] Early in Brawley's ordeal, Bill Cosby and Edward Lewis, the publisher of *Essence* magazine, offered a reward of $25,000 for information about the case, and later heavyweight champion Mike Tyson visited her, giving her his diamond-studded Rolex watch and promising that he would pay for her college education.[13] The Black Muslim leader Louis Farrakhan arrived to demonstrate in support of Brawley. While after a year the grand jury did conclude that no crime had occurred, for much of the year the Brawley story was a hot topic, persuading many African Americans that the claims of black victims would not be thoroughly investigated and making the case "a paradigm of racism in America."

At its start the incident quickly entered into racial politics. People interpreted Brawley's injuries given their own frame of reference. Noel Tepper, the attorney for the Dutchess County Committee against Racism, noted, "A good number of whites automatically suspect her story. A good number of blacks automatically believe it."[14] One *New York Times*/CBS News poll taken in July 1988 found that 62 percent of New York City residents felt that Brawley was lying, but that only about one-third of black residents felt that way.[15] One young white put it, "I think one of her own kind did it. Maybe one of her friends worked her over."[16] On the other side, supporters of Brawley claimed that Ku Klux Klan members, whom they believed had infiltrated Dutchess County law enforcement agencies, were involved in the incident.[17] Laura Blackburne, counsel to the New York State NAACP, noted, "There is so much rage and anger and frustration in the black community over the relentless racism blacks are subjected to in New York on a daily basis. It's not hard to harness that anger. If you say the right things and have the right hook, you can get people to follow you."[18] As Stanley Diamond, a Columbia University anthropologist, noted in the *Nation*, a liberal journal, "In cultural perspective, if not in fact, it doesn't matter whether the crime occurred or not. . . . False charges [frequently] rationalize the maiming and murder of countless blacks in the United States. . . . The crime that did not occur was described with skill and controlled hysteria by the black actors as the epitome of degradation, a repellent model of what actually happens to too many black women."[19] The charges made cultural sense within the African-American community. Obviously, the belief in these charges created a milieu of racial hostility and paranoia throughout Dutchess County. Even after the grand jury announced its findings, many blacks, feeling powerless, remained skeptical or even rejected them.[20] The conservative *National Review*, linking the story to Janet Cooke's fraudulent Pulitzer Prize–winning account of a nonexistent eight-year-old heroin addict, noted that "there's a ready market for these yarns of black 'victims' of Our Society."[21]

As is often the case with media-saturated stories, copycats soon emerge. Thus, "A 33-year-old black therapist at the Hudson River Psychiatric Center reported being kidnapped by two white men who tried to rape her. A quick investigation proved the story a hoax—she had spent most of the time drinking with friends."[22] Another black woman in Wappingers Falls claimed that whites were smearing excrement on her door. A police videotape eventually caught her in the act.[23] In still another case, the attorney for a white Harlem pastor, accused of sexually assaulting his black female parishioners, claimed that the pastor's main accuser filed the charges after reading about Tawana Brawley, a strategy labeled the "Tawana Brawley defense."[24] These incidents remind us that well-publicized cases may be just the tip of the iceberg of false accusations.

Interestingly, Brawley's claims may themselves have been an example of the copycat effect, based on another false claim of a racial attack:

> A friend [of Tawana Brawley], sixteen-year-old Tawana Ward
> Dempsey, had tried to conceal a late night escapade with a boy.
> Tawana Dempsey had gone to the police and told them that, as she
> was walking home one night along a quiet road in Poughkeepsie,
> two white men in a green car had pulled up, dragged her inside,
> driven her into the woods, and raped her. The police discovered
> discrepancies in the story, and an investigation revealed that she had
> fabricated the tale to cover up her rendezvous with a boy.[25]

After the Brawley grand jury report, some black commentators, such as Clarence Page, lamented that this case only served to trivialize legitimate cases of injustice, leading to suspicion of those claims.[26] Within the context of black paranoia, any charge aimed at black men can be presumed false (e.g., the claims that the rape and assault charges of the Central Park jogger were a hoax),[27] and any claim made by a black is accorded belief. For an African American to reject such racial claims is seen by some as an act of disloyalty; such skeptics are seen as "less black."[28] For whites, the problem is what *New York Times* reporter Craig Wolff refers to as "the tiptoe effect."[29] Whites are afraid, perhaps for fear of being labeled racists, to confront false accusations made by blacks. Thus, even though there was early suspicion that Brawley's story was false, officials and observers were careful to avoid saying so explicitly and were afraid to claim that this young woman who falsely accused others as rapists and torturers was "evil"—a compunction not seen in discussions of white accusers. At least in cases of white accusers, once the accusations are proven false, their previous community support is replaced by scorn and anger.

CHARLES STUART

On the night of October 23, 1989, Boston police dispatchers received a frantic call from a driver who claimed that he and his pregnant wife had been shot by a black man as they were returning home from a childbirth class at Boston's Brigham and Women's Hospital. Police traced the call to a car parked in the predominantly black Mission Hill neighborhood. Within a few hours the wife died; her baby, delivered by cesarean section, died seventeen days later. The man who made the call, Charles Stuart, had been shot in the abdomen, but after several weeks in the hospital, he recovered.[30]

With an injury that serious, at first there seemed little reason to doubt Stuart's story. Indeed, the earliest information about the family to emerge suggested that Charles and his wife, Carol, an attorney, had a storybook life. Charles had risen from working-class origins to work for a prominent Boston furrier. The couple seemed prosperous and appeared to be eagerly awaiting the birth of their first child. So, when Stuart claimed that a raspy-voiced black man had committed the crime, and provided a description of the perpetrator, the police went to work immediately, questioning men throughout the area. Boston's mayor, Raymond Flynn, ordered all available police detectives to help in the hunt. Within a day, over a hundred policemen had fanned out over the Mission Hill projects using their stop-and-search technique to confront and question (and some said to humiliate and harass) any likely looking young black man. Flynn and other Boston politicians attended the funeral of Carol Stuart. Her husband sent a moving poem from his hospital bed to his dear departed wife. At one point, after having detained several black men, the police came close to arresting one suspect, William "Willie" Bennett, a man with a record of violent crimes, who had previously shot a police officer. Stuart had identified him in a lineup, and Bennett reportedly had bragged to a relative about having robbed the Stuarts.[31]

The problem was that Stuart's story was a lie. With the help of his brother and a friend (both subsequently convicted), he had murdered his wife, shot himself, and lied about it. Stuart never directly confessed, but when he learned in January that he had become a prime suspect, he committed suicide by jumping off the Tobin Bridge. Apparently he had a lengthy conversation with his attorney immediately before his death, a conversation which the attorney, pleading lawyer-client confidentiality, has never detailed. Theories that developed included the possibility that Stuart wanted the insurance money from his wife's death, that he felt tied down by the prospect of becoming a father, and that he had a girlfriend. As more information was revealed about Stuart, particularly after his suicide, the more apparent it was that his life was built on lies. For example, although he claimed to have attended Brown University on an athletic scholarship, he actually had graduated from a vocational technical institute.

In retrospect, police should have recalled that most female homicide victims are murdered by husbands or lovers; the perpetrator often fakes an injury.[32] Yet the information Stuart provided about a black male in a black running suit with red stripes, coupled with his extensive, life-threatening injuries, made too much cultural sense. As it happened, the emergency medical technicians who discovered Stuart and his wife that night were accompanied by a television crew from the CBS program *Rescue 911*. Within days Stuart had become a media icon, a symbol of the danger of street crime and urban decay.

Shortly after the shooting, the *Boston Globe* noted, "Coming after a recent wave of shootings that have involved innocent bystanders, the attack on the Stuarts . . . sparked particular outrage yesterday in Boston."[33] A radio station set up a tip line for information, and a Boston businessman offered a $10,000 reward for the arrest of the killer. The police were convinced that the attacker lived in or routinely committed crimes around the Mission Hill housing project.[34] Boston politicians hurried to provide support to the Stuarts and to assure the Boston public that they supported the police. Others advocated reinstating the death penalty. One councilman proposed to provide the police with a $10 million supplement. A black councilman noted that the Stuarts had "become a symbol" of the "carnage" on the streets of Boston.[35] The city was fascinated by the story, as newspaper circulation and television ratings increased dramatically and the media competed to describe the Stuarts' idyllic life and to contrast it with the evil on the streets. Despite the reduction in the Boston crime rate the previous year, there was talk of the need to call a "crime emergency."[36]

After Stuart's suicide the holes in his story became clear.[37] Perhaps a circulation war among Boston newspapers was responsible for the massive attention given to the story. Perhaps the situation was exacerbated by Boston police pressuring witnesses to provide false statements to the police and the grand jury, a claim made in a 1991 report by U.S. Attorney Wayne Budd and subsequently admitted to by the police.[38]

Nearly half of all Bostonians polled in the aftermath of the case felt that race relations had declined, and that both blacks and whites used the case to support their own racial attitudes.[39] However, it must be recognized that in this instance it was a white criminal who made the false accusation, and it was quickly accepted by a largely white power structure. While no black man was charged, several were targets of the investigation, and many were viewed with increased suspicion.

Stuart's story made sense culturally, as Robert Maynard noted:

> Stuart knew America and Americans better than we know ourselves. He knew he could rely on two key institutions, the police and the news media, to swallow his lurid story hook, line and sinker. . . . It was based on his understanding of racism in American society. He knew he could rely on the police and the press to ignore any nagging inconsistencies in his story. . . . This entire dreadful fiasco would have been virtually impossible to have even been hatched in a society not conditioned in advance to believe the worst of black urban society. . . . Our perceptions of pathology are almost unlimited where certain groups are concerned. The urban black underclass leads the list in that respect.[40]

Or as Harvard law professor Christopher Edley commented:

> The reaction of politicians and the press to the Boston murder/hoax of Charles Stuart is a case in point. Here's how it works: Police, politicians, and commentators try to avoid facing their own racism by saying that they were fooled by Stuart and that he manipulated us all. The whole episode—from murder to strip-searches to false grand-jury testimony—becomes Stuart's fault. . . . *Washington Post* columnist Mary McGrory wrote, "Racism has its fleeting users." The reality is far worse. It is indeed cynically manipulative and effective for a Charles Stuart or a Tawana Brawley to play on fears and bigotry. But it is also cynical and worse to say that only the tricksters are to blame; our easy gullibility is not so innocent.[41]

The apologies eventually issued to Willie Bennett's mother and to the citizens of Mission Hill did little to compensate for the bitterness caused by the false accusation.

As in the case of Tawana Brawley, the charges used by Stuart were not unique. At about the same time as the Stuart murder, David Craig, a former leader of the True Knights of the Ku Klux Klan, was convicted of murder in the death of a fellow Klan member. He and his partner (the deceased's widow) had previously blamed the murder on black men.[42] In Milwaukee in 1992, Jesse Anderson claimed that two young black men had stabbed him and killed his wife in the parking lot of a local restaurant. At first the police stopped and checked black men in connection with the case, but eventually Anderson was convicted of killing his wife and was sentenced to sixty years in prison. Milwaukee alderman Marvin Pratt noted, "Based on the racist climate, if you say a black male or two black males assaulted you, you would be believed."[43] We must note that in each of these cases the white accusers were eventually discovered; however, it is also fair to ask how many black men are in prison or have been executed because of false accusations that have never been disproved.

SUSAN SMITH

In late 1994 the nation was once again stunned by a vicious crime. A young mother in the small town of Union, South Carolina (population ten thousand), reported to police on October 25 that her automobile, with her two young children in the backseat, had been carjacked by a black man.[44] She claimed to have been forced to leave the car, while the black man drove off with her children, promising not to hurt them. Susan Smith caught the attention of the nation as she appeared on national television to plead for the return of her children, Michael and Alex, ages three years and fourteen months.

From early on, the police in Union, led by Sheriff Howard Wells, were suspicious of Smith's story, and while they searched for the kidnapper, they meticulously built a case against Smith. What, after all, would a black criminal want with two young white children or an older-model Mazda? Within nine days Susan Smith had confessed and led police to a lake dock where she had rolled her car into the lake, with her two young children strapped inside. Eventually she was tried and convicted of murder and was given a life sentence. She had led a troubled life, sexually abused by her stepfather when she was a teenager, and separated from her husband. Her boyfriend did not wish to be tied down with her children, and he had ended their relationship the previous week.

Although this incident was likened to the Stuart case, in South Carolina the criminal justice system worked properly, even if the media sensationalized the story. The police took Smith's statements seriously, but they were skeptical from the start and did not conduct an indiscriminate search of the African-American community, particularly after Smith failed a lie detector test. The sheriff recognized that just as he needed to search for a suspect, he needed to consider the welfare of his black community, which represented 29 percent of the population.[45] Only a few black men were brought in for questioning, and those who were, were questioned with respect.[46] Indeed, the description that Smith provided could have matched nearly any black man between twenty and thirty years old:[47] an image of white America's worst nightmare, "a surly black man wearing a dark knit cap."[48] Smith's story did not add up; it seemed to reflect television and film plots rather than life in rural South Carolina. Bureau of Justice statistics indicate that there are three carjackings per hundred thousand residents in rural areas, compared with ten times that number for urban residents. The image of the violent black man is often seen in popular culture (and in urban crime statistics), and so it is available to draw upon. For many Americans, Smith's claim, coupled with the romantic image that we give to the mother-child bond, worked, if only briefly.

Yet African Americans remained troubled by the fact that a "sketch of a nondescript black man drawn according to Smith's specifications cast a nationwide cloud of suspicion over thousands of black men."[49] Black men noticed whites staring at them as they went about their business. As Jesse Glen, a thirty-eight-year-old black man who owned a

Mazda that looked like Smith's, noted, "The white people's necks were all turning as we drove by. You see the look. You know what it means. . . . That look is what racism is all about."[50]

Given that this was the rural South, many Americans remembered when black men were lynched on little more than the claims of a Susan Smith. As a North Carolina newspaper, the *Durham Herald-Sun*, noted: "The convenient but outrageous use of a fictitious black perpetrator does enormous damage to fragile relations between the races. . . . African Americans in Union and elsewhere are mad as hell about this backward tumble into old-time racism, and they should be. . . . The truth, as in the Smith and Stuart cases, is usually more horrid than fiction."[51] Of course, the fact that Smith's crime and trial occurred during the same period in which Americans were fascinated with the trial of O. J. Simpson, and the claims by his supporters that two unknown white men had murdered his ex-wife and Ron Goldman, gave extra piquancy to the charge.

Charges of attacks on white women by black men generate greater incendiary power than most false accusations. The image of interracial sexual assault dies hard. At times white women—not just Susan Smith—have resorted to these charges, perhaps to manage their relationships with husbands and lovers. Accusations are gendered as well as racial (as false accusations of rape indicate), but when the two are combined, the dynamics are explosive. In fact, the year before the Smith case, a white woman had falsely accused a black man of robbing her of her cash, a story created to appease a husband who would have been furious had he known she had lost the money gambling.[52] In a period of heightened racial tension at Olivet College in Michigan in 1992, a white female student claimed that she had been attacked by four African-American students and had been left unconscious in a field near the campus. College officials were skeptical of her charges, and no arrests were made. However, gossip spread, and that night two trash cans were set on fire outside the rooms of black student leaders.[53] In 1994, in a case that reminds us of the Sabrina Collins incident, a white student at the State

University of New York at Old Westbury claimed that she had been slashed across the face and stabbed in the stomach by a black man. Later she admitted that she had wounded herself.[54] Even if these incidents did not lead to arrests and convictions, they remind us of the delicate relations between white women and black men.

CONCLUSION

The material reported in this chapter is dispiriting. Both black and whites are willing to use racial suspicion to direct blame for their actions The social structure, both institutional (notably the role of law enforcement and mass media) and racial, provides the basis in which narrators create their lies and the settings in which the accusations are narrated and spread. As the folklore diamond suggests, the motivations of the narrators (their personal imperatives) and the conditions under which narration is spread (the performance dynamics) contribute to the content of which false accusations are likely to be taken as true.

Recounting these stories, while saddening, may *sensitize* us the next time a charge is made: perhaps we will remember Tawana and Susan, and look at the claims of their successors with more skepticism. Perhaps we will recognize that their stories are similar to the rumors covered in previous chapters. Perhaps some of the accusations were motivated by knowledge of racial rumors. Of course, not every accusation is a false accusation; many horrid crimes demonstrate this point. Some accusations are true, just as some rumors turn out to be accurate.

The media, here as elsewhere, play a critical role. These cases gain their resonance through the use to which the mass media put them. While the media wish to report the "truth," they also wish to gain audiences. We do not claim that these four cases gained the prominence they did because the media "lied," but it is reasonable to suggest that, particularly in the early days of public concern, due diligence was not always evident. The stories seemed "too good" to be burdened by doubts about the veracity of the claims. In such racially charged claims, the media must do more than be a conduit or a magnifying glass; it must present cautions when racial passions threaten to explode.

Throughout this book we have emphasized that rumor should not be dismissed but should be viewed carefully in light of previous stories. So it is with these accusations. When one hears of a crime that seems to be too sad, it may well be so. When responding to accusations, whites rely on their history of racial stereotypes and blacks on their history of racial injustice. Crafty criminals use these images to their advantage. Ultimately we, the public, are the agents of justice, and we must strive not to be blind.

EIGHT

Coming Clean

A group of elderly white women enter a big-city hotel elevator. As the doors are closing, a large black man and his dog enter. The man orders the dog to sit, and the frightened women, thinking he is addressing them, collapse to the floor. He apologizes, and at dinner that night the black man, a celebrity, has the check paid for them.

The programmers who designed Microsoft Word have created a program whereby if one types in "I'd like all niggers to be killed," the thesaurus will respond, "I'll drink to that."

The preceding chapters do not lend themselves to easy conclusions. In fact, in writing this volume, we, the authors, continually debated the conclusions that we should draw. Like most Americans, we believe that sorting out the state of race relations in this country is much more complicated than it has ever been. With all our training, teaching, reading, talking, and interviewing, our own individual backgrounds steer us toward those stories we hear and the ones we tell. Fine is eager to embrace evidence that suggests that white Americans have in considerable measure abandoned the overt prejudices and biases of the past. He points to the widespread popularity of Colin Powell, Sammy Sosa, and Oprah Winfrey. Turner seizes the evidence that suggests that African

Americans are wise to remain cautious about their status in American society. She points to the record of discriminatory practices recently documented at Texaco and Denny's, as well as the continued "racial profiling" of drivers on the nation's highways. The truth is that it is easy to sympathize both with those who argue that racism is endemic in American society and with those who praise the dramatic increase in tolerance and optimistically contrast the barriers to African-American achievement today with those of two generations ago. The challenge, thus, is to determine how, given these contradictory perspectives and our heightened racial sensitivity, we can better understand each other. That we as authors do not fully agree, even when we understand each other, represents the frustration and hope of racial dialogue.

Readers will be similarly influenced by how the evidence we have presented fits into their overall perspectives. The rumors, contemporary legends, and truth claims we have examined are credible because they reinforce the worldviews of those who share them. As the previous chapters indicate, rumors are evidence of a problem or perception deeper than the "facts" on the surface of the texts reveal. People err by listening and responding to what the texts say directly. Truth and fiction blend in ways that are difficult to unravel. But unless we examine all levels of rumors, the deeper ones that whisper as well as the superficial ones that shout, the dilemmas that stimulated the initial texts will persist. Debunking one rumor about a gang initiation will not result in whites trusting African-American teenagers. Demonstrating that a white supremacist group did not seize control of a fast-food chain will not result in blacks trusting corporate America. To diminish the circulation of rumors that reflect persistent racial mistrust, white and black Americans must participate in the painful process of coping with the past and conducting themselves forthrightly and honestly in the present. Both races need to listen attentively to their own stories as well as those of others. After working together for the better part of a decade, we as coauthors do not agree completely. But our understanding of each other's views has been enhanced by our willingness to listen to the other.

It is a fact of life that most people relish the opportunity to debunk a rumor believed by someone else while they are loathe to acknowledge their own susceptibility. African-American informants are quick to disabuse whites of the belief that a gang initiation requires the rape of a white woman or that the Black Panthers armed themselves and hid in the mountains of Utah, planning to invade Salt Lake City. White informants are just as eager to demonstrate that no prominent fashion designer ever professed white supremacist support on *The Oprah Winfrey Show* or on *Montel Williams*. If we probed our own beliefs with the rigor we apply to others, we would all be better off. This impulse to correct others' misapprehensions while assuming we have none of our own is understandable, although unfortunate.

Rumors serve as a gauge for the state of race relations in American society. Judging by the rumors and false accusations we described in the previous chapters, all too often we find a distressing absence of trust. Both blacks and whites attempt to deflect attention from their troubles by blaming their victims. While some rumors are based in fact and some accusations are accurate, enough are spread to gain attention, defuse fears, justify prejudice, or deflect blame—often with the narrators not being fully conscious of their motives. Did the white husband who claimed to have been mugged by a black man only wish to prevent his wife from learning that he spent money on a prostitute? Did the black student pointing to a piece of racial hate mail create it herself, craving attention? While these false accusations are rare, the belief that they could represent racial politics is becoming increasingly common. Truth claims operate in a climate of plausibility, and our racial misunderstandings admit a wide range of beliefs.

Claiming that one's hidden concerns actually are real transforms a prejudice into a social problem. Even threatening rumors carry a certain measure of comfort as they justify beliefs. With many of the stories being reported—and sometimes magnified—by the media, the claims gain credibility by having been published or broadcast. The media have a special role in this regard because their reports constitute the "confirmation" that many seek, even when the stories themselves merely report the existence of the rumor's spread.

The most compelling stories feature ominous villains. As we pointed out in chapter 3, for many African-American consumers, rejecting an appealing commodity may entail linking it to an individual or group that represents evil. Corporate executives—white men with great power and with little sympathy for poorer consumers—fill this position well. Until corporate America assumes a proactive role in diminishing the opportunity imbalance between whites and blacks and ensures that its advertisements are not racially insensitive, it can expect to face racial rumors. Likewise, rumors about government conspiracies, such as those described in chapter 4, are likely to continue until the white patina of high government office and law enforcement changes.

For their part, whites voluntarily limit their leisure activities, often refusing to visit downtown areas during the evening for fear of evil and animalistic black criminals and rampant gangs, a process we described in chapters 5 and 6. Both blacks and whites punish themselves because of their perverse fears. Here governments must endeavor to make all citizens safe and welcome in public spaces. Statistically, blacks are the overwhelming victims of violent crimes, and black leaders should vigorously address the public safety concerns of all citizens, which they have not always done emphatically or frequently. As evidence from both whites and blacks attests, those who believe the rumors become their victims, limiting their choices.

To cope with the truth claim behind a rumor requires us to be aware of those features of our belief systems that decrease our critical ability. Rather than denying and hiding our beliefs in the name of tolerance or attempting to cobble together evidence to support our claims, we must critically examine those beliefs and then question claims that seem "too good to be false."

In many ways it has never been easier to determine that particular claims are false. This is easiest in the case of the consumer texts. Within days after the circulation of texts alleging that Tommy Hilfiger made racist comments on a talk show, the Internet and news broadcasts carried evidence to the contrary. Becoming an informed consumer of rumors about the government is harder. While the evidence that Hilfiger did not appear on a talk show is compelling, determining whether or not anyone with U.S. government credentials facilitated the movement of drugs into black communities is tricky. Given the quasi-legitimate and even illegal activities by some government officials, it sometimes seems wise to assume the worst. But just as the government has a spotty record when it comes to functioning above the law, it also has a poor track record when it comes to secrecy. Most of those who work for the government are probably insufficiently organized to execute successfully a complex conspiracy, and, to be fair, most are thoroughly moral and upstanding.

Judging rumors and truth claims about criminal activity poses particular challenges. After all, black and white criminals inhabit our world. The more heinous their crimes, the more news time they garner. The media suggest that serial killers and murderers lurk on every street and country road. But as statistics indicate, most Americans are in far less danger from strangers than we have been led to believe. If we do become a victim of a violent act, someone of our own race, indeed of our own family, is most likely to be the perpetrator. The expression "isolated incident" has become a very charged one. But many crimes in which a black criminal assaults a white victim are just that: reprehensible acts committed by one individual. He or she is to blame, not all members of a larger group. In turn, individuals associated with virulent white supremacist groups do commit deplorable crimes. These groups tend to attract disenfranchised, poorly educated individuals, quite similar in many ways to black gang members.

Ultimately people cannot magically wish away uncomfortable, stereotypical beliefs that judge an entire racial group. These beliefs will remain, only gradually dissipating if we work diligently. Stripping away the artifice to come to grips with the underlying truth is not easy, but it is necessary. Denial is not the means to this end. Assuring oneself that it is wrong to hold these beliefs no more eliminates them than continually reminding oneself not to think about elephants drives these beasts from our mind.

Further, informing another person that he or she has an offensive or paranoid perspective does little to promote mutual understanding. While charges of racism or paranoia may have some legitimacy, they often lead to withdrawal from contact. To the extent that all dialogue about racial issues becomes a discussion of the problem of racism, while understandable, this ignores the fears and concerns of whites. Whites worry about crime and affirmative action, particularly those programs that affect the life chances of one's offspring, such as college admissions decisions. The absence of these topics in racial discussions keeps the exchange unbalanced. Discussions about race must be balanced, sympathetic to perceived grievances and fears among all groups.

In the appreciation of rumor, African Americans are likely to embrace those stories that reveal in dramatic fashion the oppression they know from their lived experience. In turn, in their rumors, whites feel burdened by blacks. While whites are not oppressed by black institutions, all too often these rumors suggest that they feel attacked or displaced by black individuals. While it is easy to dismiss these two perspectives as ill-founded, they do explain much about the difficulties of mutual understanding.

Social psychologist Claude Steele, in a provocative essay in the *Atlantic Monthly* that explains conditions under which black school achievement occurs, speaks of the importance of identifying with the institution.[1] For success, one's self-definition must be linked to a belief that the institution will act equitably. In this way the belief in pervasive racism is especially pernicious: the belief, perhaps accurate, harms the believer more than the perpetrator. Some suspect that the best way to defeat racism is simply not to believe in its existence. For their part, most whites realize that something needs to be done to overcome the problems that blacks face, but it is by no means certain what this something should be. Yet there is a desire to transcend the past and to create a world of justice, one in which all can succeed on their own merit.

Despite the difficulty of racial understanding, there are some signs of hope—hope found in a rumor complex that simultaneously presents racism but may also present directions to a way free.

GIVING BENEDICTION

One arena in which blacks have achieved some measure of public esteem is the sports and entertainment industry. Whites seem especially willing to accept and even cherish black superstars, whose finely honed physical abilities are so evident. Although many whites still have difficulty accepting blacks as intellectual equals, the physical skills of blacks are widely acknowledged. Yet when black celebrities are praised (as a "credit to their race"), the praise often implies that brutality and incompetence are the standard from which the celebrity deviates.

In the realm of rumor, one major narrative—"The Elevator Incident"—particularly captures this racial ambivalence. This rumor attaches itself to an African-American celebrity (although the figure changes, the celebrity named is always black). The story describes how a black sports or music celebrity—most often Reggie Jackson or Lionel Ritchie but sometimes boxer Larry Holmes, Wilt Chamberlain, "Magic" Johnson, O. J. Simpson, Jackie Robinson, or "Mean" Joe Greene—frightens white women on a elevator by giving instructions to his dog. The women make an incorrect and racially insensitive assumption that he is talking to them. Later—and this is the dramatic and significant part—the celebrity rewards them by buying them a meal or sending them champagne. He undermines their thinly veiled racism.

Jan Harold Brunvand presents a version, originally from a January 5, 1982, column by Jack Jones of the *Rochester (N.Y.) Democrat and Chronicle*. It describes an incident involving three unidentified women from Rochester who had recently visited New York City.

The women were on an elevator. A black man got on the elevator with a dog.

The elevator door closed.

"Sit!" the man commanded.

The three women sat.

The man apologized and explained to the women that he was talking to his dog.

The women then nervously said that they were new to New York, and asked the nice man if he knew of a good restaurant.

The women went to the restaurant recommended by the man. They had a good meal, and called for their check. The waiter explained that the check had been paid by Reggie Jackson—the man they had met on the elevator.[2]

Reggie Jackson himself claims to have heard the story "a thousand times." It has become an old chestnut, seemingly innocuous, and found around the country. It was described in the august *New York Times* as having happened to four doctors' wives from York, Pennsylvania, who misunderstood Jackson's command to his Doberman. Jackson's agent, Matt Merola, explained to the *Boston Globe*, "I tell everyone it's true. It's a nice story, a good story, if you want it to be true, it's true." He later explained that the story is false, but whites typically assume that it is a "nice story." Indeed, the story is much nicer than much of what we have described in previous chapters.

To appreciate the meaning of this story, one must recognize the context in which the incident occurs. The victims are always white women, the "perpetrator" is always a large black man. In many cases, the women are specifically warned about the dangers of the big city— dangers that must be taken as racial. In one story the women are warned by the son of one of them: "Never resist a mugger . . . do whatever he wants. It's better than dying." Another version from "Darling" in the *Detroit Free Press*, again not mentioning a racial warning, notes that "four Cottage Hospital Pink Ladies [hospital volunteers from Detroit] . . . wanted to go to a convention in New York. Their husbands agreed only if the little women promised not to visit Times Square or any other nasty areas."[3]

Sometimes the images of dangerous hands "violate" the closing elevator door. The story from the *Detroit Free Press* continues: "The first evening, as they were boarding the hotel elevator, a large hand reached in and held the door open. Then the rest of a large, muscular man, accompanied by a big dog, got on the elevator." Another text collected by folklorist Ervin Beck reports, "Just before the elevator door closed, they saw a pair of hands grab the doors and open them again. There stood a big, black man—and his equally big dog." A sketch depicting this story appeared on *The Bob Newhart Show* (we are unsure if the show was based on the legend or vice versa), in which the command to the white dog was "Sit down, Whitey," clearly indicating the racial threat involved.

The women depicted in "The Elevator Incident" often hail from the whitest and most "innocent" regions and find themselves "trapped" with a fierce, invading black man with a large "snarling and tugging" dog. In published accounts the women are often Mennonite or Amish, which only makes the contrast more dramatic.

Reggie Jackson's agent is not the only one who finds the story "nice." John Mooney, a sports reporter for the *Salt Lake Tribune*, commented that the story represented the "good aspects of sports," adding, "Now doesn't that make you feel better this morning, realizing that most of the athletes are really decent folks underneath all the bickering and scandals?"[4]

In debunking the story, the late Herb Caen, a longtime columnist for the *San Francisco Chronicle*, notes that "even Reggie can't figure out how this fable got started, but since he comes out the hero, who cares." Jan Harold Brunvand, who, in fairness, notes the racial stereotypes and fear of crime, reports, "Well, wouldn't *you* sit down when the big man commanded 'Sit!' and wouldn't you be relieved the next morning to find the bill paid and a nice note of apology from the baseball star?"[5] Brunvand's "you" is evidently a white "you," just as the "big man" is a black "stranger." The story concerns the fearful otherness of the black celebrity and *his* attempt to overcome *white* bias through apology and gifts. Perhaps the white women should send the champagne. Even though this story is about misguided racism, and thus is the "nice" story that proponents believe, it depends on the black man to forgive whites for their beliefs, a not entirely happy conclusion.

Yet the fact that the story is spread widely among whites sends a message that perhaps whites are coming to recognize their prejudices. The story would not be narrated if there were not some recognition of embarrassment and some willingness to enshrine a black man as a moral exemplar. Indeed, some blacks, recognizing this, wish to use the opportunity of interpersonal closeness and likely misunderstanding to underline the discomfort of whites, such as the practical joker who admits to thinking about saying "Boo!" when he is alone in an elevator with whites.[6]

This story mirrors a string of personal experience narratives in which African-American celebrities describe how they were approached by well-meaning whites who were convinced that they were service workers, such as bellhops and porters. These racial misunderstanding tales, told as actual experiences, although possibly embellished, reveal deeply held misinterpretations. One version, told by Jesse Jackson, reveals such a mistake:

> [Jackson] told the story of how he was at a glitzy New York hotel, waiting at the elevator just after a meeting with Zimbabwe Prime Minister Robert Mugabe, just before he was heading out for dinner at Bill Cosby's house. Jackson was waiting there, undoubtedly in his handsome suit with the gold collar stickpin under the silk tie with the matching handkerchief in the coat pocket, looking, you just know, about as elegant and successful as a man can look, when a finely dressed elderly white woman walked up and said, "I couldn't have made it downstairs without you," and pressed a dollar in his

hand. Jackson was confused for an instant, until he realized she had mistaken him for the bellman. The woman's middle-aged daughter was mortified, but Jackson shrugged it off.[7]

One, of course, is not told the condition of the older woman; if she had failing eyesight or memory, the story would have had a different moral. Further, the word "undoubtedly" suggests that the elaborate description of Jackson's wardrobe came from the reporter, not Jackson. This story is already showing signs of becoming traditional (either in Jackson's retelling two years later or through a reporter's revisions of the earlier version):

> A speech on apartheid before the United Nations, a reception hosted by several foreign ambassadors and finally dinner with Zimbabwe President Robert Mugabe and his wife at the home of Bill and Camille Cosby—the day's schedule promised to be a heady one, even for a man as prominent as the Rev. Jesse Jackson. But as he stood outside of a hotel waiting for a limousine, it happened. Out of nowhere came the seemingly innocent yet ugly reminder that some people in this day and age still judge a person's station in life by the color of his skin. "This White lady walked up to me," Rev. Jackson recalls. "She said, 'Oh, I'm so glad to see you. You really saved me. If you hadn't helped me get those bags off the elevator, I couldn't have made it.'" Having said all that, she then gave him a dollar. Startled, Rev. Jackson—a two-time candidate for the presidency of the United States—took the dollar, thanked the woman and climbed into his waiting stretch limousine, which was driven by a White chauffeur.[8]

In this version, the event occurs outside the hotel, not at the elevator. The mortified white daughter is eliminated, the woman's statement is elaborated, and the stretch limo, *driven by a white man,* arrives at the proper moment. Whether Jesse Jackson has become a better narrator or the reporters are improving the story is uncertain. This narrative is sufficiently dramatic that it has entered the academic literature as an example of how prominent black Americans may be treated.[9]

One regional version targeted Karl Malone of the Utah Jazz, who was waiting in the baggage claim area at the Salt Lake International Airport for his brother to arrive. A white woman approached him, thinking he was the "porter-boy." According to the original account by Malone himself, making it a personal experience narrative—before it became transformed in retelling—Malone refused the tip, telling the woman that he played professional basketball. Malone explained to a sportswriter, "It was really . . . funny. I was having a good time."[10]

We believe that these stories capture an important aspect of American race relations. The narratives represent the confusion that we often feel in trying to understand each other. In these texts, unlike others that we discuss, all participants are people of goodwill, even if misguided. Undeniably the stories report prejudicial behavior of whites and, in the case of "The Elevator Incident," behavior that could reasonably be interpreted as provocative. Yet the outcome represents a triumph of goodwill over grievance. In these stories the black man makes amends for the prejudices of the whites, but at the same time whites return the favor by telling the story on themselves. These narratives are ultimately about misplaced racism and about goodwill, even if some blacks find the legends vexing and the actions of the celebrities demeaning. For whites to share these rumors presents the moral that they should not rely on skin color to judge those with whom they come into contact. If nothing else, this is a hopeful place to begin.

Of course, many African-American informants find this legend frustrating. They often denigrate the black celebrity who opts to reward whites for their biases. Many blacks perceive this as the conduct of a sellout. Yet, just as we have debated the meanings of this legend, others might find that talking about it and other legends across racial lines might help mutual understanding.

COPING WITH RUMOR

Describing the rumors and beliefs that bedevil our attempts to communicate across racial boundaries is necessary but not sufficient. If we hope to understand each other and appreciate each other's concerns, how should we proceed? We claim that five steps are necessary to begin the uncertain process of racial healing.

ACCEPT ONESELF

First, we believe that to engage in a racial dialogue, we must accept who we are, warts and all. While ridding oneself of racism, paranoia, bias, and misinformation is an admirable goal—few would disagree that these ends are desirable—it is not easy. In some measure it may even be impossible. Wishing that one did not accept stereotypes does not make it so. To decide consciously to reject the belief that African Americans are substantially less intelligent or that whites are trying to practice genocide may work on a conscious level, but these beliefs, along with their historical grounding, are so ingrained that the decision may alter only what one says, not how one dreams. Indeed, it may not entirely matter what one believes. What is more important is that black and white citizens recognize that they cannot escape from the force of a set of historical understandings. One need not be ashamed of the fact that some beliefs cannot easily be erased. Feeling shame over one's own racism or paranoia may be as detrimental to the process of healing as the beliefs themselves. Accepting the existence of uncomfortable beliefs may be legitimate in that we can recognize that they do not necessarily affect behavior.

DIRTY HANDS

Given our argument that uncomfortable beliefs are endemic in discussions of race relations, it is critical that we not expect moral perfection of others. We come to the table with our hands (and minds) dirty. Perhaps we are racists and paranoids, but we must be good-hearted racists and paranoids. We do not mean to be flippant because it is obvious that both racism and racial paranoia are destructive; yet we cannot wait until these feelings have vanished, nor can we use our failings as a means of discrediting others. We must not make those we hope to understand so ashamed of their beliefs that they will engage in self-censorship or intense self-monitoring. This will only make our contacts artificial; or, even worse, as so often happens today, it may destroy any pretense of honest communication. If one is afraid that one's moral standing—or one's career—is at risk with the expression of a sudden, thoughtless remark, one will surely avoid those situations in which such remarks are likely. As a result, we worry about the implications of a "culture of tolerance," one in which people have intolerant thoughts but are afraid that these views may slip out, with dire consequences. Tolerance is a virtue, especially when directed toward those with dirty hands. The situations that we confront have been constructed by whites and blacks, together with self-fulfilling prophecies arising from the images of both groups.

QUESTION EASY TRUTH CLAIMS

After describing the power of rumor to create and bolster images of the social order, we hope to change how people think about rumor. Rumor is not a statement that is true or false; it is a truth claim with variable amounts of credibility. The structure of plausibility determines whether an audience accepts an account. Both blacks and whites take for granted claims that demand more skepticism. Such a demand is often easier said than done because it is precisely the "obvious truth" of rumors that makes them credible. We do not demand proof for most of the things that we are told, and we typically do quite well accepting what we hear. Our suggestion is challenging in that—at least as far as race is concerned—we propose that those things that we are most ready to accept are the ones that should be most deeply questioned.

Perhaps the best rule of thumb is that one should be wary of accepting stories that condemn those of another race or institutions affiliated with that race. Such stories are too good to be false, and our credibility impels us to believe. Even when the information is highly specific and detailed, it may still be incorrect. Rumor often presents a detailed account, even though the details may have no grounding in reality. Asking from where the story derives often does not help. Narrators recall having read a rumor told as truth in a responsible media outlet, even though the information may have been debunked or heard orally from a friend or colleague. Sometimes the stories are from the mass media but have not been checked fully or have been exaggerated. We do not assume rumors are altered maliciously; more likely, they are altered in an unconscious attempt to bolster the credibility of the story. Thus we might hear that a racial rumor was reported in the *New York Times*, whereas the *Times* had attempted to discount the very same story.

While we do not deny the value of critically examining narratives about race, this alone is not sufficient. In addition, we should accept negative racial information provisionally. We do not suggest that one can simply ignore negative and compelling stories, but the information should be treated as unproven. Further, listeners who are aware of the range of rumors that have dealt with race will find that they have heard the story before. The volumes on contemporary legends authored by Jan Harold Brunvand have led otherwise gullible listeners to note that a particular story sounds like a legend, increasing their critical ability. The awareness that a story seems like a rumor, coupled with the stories' traditional content, permits a healthy skepticism of why we are so prone to believe.

TAKE UNCOMFORTABLE BELIEFS SERIOUSLY

To be suspicious of claims about racial matters is not equivalent to denigrating those beliefs. While it is easy and perhaps satisfying to label particular beliefs as paranoid or racist, doing so does not address the empirical basis of these beliefs. Racist and paranoid claims do not appear from nowhere. The belief that the United States government has deliberately manufactured the HIV virus is linked to the Tuskegee syphilis experiment, in which black men were denied medical treatment, to accounts of whites giving American Indians infected blankets, and to actual experiments in biological and chemical warfare. Similarly, the beliefs that gangs initiate new members by having them rape white virgins are bolstered by the brutality of gang violence, the statistically higher proportion of rapes by young black men, and the patterns of urban violence against women. These stories may be false, but they are not mad.

As a result, it is critical that we recognize that these racial rumors are not the product of maliciousness or irrationality. People take these claims seriously, and they have reasonable reasons for doing so. People are not hostile toward racial others because they are evil but because they believe that they have justification to hold such views. To overcome these stories, we must listen sympathetically and then propose alternative explanations. When necessary, we must challenge those beliefs by presenting other stories with better empirical grounding, which contribute to a more accurate racial understanding.

PAINFUL FORGIVENESS

From the recognition that we should respect painful beliefs and that none of us come to the table with our hands clean, we need to forgive others for their sins of misinterpretation. It is understandable to wish to punish racism and hostile paranoia. Yet, if our goal is a better future, rather than justice for an imperfect past, forgiveness is necessary. Of course, we would be excessively optimistic if we assumed that this forgiveness will be easy. People—particularly African Americans—have suffered deeply from beliefs and rumors about race.

We do not call for a collective amnesia about the past, nor do we demand that we embrace those racial warriors who have enacted discriminatory practices. We propose no amnesty for those with explicitly bigoted ideologies. Fortunately, the number of those who are consciously committed to a program of ethnic and racial hostility is small. Most prejudicial beliefs are not consciously filled with hate; in contrast, they are attempts to appreciate truth claims about the real world. To transcend these beliefs is ultimately to recognize the humanness of those who hold them.

MEDIATED RUMORS

One of the themes that has become clear during our writing of this book is that rumor transmission has changed significantly during the past decade as a result of the rise of the Internet. Rumors can spread much more rapidly and widely than ever before, and simultaneously they can be debunked more quickly. Surely the popularity of books that deal with "urban legends" contributes to this sensitivity.

While some commentators have lamented the fact that this new technology is being used to disseminate misinformation and recognize that at present more whites and males use the Internet than women and minorities, we have a more optimistic view. We have come to suspect that the anonymity with which individuals can flesh out their beliefs in cyberspace without being certain about the race and gender of one's partners may ultimately result in improved racial discourse. While the growth in Internet usage is considerable, the racial composition of users at this point does not suggest a fully open dialogue; as Internet usage becomes more widespread (currently about a third of the population uses it), these opportunities will be increasingly present.

Let us provide an example. In the late 1990s a text began to circulate almost exclusively on the Internet. In the early hours of its dissemination, it was posted primarily to African-American discussion lists, but before long it spread far beyond those corridors. Most versions resembled the following:

> I did this on my system at work and it's true! I don't believe it!
> You won't believe your eyes:

1. Go into Microsoft Word
2. Type: I'd like all niggers to die
3. Highlight the sentence
4. Go into the Tools > Language> Thesaurus

I know you may not have MS Word but what happens is you get a message saying, "I'll drink to that."

Lesson learned: Don't be fooled into thinking racism isn't alive and well—it has just taken a different form. I wonder if Bill Gates knows what his programmers have put into the system. NOW might be the time to let him know! Pass it on!!

Understandably, such a claim was first spread by and to African Americans, although it is puzzling why a black person would opt to type "I'd like all niggers to die" in the first place. However, such logical inconsistencies are rarely considered.

The text as spread exhibits several components of classic contemporary legends. The speaker enhances his or her own status by claiming to have participated in the discovery of this previously unrevealed racism. Specifying the motivation of Microsoft Word and its programmers, the text targets the biggest company and its prominent leader in a particular industry. The sender editorializes and encourages recipients to seize power over the information by sharing it.

But what we find compelling and believe serves as grounds for optimism is the aftermath of the proliferation of the original text. Needless to say, many recipients followed the instructions and received the "I'll drink to that" message, as Fine was shocked to discover. But some experimenters took it a step further. They modified the original prompt and discovered that the "I'll drink to that" message comes up if one replaces "nigger" with any word or phrase, or simply highlights any sentence beginning with the word "I'd" ("I'd like there to be racial equality"). This information was then circulated through cyberspace channels. Numerous details about the thesaurus were provided. While it is true that some computer users received only the original claim and not the explanation, many received both. Numerous messages were accompanied by tag lines about the claims of the intent of Microsoft programmers being "one of those cybermyths" or "just another urban legend." Each time one of these exchanges occurs, recipients increase their understanding of how beliefs operate, as well as how members of minority groups think about their position in the world. The claim and the response to it suggest the possibility for better racial understanding as well as collaboration against racism.

BEYOND A CULTURE OF RUMOR

Despite our unwillingness to condemn, we are not penning a manifesto that supports the status quo. In this culture, rumor is too often taken as fact, and supposition is seen as equivalent to demonstration. We wrote this volume because we concluded that the relations between blacks and whites were often desperately misguided and dishonest. Rather than becoming closer, in some respects blacks and whites have drifted farther apart. Such divisions are evident in the social structure, the locations of performance, the characteristics of the narrators, as well as the content of the rumors that are spread—in short, in all corners of the folklore diamond.

The effects of these multiple divisions are demonstrated in the responses of many of those to whom we have shown this material. These friends have been profoundly surprised and dismayed by the beliefs held by members of the other race. White Americans, in particular, are largely unaware of beliefs within the black community, perhaps because whites are not exposed to black media, whereas the reverse is far more common. Perhaps changes brought about by the Internet will alter this situation, but perhaps not.

We have not attempted to provide our own vision for what future race relations might look like. There are solutions aplenty from those who have been active in the fight for racial justice and social equality. Our goal is to describe some of the barriers on the road to this goal. Given the prominence of race in American society and the importance that we attach to it, the rumors that blacks and whites develop about each other seem inevitable.

This proliferation of rumors, and our belief in them, contributes to a situation in which racial understanding becomes a considerable challenge. By recognizing the range of rumor and then confronting our own beliefs and justifications, we can begin to confront the beliefs of others. As a first step, blacks and whites can listen to themselves and each other more carefully and critically, clinging to the possibility of good faith. Race affects many things, but one's humanity and morality should not be among them.

NOTES

INTRODUCTION

1. Folklorist Janet Langlois presented an excellent study of the film at the International Society for Contemporary Legend Research Conference in Bloomington, Indiana, in 1993.

2. Linda Degh, *Folktales and Society* (Bloomington: Indiana University Press, 1969); Alan Dundes, "On the Psychology of Legend," in *American Folk Legend*, ed. Wayland Hand (Berkeley and Los Angeles: University of California Press, 1971), 92–100.

3. William Wells Newell, "On the Field and Work of a Journal of American Folk-Lore," *Journal of American Folklore* 1 (1888): 3–7.

4. Barbara Myerhoff, *Number Our Days* (New York: Simon and Schuster, 1980), 272.

5. Tom Morgenthau, "What Color Is Black?" *Newsweek*, February 13, 1995, 63.

6. Victoria Benning and Philip Bennett, "Questions of Race Confound Anew," *Boston Globe*, September 14, 1992, 6.

7. Victoria Benning and Philip Bennett, "Racial Lines Shadow New Generation," *Boston Globe*, September 13, 1992, 31.

8. Ruth Frankenberg, *The Social Construction of Whiteness: White Women, Race Matters* (Minneapolis: University of Minnesota Press, 1993), 3.

9. Joe Feagin and Melvin Sikes, *Living with Racism* (Boston: Beacon Press,

1994), 53. See also Theodore Sasson, "African American Conspiracy Theories and the Social Construction of Crime," *Sociological Inquiry* 65 (1995): 265–85; Anita Waters, "Conspiracy Theories as Ethnosociologies: Explanation and Intention in African American Political Culture," *Journal of Black Studies* 28 (1997): 112–25.

10. Studs Terkel, *Race: How Blacks and Whites Think and Feel about the American Obsession* (New York: Anchor, 1993), 5.

11. Ibid., 6.

12. John Fiske, *Media Matters: Everyday Culture and Political Change* (Minneapolis: University of Minnesota Press, 1994), 191.

13. Terkel, *Race*, 328.

14. Frederick R. Lynch, *Invisible Victims: White Males and the Crisis of Affirmative Action* (New York: Praeger, 1989), xiii.

15. Ellis Cose, *The Rage of the Privileged Class* (New York: HarperCollins, 1993), 12.

16. Dundes, "On the Psychology of Legend," 92–100.

17. Marilyn Rosenthal, "When Rumor Raged," *Trans-Action* 8, no. 4 (1971): 34–43.

18. Janet Langlois, "The Belle Isle Bridge Incident: Legend, Dialectic and Semiotic System in the 1943 Detroit Race Riots," *Journal of American Folklore* 96 (1983): 183–96.

1. RUMOR IN THE LIFE OF AMERICA

1. Stacey Koon, *Presumed Guilty: The Tragedy of the Rodney King Affair* (Washington, D.C.: Regnery Gateway, 1992).

2. K. W. Lee, "Goodbye Hahn, Good Morning Community Conscience," *Currents* 12, no. 2 (May 1999): 1.

3. What began as a black protest spread quickly, with more arrests of Latinos than of blacks. Melvin L. Oliver, James H. Johnson Jr., and Walter C. Farrell Jr., "Anatomy of a Rebellion: A Political-Economic Analysis," in *Reading Rodney King, Reading Urban Uprising*, ed. Robert Gooding-Williams (New York: Routledge, 1993), 119–21.

4. *CovertAction* Information Bulletin, "Uprising and Repression in L.A.: An Interview with Mike Davis," in *Reading Rodney King, Reading Urban Uprising*, ed. Robert Gooding-Williams (New York: Routledge, 1993), 144.

5. Staff of *The Los Angeles Times*, op.cit., 130.

6. Ibid.

7. *CovertAction* Information Bulletin, "Uprising and Repression in L.A.," 145.

8. One account suggests that a "mentally retarded 14-year-old . . . is believed to have been deported to Mexico." Mike Davis, "Burning All Illusions in L.A.," in *Inside the L.A. Riots*, ed. Don Hazen (New York: Institute for Alternative Journalism, 1992), 98.

9. Staff of the *Los Angeles Times*, 67.

10. *CovertAction* Information Bulletin, "Uprising and Repression in L.A.," 148.

11. Davis, "Burning All Illusions in L.A.," 98.

12. *CovertAction* Information Bulletin, "Uprising and Repression in L.A.," 153.

13. Davis, "Burning All Illusions in L.A.," 99.

14. Joe Domanick, "Police Power," in *Inside the L.A. Riots*, ed. Don Hazen (New York: Institute for Alternative Journalism, 1992), 22; Koon, *Presumed Guilty*.

15. *CovertAction* Information Bulletin, "Uprising and Repression in L.A.," 150. This is reported as a true account, which it may be, but it has the feel of an unsupported allegation.

16. Staff of the *L.A. Weekly*, "Riot Chronology," in *Inside the L. A. Riots*, ed. Don Hazen (New York: Institute for Alternative Journalism, 1992), 36.

17. Quoted in John Fiske, *Media Matters: Everyday Culture and Political Change* (Minneapolis: University of Minnesota Press, 1994), 148.

18. Douglas Massey and Nancy Denton, *American Apartheid* (Cambridge, Mass.: Harvard University Press, 1993).

19. Josh Gamson, *Claims to Fame* (Berkeley and Los Angeles: University of California Press, 1994); John Caughey, *Imaginary Social Worlds* (Lincoln: University of Nebraska Press, 1984).

20. Anna Deavere Smith, *Twilight Los Angeles, 1992 on the Road: A Search for American Character* (New York: Anchor, 1994), 152–53.

21. Ibid., 155.

22. Frank Chin, "Hello USA, This is LA.," in *Inside the L.A. Riots*, ed. Don Hazen (New York: Institute for Alternative Journalism, 1992), 40.

23. Davis, "Burning All Illusions in L.A.," 100.

24. L. A. Kauffman, "Panic in New York," in *Inside the L.A. Riots*, ed. Don Hazen (New York: Institute for Alternative Journalism, 1992), 60–61.

25. *CovertAction* Information Bulletin, "Uprising and Repression in L.A.," 148. These numbers led the police to create many anti-gang strategies, keeping rosters of gang members, as in the LAPD's Operation Hammer: a total of some 150,000 files. California's Street Terrorism Enforcement and Prevention Act labels membership in a gang a separate felony count in conjunction with a crime.

26. For example, college students often talk about a prediction made about a maniac who will attack female students attending a state school in New York whose name starts with an "O." Identifying those schools that fit whatever formula is used is fairly simple. Upstate New York college students know that Oneonta and Oswego are the schools that start with an "O".

27. *CovertAction* Information Bulletin, "Uprising and Repression in L.A.," 147. In this interview, Mike Davis suggests, without providing proof, that this is "obvious police disinformation," reminiscent of the COINTELPRO strategy of the 1960s, aimed at the Black Panthers and other radical groups. Perhaps the claim of disinformation, too, is rumor.

28. In a similar vein, in the controversy over integration in Dubuque, Iowa, armed blacks were supposed to arrive from Chicago. Joe Feagin and Hernan Vera, *White Racism* (New York: Routledge, 1995), 26.

29. Gordon Allport and Leo Postman, *The Psychology of Rumor* (New York: Holt, 1947), vii; see Neil Smelser, *Theory of Collective Behavior* (New York: Free Press, 1962), 80–83.

30. Albert Hastorf and Hadley Cantril, "They Saw a Game: A Case Study," *Journal of Abnormal and Social Psychology* 49 (1954): 129–34.

31. Tamotsu Shibutani, *Improvised News: A Sociological Study of Rumor* (Indianapolis: Bobbs-Merrill, 1966).

32. Stanley Cohen, *Folk Devils and Moral Panics: The Creation of the Mods and Rockers* (London: MacGibben and Kee, 1972), 154–55.

33. Terry Ann Knopf, *Rumor, Race, and Riots* (New Brunswick, N.J.: Transaction, 1975), 159.

34. Ibid., 201.

35. Ibid.

36. Andrew Hacker, *Two Nations: Black and White, Separate, Hostile, Unequal* (New York: Ballantine, 1995), 201.

37. Knopf, *Rumor, Race, and Riots*, 16.

38. J. T. Headley, "Pen and Pencil Sketches of the Great Riots," in *Mass*

Violence in America, ed. Robert Fogelson and Richard E. Rubenstein (New York: Arno Press, 1969), 28–29, cited in Knopf, *Rumor, Race, and Riots*, 16.

39. Ibid.

40. Elliot Rudwick, *Race Riot at East St. Louis, July 2, 1917* (Urbana: University of Illinois Press, 1982).

41. Janet Langlois, "The Belle Isle Bridge Incident: Legend, Dialectic and Semiotic System in the 1943 Detroit Race Riots," *Journal of American Folklore* 96 (1983): 183–98.

42. David J. Jacobson, *The Affairs of Dame Rumor* (New York: Rinehart, 1948), 75.

43. Ruth Frankenberg, *The Social Construction of Whiteness: White Women, Race Matters* (Minneapolis: University of Minnesota Press, 1993), 154.

44. Marilyn Rosenthal, "Where Rumor Raged," *Transaction* 8, no. 4 (1971): 34–43.

45. Howard W. Odum, *Race and Rumors of Race* (Chapel Hill: University of North Carolina Press, 1943).

46. Jacobson, *The Affairs of Dame Rumor*, 75.

47. Shibutani, *Improvised News*, 150.

48. Fred. C. Shapiro and James W. Sullivan, *Race Riots: New York, 1964* (New York: Thomas Y. Crowell, 1994), 151.

49. Knopf, *Rumor, Race, and Riots*, 204.

50. Oliver, Johnson, and Farrell, "Anatomy of a Rebellion," 119.

51. Michael Lerner and Cornel West, *Jews and Blacks: Let the Healing Begin* (New York: Grosset/Putnam, 1995), 103.

2. HOW RUMOR WORKS

1. Linda Degh and Andrew Vazsonyi, "The Hypothesis of Multi-conduit Transmission in Folklore," in *Folklore: Performance and Communication*, ed. Dan Ben-Amos and Kenneth Goldstein (The Hague: Mouton, 1975), 207–51.

2. Ralph L. Rosnow and Gary Alan Fine, *Rumor and Gossip: The Social Psychology of Hearsay* (New York: Elsevier, 1976), 11.

3. Jan Harold Brunvand, *The Mexican Pet* (New York: Norton, 1986), 9.

4. L. Flem (1982), cited in Jean-Noel Kapferer, *Rumors* (New Brunswick, N.J.: Transaction, 1990), 10.

5. Kapferer, *Rumors*, 5.

6. Michael J. Colligan, James W. Pennebaker, and Lawrence R. Murphy, eds., *Mass Psychogenic Illness: A Social Psychological Analysis* (Hillsdale, N.J.: Erlbaum, 1982).

7. Alan Kerckhoff and Kurt Back, *The June Bug* (New York: Appleton-Century-Crofts, 1968).

8. D. M. Johnson, "The Phantom Anesthetist of Mattoon: A Field Study of Mass Hysteria," *Journal of Abnormal and Social Psychology* 40 (1945): 175–86.

9. Quoted in Rosnow and Fine, *Rumor and Gossip*, 2.

10. Smedley D. Butler, "Dame Rumor: The Biggest Liar in the World," *American Magazine* 111 (June 1931): 156.

11. Otto Kerner et al., *Report of the National Advisory Commission on Civil Disorders* (New York: Bantam, 1968), 326.

12. Tamotsu Shibutani, *Improvised News: A Sociological Study of Rumor* (Indianapolis: Bobbs-Merrill, 1966), 17.

13. Ibid.

14. Keith Davis, "Grapevine Communication among Lower and Middle Managers," *Personnel Journal* 48 (1969): 269–72.

15. David Maines, "Information Pools and Racialized Narrative Structures," *Sociological Quarterly* 40 (1999): 317–26.

16. John P. Kisler, Kenneth W. Yarnold, Jean M. Daly, Frank I. McCabe, and Jesse Orlansky, "The Use of Rumor in Psychological Warfare," in *A Psychological Warfare Casebook*, ed. William E. Daugherty and Morris Janowitz (Baltimore: Johns Hopkins University Press, 1960), 657–66.

17. D. Sinha, "Rumors as a Factor in Public Opinion During Elections," *Eastern Anthropologist* 8 (1955): 63–73.

18. Edgar Morin, *A Rumor in Orleans* (New York: Pantheon, 1971). A similar story is now spreading in the United States. Women are lured into the parking lots of shopping centers in the belief that they will be participating in a commercial or a public service announcement, and they are abducted. Personal communication, Thomas C. Hood, 2000.

19. John A. Irving, "The Psychological Analysis of Wartime Rumor Patterns in Canada," *Bulletin of the Canadian Psychological Association* 3 (1943): 40–44; Warren Peterson and Noel Gist, "Rumor and Public Opinion," *American Journal of Sociology* 57 (1951): 159–67; Jamuna Prasad, "The Psychology of Rumor: A Study Relating to the Great Indian Earthquake of 1934," *British Journal of Psychology* 26 (1935): 1–15.

20. Robert H. Knapp, "A Psychology of Rumor," *Public Opinion Quarterly* 8 (1944): 23–37.

21. A sample collected during the Nigerian civil war of 1967–70 found a much higher proportion of pipe-dream rumors. N. K. U. Nkpa, "Rumor Mongering in War Time," *Journal of Social Psychology* 96 (1975): 27–35.

22. R. H. Blake, "The Relationship between Collective Excitement and Rumor Construction," *Rocky Mountain Social Science Journal* 6 (1969): 119–26.

23. These models originated to explain the role of gossip, but they are clearly relevant to rumor, recognizing the often hazy line between the two forms of talk.

24. Robert Paine, "Gossip and Transaction," *Man: The Journal of the Royal Anthropological Institute* 3 (1968): 305–8; John Szwed, "Gossip, Drinking, and Social Control: Consensus and Communication in a Newfoundland Parish," *Ethnology* 5 (1966): 434–41.

25. Richard J. Hill and Charles M. Bonjean, "News Diffusion: A Test of the Regularity Hypothesis," *Journalism Quarterly* 41 (1964): 336–42.

26. Ibid.

27. Tamotsu Shibutani, "Reference Groups as Perspectives," *American Journal of Sociology* 60 (1955): 556.

28. Stuart Dodd, "A Test of Message Diffusion by Chain Tags," *American Journal of Sociology* 61 (1956): 425–32.

29. Degh and Vazsonyi, "The Hypothesis of Multi-conduit Transmission in Folklore."

30. Neil Smelser, *The Theory of Collective Behavior* (New York: Free Press, 1962).

31. Frederick Koenig, *Rumor in the Marketplace: The Social Psychology of Commercial Hearsay* (Dover, Mass.: Auburn House, 1985).

32. Otto Larsen, "Rumors in a Disaster," *Journal of Communication* 4 (1954): 111–23.

33. Frederick Bartlett, *Remembering* (London: Cambridge University Press, 1932).

34. Allport and Postman, *The Psychology of Rumor.*

35. Ibid., 111.

36. Gary Alan Fine, "Folklore Diffusion through Interactive Social Networks," *New York Folklore* 5 (1979): 99–125.

37. Terry Ann Knopf, *Rumor, Race, and Riots* (New Brunswick, N.J.: Transaction, 1975).

38. In the African-American community the belief appears each generation that the mass media is controlled by Jews—a wedge-driving rumor.

39. Koenig, *Rumor in the Marketplace*; H. T. Buckner, "A Theory of Rumor Transmission," *Public Opinion Quarterly* 29 (1965): 54–70.

40. John Caughey, *Imaginary Social Worlds* (Lincoln: University of Nebraska Press, 1984).

41. J. L. Austin, *How to Do Things with Words* (Cambridge, Mass.: Harvard University Press, 1975).

42. C. Wright Mills, "Situated Actions and Vocabularies of Motive," *American Sociological Review* 5 (1940): 904–13; Marvin Scott and Stanford Lyman, "Accounts," *American Sociological Review* 33 (1968): 46–62.

43. Shibutani, *Improvised News*, 31.

44. Linda Degh and Andrew Vazsonyi, "Legend and Belief," in *Folklore Genre*, ed. Dan Ben-Amos (Austin: University of Texas Press, 1976), 93–123.

45. Deirdre Boden, "The World as It Happens: Ethnomethodology and Conversation Analysis," in *Frontiers of Social Theory: The New Synthesis*, ed. George Ritzer (New York: Columbia University Press, 1990), 185–213.

46. Degh and Vazsonyi, "Legend and Belief"; Robert Georges, "Feedback and Response in Storytelling," *Western Folklore* 38 (1979): 4–10.

47. Gary Alan Fine, *Manufacturing Tales: Sex and Money in Contemporary Legends* (Knoxville: University of Tennessee Press, 1992), 5.

3. MERCANTILE RUMOR IN BLACK AND WHITE

1. James C. Scott, *Domination and the Arts of Resistance* (New Haven, Conn.: Yale University Press, 1990).

2. Gary Alan Fine, "The Kentucky Fried Rat: Legends and Modern Society," *Journal of the Folklore Institute* 17 (1980): 222–43.

3. Patricia A. Turner, *I Heard It through the Grapevine: Rumor in African-American Culture* (Berkeley and Los Angeles: University of California Press, 1993), 68.

4. Gary Alan Fine, "The Goliath Effect: Corporate Dominance and Mercantile Legends," *Journal of American Folklore* 98 (1985): 63–84.

5. Turner notes that in the African-American community when she was growing up, fried food was considered healthy; these attitudes have changed over the decades.

6. Joe R. Feagin and Melvin Sikes, *Living with Racism: The Black Middle-Class Experience* (Boston: Beacon Press, 1994).

7. Barbara Grizutti Harrison, "Spike Lee Hates Your Cracker Ass," *Esquire*, October 1992, 137.

8. Kathleen Deveny, "Can Ms. Fashion Bounce Back?" *Business Week*, January 16, 1989, 64.

9. Ibid.

10. Katherine Weisman, "Mr. Liz," *Forbes*, December 10, 1990, 302.

11. Teri Agins, "Claiborne Reveals Its First Big Campaign," *Wall Street Journal*, September 26, 1991, B1.

12. Ibid.

13. Jeffrey A. Trachtenberg and Teri Agins, "Can Liz Claiborne Continue to Thrive When She Is Gone?" *Wall Street Journal*, February 28, 1989, A1.

14. Joshua Gamson, *Claims to Fame* (Chicago: University of Chicago Press, 1994), 57–75; Irving Rein, Philip Kotler, and Martin Stoller, *High Visibility: The Making and Marketing of Professionals into Celebrities* (Lincolnwood, Ill.: NTC Business Books, 1997), 1–11.

15. We have heard that when a customer wears down the soles of a British Knights sneaker, he will see the letters "KKK."

16. http://www.sltrib.com:80/96/FEB/25/sat/20213601.htm.

17. Turner, *I Heard It through the Grapevine*, 59–74.

18. Gary Alan Fine, *Manufacturing Tales: Sex and Money in Contemporary Legends* (Knoxville: University of Tennessee Press, 1992).

4. THE ENEMY IN WASHINGTON

1. Of course, not all attitudes toward the government are negative and filled with suspicion, often without citizens noting the contradiction. It is ironic that despite the mistrust of African Americans toward the government, they simultaneously push for a more activist government. Many whites similarly demand that the government continue to play a significant role in their lives.

2. Frederick Lynch, *Invisible Victims: White Males and the Crisis of Affirmative Action* (New York: Greenwood Press, 1989), 3.

3. Ibid., 51.

4. Ibid., 7.

5. Blacks, of course, equally feel themselves victims of discrimination. One

study by the sociologists Elizabeth Higginbotham and Lynn Weber ("Workplace Discrimination for Black and White Professional and Managerial Women," in *Women and Work*, ed. Elizabeth Higginbotham and Mary Romero [Newbury Park, Calif.: Sage, 1997]) found that 42 percent of their informants had personally experienced discrimination, notably with regard to salary and promotion. Anyone who has been rejected for a position can use race (or gender) as an excuse, and some of these excuses are correct.

6. Joe Klein, "The End of Affirmative Action," *Newsweek*, February 13, 1995, 36.

7. Cited in Leon Kamin, "Behind the Curve," *Scientific American*, February 1995, 103.

8. Cited in Lynch, *Invisible Victims*, 31.

9. Joe Feagin and Hernan Vera, *White Racism* (New York: Routledge, 1995), 55.

10. Jan Harold Brunvand, *The Baby Train and Other Lusty Urban Legends* (New York: Norton, 1993), 126.

11. Studs Terkel, *Race: How Blacks and Whites Think and Feel about the American Obsession* (New York: Anchor, 1993), 106.

12. Jan Harold Brunvand, *Curses! Broiled Again! The Hottest Urban Legends Going* (New York: Norton, 1989), 236–39.

13. Alan Dundes and Carl Pagter, *Urban Folklore from the Paperwork Empire* (Austin: University of Texas Press, 1975), 125–26.

14. Brian Doherty, "Affirmative Reaction," *Reason* 26 (October 1994): 6.

15. Jan Harold Brunvand, *The Choking Doberman and Other "New" Urban Legends* (New York: Norton, 1984), 195.

16. Max Hall, "The Great Cabbage Hoax: A Case Study," *Journal of Personality and Social Psychology* 2 (1965): 563–69.

17. Andrew Hacker, *Two Nations: Black and White, Separate, Hostile, Unequal* (New York: Ballantine, 1995), 54.

18. John Fiske, *Media Matters: Everyday Culture and Political Change* (Minneapolis: University of Minnesota Press, 1994), 191. Fiske also terms this "counterknowledge."

19. James H. Jones, *Bad Blood: The Tuskegee Syphilis Experiment* (New York: Free Press, 1981). Information has recently come out that the government actually did run experiments using radiation on unknowing white patients, possibly contributing to unnecessary cancers—information that surely contributes to the general mistrust of government action.

20. Indeed, attorneys for Wayne Williams, the black man who was eventually convicted of the murders, have appealed his case, as yet unsuccessfully, claiming that the crimes were really committed by white supremacists.

21. Walter Leavy, "The Case of the Disappearing Blacks," *Ebony*, December 1980, 136–38.

22. James Baldwin, *The Evidence of Things Not Seen* (New York: Holt, Rinehart and Winston, 1985), 87.

23. It is stretching the data to some degree to point to the possibility of an anti-Semitic theme here. What could be special about the end of black penises? The link between Jewish doctors and uncircumcised black youngsters is speculative, but it would fit a cultural logic.

24. Steven Hahn, " 'Extravagant Ideas of Freedom': Rumor, Political Struggle, and the Christmas Insurrection Scare of 1865 in the American South" (unpublished manuscript, 1992).

25. "IRS Rejects '40 Acres' Argument of Slaves' Kin," *Phoenix Gazette*, October 20, 1994, A10.

26. Brunvand, *Curses! Broiled Again!* 261–64.

27. See also Feagin and Vera, *White Racism*; Boris Bittker, *The Case for Black Reparations* (New York: Random House, 1973).

28. Christopher Ruddy and Hugh Sprunt, "Questions Linger about Ron Brown Plane Crash," *Pittsburgh Tribune-Review*, November 24, 1997.

29. Peter Garrison, "Minor Deviations," *Flying*, February 1997, 92.

30. Jason DeParle, "Talk of Government Being Out to Get Blacks Falls on More Attentive Ears," *New York Times*, October 29, 1990, B7. Four percent of whites also felt that the statement was true, and another 12 percent felt that it might possibly be true—approximately one of every six whites.

31. Gary Webb, *Dark Alliance: The CIA, The Contras, and the Crack Cocaine Explosion* (New York: Seven Stories Press, 1998).

32. DeParle, "Talks of Government Being Out to Get Blacks," A12.

5. THE WAGES OF SIN

1. For instance, some claim that a biological means of determining whether a person has African ancestry is the presence of a distinctive half-moon shape in the cuticles of the fingers, a technique of identification apparently used by racist groups, such as investigators for the Mississippi State Sovereignty Com-

mission in the 1960s. Calvin Trillin, "State Secrets," *New Yorker*, May 29, 1995, 54.

2. Christie Davies, *Ethnic Humor around the World: A Comparative Analysis* (Bloomington: Indiana University Press, 1990).

3. Joe R. Feagin and Hernan Vera, *White Racism* (New York: Routledge, 1995), 12.

4. Ibid., 14.

5. Joel Kovel, *White Racism*, rev. ed. (New York: Columbia University Press, 1984), 8–9.

6. Ibid., 68.

7. William J. Wilson, *The Truly Disadvantaged* (Chicago: University of Chicago Press, 1987).

8. Mary Pattillo McCoy, *Black Picket Fences* (Chicago: University of Chicago Press, 1999).

9. Peter T. Kilborn, "A Family Spirals Downward in Its Wait for Federal Bias Agency to Act," *New York Times*, February 11, 1995, 7.

10. The existence of racial jokes poses very delicate problems of tact. After Tiger Woods won the Masters Golf Tournament in 1997, fellow golfer Fuzzy Zoeller suggested that Woods would select fried chicken for the banquet at the 1998 tournament. While teasing a colleague about ethnic food preferences would seem to be about as innocuous a joke as possible, the remark raised enormous controversy and led to Zoeller being denounced as a racist. Of course, the stereotype that the joke referred to connected to other less innocuous ones, and such remarks were not made about the tastes of German-American golfers (or, if they were, were not judged as newsworthy). The attack on Zoeller provoked an Internet counterattack: a call to boycott KMart on behalf of "white shoppers," who objected to the store's decision to release Zoeller as the spokesperson for its golf equipment. This decision was taken as a capitulation to black consumers. Thus, a mild, if tasteless, joke aimed at a talented mixed-race golfer has become yet another instance in which the divisions between blacks and whites have become inflamed.

11. Some African Americans may, in fact, be able to accept these jokes and may give back as good as they get, participating in a racial jocularity with their coworkers (in which insults such as "nigger" and "honky" are traded back and forth). These friendships may be real and based on trust; however, in most instances they depend on the black being willing to accept the work conditions

of the white coworkers. Fine noted a similar phenomenon when women who can "take it" are fully accepted in male-dominated workplaces. Still, these women must accept the definitions of the workplace put forth by their male coworkers; they must agree to be "one of the boys." Those women who are unable or unwilling to accept these rules are seen as "problems."

12. David Jacobson, *The Affairs of Dame Rumor* (New York: Rinehart, 1948), 78–79.

13. Ibid., 79.

14. Collected from Renee Kornbuth, March 11, 1993.

15. Jan Harold Brunvand, *The Baby Train and Other Lusty Urban Legends* (New York: Norton, 1993), 50–52.

16. Joe Feagin and Melvin Sikes, *Living with Racism* (Boston: Beacon Press, 1994), 48.

17. Collected by Xenia Cord, reported in Jan Harold Brunvand, *The Choking Doberman and Other "New" Urban Legends* (New York: Norton, 1984), 27.

18. Brunvand, *The Baby Train*, 54–55.

19. John Fiske, *Media Matters: Everyday Culture and Political Change* (Minneapolis: University of Minnesota Press, 1994), xvi.

20. Ibid., viii.

21. Ibid., xix.

22. Mark Gerson, "Race, O. J. and My Kids," *New Republic*, April 24, 1995, 28.

23. Tamotsu Shibutani, *Improvised News: A Sociological Study of Rumor* (Indianapolis: Bobbs-Merrill, 1966), 60.

24. Fiske, *Media Matters*, 191.

25. Hanna Rosin, "The Homecoming," *New Republic*, June 5, 1995, 14.

26. Jason DeParle, "Talk of Government Being Out to Get Blacks Falls on More Attentive Ears," *New York Times*, October 29, 1990, B7.

27. Rosin, "The Homecoming," 23.

28. One treatise (Alan Cantwell, *Queer Blood: The Secret AIDS Genocide Plot* [Los Angeles: Aries Rising Press, 1993]) links the AIDS virus with the hepatitis B vaccine that was tested on gay men in the late 1970s. The author, a physician, noting the remarkable temporal coincidence, sees the virus as a biological weapon developed by the American government. As a gay man, he finds himself as the target.

29. Patricia A. Turner, *I Heard It through the Grapevine: Rumor in African-American Culture* (Berkeley and Los Angeles: University of California Press, 1993), 157.

30. DeParle, "Talk of Government Being Out to Get Blacks," B7.

31. Gary Thatcher, "Genetic Weapon: Is It on the Horizon?" *Christian Science Monitor*, December 15, 1988, B11–B12; Carl A. Larson, "Ethnic Weapons," *Military Review* 50 (1970): 3–11; Fiske, *Media Matters*, 196–97.

32. Thatcher, "Genetic Weapon," B12.

33. Personal correspondence to Patricia Turner from Arthur S. Hulnick, coordinator for Academic Affairs, Central Intelligence Agency, August 23, 1988.

34. "Soviet Active Measures in the Era of Glasnost," report prepared at the request of the U.S. House of Representatives Committee on Appropriations (Washington, D.C., 1988), 12.

35. DeParle, "Talk of Government Being Out to Get Blacks," B7.

36. Rosin, "The Homecoming," 26.

37. Gladys-Marie Fry, *Night Riders in Black Folk History* (Knoxville: University of Tennessee Press, 1975).

38. DeParle, "Talk of Government Being Out to Get Blacks," B7.

39. Black Liberation Radio, March 18, 1992, cited in Fiske, *Media Matters*, 204.

40. Some believe that AIDS was spread in Africa through the World Health Organization's immunization program against smallpox, either because the smallpox vaccine awakens the dormant HIV virus or because the vaccine was laced with the virus. It has not passed unnoticed that there is a strong correlation between those countries in which WHO vaccinated children and the spread of AIDS. See Fiske, *Media Matters*, 198–201.

41. DeParle, "Talk of Government Being Out to Get Blacks," B7.

42. Some AIDS drugs, such as Kemron, are popular in the African-American community, but scientific evidence has suggested that they are not effective. However, the claims of the World Health Organization and the National Institutes of Health are seen as further examples of racist manipulation. Rosin, "The Homecoming," 22.

43. Ibid., 26.

44. Susan Sontag, *AIDS and Its Metaphors* (New York: Farrar, Straus and Giroux, 1988), 52.

45. Cindy Patton, *Sex and Germs: The Politics of AIDS* (Boston: South End Press, 1985), 7.

6. ON THE ROAD AGAIN

1. Joel Best and Gerald T. Horiuchi, "The Razor Blade in the Apple: The Social Construction of Urban Legends," *Social Problems* 32 (1985): 488–99.

2. By no means a new phenomenon; see Richard D. Altick, *Deadly Encounters: Two Victorian Sensations* (Philadelphia: University of Pennsylvania Press, 1986); and Michael Schudson, *Discovering the News* (New York: Basic Books, 1978).

3. Maureen T. Reddy, *Crossing the Color Line: Race, Parenting, and Culture* (New Brunswick, N.J.: Rutgers University Press, 1994), 16.

4. The white feminist author, wife of a black man, to whom this letter was addressed found the letter creepy and frightening, and she wonders whether the letter writer's "hatred" would "be satisfied by the mere writing of letters." We wonder, too. Such concerns are real (and not found only among elderly *white* women) and are the types of issues that insults only submerge.

5. Quoted in Ellis Cose, *The Rage of the Privileged Class* (New York: HarperCollins, 1993), 96.

6. For a dialogue on this point, see Michael Lerner and Cornel West, *Jews and Blacks: Let the Healing Begin* (New York: Putnam, 1995), 140–41.

7. David J. Jacobson, *The Affairs of Dame Rumor* (New York: Rinehart, 1948), 62.

8. We are grateful to our Utah colleagues William "Bert" Wilson and Barbara Walker for sharing research conducted by Utah college students on these rumor cycles.

9. Cited in Newell G. Bringhurst, *Saints, Slaves, and Blacks: The Changing Place of Black People within Mormonism* (Westport, Conn.: Greenwood Press, 1981), 230.

10. Ibid., 231.

11. Eleanor Wachs, *Crime-Victim Stories* (Bloomington: Indiana University Press, 1988), 84–85.

12. Jan Harold Brunvand, *The Baby Train and Other Lusty Urban Legends* (New York: Norton, 1993), 125.

13. Xenia Cord, "Further Notes on 'The Assailant in the Back Seat,'" *Indiana Folklore* 2 (1969): 47.

14. Carlos Drake, "The Killer in the Backseat," *Indiana Folklore* 1 (1968): 107–9; Cord, "Further Notes," 47–54; Jan Harold Brunvand, *The Vanishing Hitchhiker* (New York: Norton, 1981), 52–53.

15. Cord, "Further Notes," 50.

16. April 20, 1982, cited in Jan Harold Brunvand, *The Choking Doberman and Other "New" Urban Legends* (New York: Norton, 1984), 3.

17. Brunvand *The Choking Doberman*, 11; Jan Harold Brunvand, *The Mexican Pet* (New York: Norton, 1986), 43.

18. Eli Anderson, in *Streetwise* (Chicago: University of Chicago Press, 1991), 222–28, points to the fear that black men have of strange dogs and notes that whites may choose to use dogs for protection.

19. Mary Cerney, "Many Dubuquers Afraid to Speak Out," letters, *Telegraph Herald*, August 20, 1991, 3A, cited in Joe Feagin and Hernan Vera, *White Racism* (New York: Routledge, 1995), 26.

20. Ralph Turner and Samuel J. Surace, "Zoot-Suiters and Mexicans: Symbols in Crowd Behavior," *American Journal of Sociology* 62 (1956): 14–20.

21. Howard S. Becker, *Outsiders* (New York: Free Press, 1963).

22. Malcolm Spector and John Kitsuse, *The Construction of Social Problems* (Chicago: Aldine, 1977); Joseph W. Schneider, "Social Problems Theory: The Constructionist View," *Annual Review of Sociology* 11 (1985): 209–29.

23. Stanley Cohen, *Folk Devils and Moral Panics* (London: MacGibbon and Kee, 1972).

24. Lewis Yablonsky, *The Violent Gang* (New York: Macmillan, 1962).

25. Steve Rubenstein, "Rumors Fly on Computer Networks: San Jose Police Deny Persistent Tale of Gang Violence," *San Francisco Chronicle*, September 23, 1993, A19.

26. Brian West and Amy Donaldson, "Gang Rumor Has Police and Schools Scrambling," *Deseret News*, September 18, 1993, A5.

27. Richard Dorson, *Land of the Millrats* (Cambridge, Mass.: Harvard University Press, 1981), 228–29.

28. Michael Carroll, "The Castrated Boy: Another Contribution to the Psychoanalytic Study of Urban Legends," *Folklore* 28 (1987): 216–25; Charles Clay Doyle, "The Avenging Voice from the Depths," *Western Folklore* 47 (1988): 21–37.

29. Barre Toelken, *The Dynamics of Folklore* (Boston: Houghton Mifflin, 1979), 178.

30. Alan Dundes, "Projection in Folklore: A Plea for Psychoanalytic Semiotics," *Modern Language Notes* 91 (1976): 1524–25.

7. CRIES AND WHISPERS

1. Kim Lersch, "Current Trends in Police Brutality: An Analysis of Recent Newspaper Accounts" (master's thesis, University of Florida, Gainesville, 1993), cited in Joe Feagin and Hernan Vera, *White Racism* (New York: Routledge, 1995), 69–70.

2. Studs Terkel, *Race: How Blacks and Whites Think and Feel about the American Obsession* (New York: Anchor, 1993), 9; for a similar story, see page 352. One wonders whether Terkel could have gotten away with the story if both boys were black and if he referred to their vandalism not as "mischief" but as "crime."

3. See Feagin and Vera, *White Racism*, 70; Steven Yates, *Civil Wrongs: What Went Wrong with Affirmative Action* (San Francisco: Institute for Contemporary Studies Press, 1994), 27–30; Shawn Donnan, "Dad Lied, Police Say in Slaying of Girl, 2," *Atlanta Journal/Constitution*, July 31, 1996, A8.

4. Richard Nicolas, a black Baltimore man, was accused of killing his two-year-old daughter. He had blamed a white driver for shooting his child. The story received little media attention, and the outcome of the trial was not reported. See Donnan, "Dad Lied."

5. "Campus Life: Emory; Racial Attacks Leave Freshman in Severe Shock," *New York Times*, April 22, 1990, 44.

6. Reports from United Press International, June 2, 1990; Associated Press, June 3, 1990.

7. Events at Olivet College in 1992 in which white female students accused black male students indicate that blacks are not the only ones making racially motivated claims, as shall be discussed later.

8. For discussion of the case, see Robert D. McFadden, Ralph Blumenthal, M. A. Farber, E. R. Shipp, Charles Strum, and Craig Wolff, *Outrage: The Story behind the Tawana Brawley Hoax* (New York: Bantam, 1990); and Mike Taibbi and Anna Sims-Phillips, *Unholy Alliances: Working the Tawana Brawley Story* (San Diego: Harcourt Brace Jovanovich, 1989).

9. Rhea Mandulo, "Tawana Brawley's Mother Attends Subpoena-Shredding News Conference," *United Press International*, May 21, 1988.

10. William Tucker, "The Mystery of Wappingers Falls: The Tawana Brawley Case," *New Republic*, March 21, 1988, 19.

11. "It's Time to Show Concern for Tawana Brawley," *Newsday*, February 28, 1988, 3.

12. See McFadden et al., *Outrage*, 227 ff.

13. James S. Kunen, "Incident at Wappingers Falls: The Case of Tawana Brawley Puts New York Justice on Trial," *People*, March 7, 1988, 42.

14. Ibid.

15. Dan Hurley, "Beyond Zealous Advocacy? Lawyers' Tactics in Tawana Brawley Case Draw Skepticism," *American Bar Association Journal* 74 (September 1, 1988): 28. However, when asked whether they believed the story, only 7 percent of whites and 18 percent of blacks accepted it as true. Obviously they were distinguishing between whether the story was true and whether Brawley herself, who never testified and was never extensively questioned, was lying. Taibbi and Sims-Phillips, *Unholy Alliances*, 359.

16. Taibbi and Sims-Phillips, *Unholy Alliances*, 359.

17. Jeff Jones, "Brawley and Others: Justice in the Hudson Valley," *Nation*, March 19, 1988, 376; Tucker, "The Mystery of Wappingers Falls," 19.

18. Howard Kurtz, "Al Sharpton, into the Maelstrom: The Outspoken N.Y. Preacher and His Notoriety in the Tawana Brawley Case," *Washington Post*, July 14, 1988, D1.

19. Stanley Diamond, "Reversing Brawley: Tawana Brawley Case," *Nation*, October 31, 1988, 409.

20. Don Wycliff, "Blacks and Tawana Brawley," *New York Times*, October 13, 1988, A26.

21. "The Brawley Gang vs. Us: Tawana Brawley Case," *National Review*, October 28, 1988, 18.

22. Tucker, "The Mystery of Wappingers Falls."

23. Taibbi and Sims-Phillips, *Unholy Alliances*, 374.

24. Barbara Goldberg, "Pastor Invokes 'Tawana Brawley' Defense," United Press International, May 22, 1989.

25. McFadden et al., *Outrage*, 103. According to Taibbi and Sims-Phillips (*Unholy Alliances*, 96), who report a suspiciously similar story, the girl was attempting to cover up sexual abuse by a black neighbor.

26. Clarence Page, "Tawana Brawley and the Exploiting of Racial Problems," *Chicago Tribune*, October 5, 1988, 29.

27. Jim Sleeper, "New York Stories: The Racial Wages of Misogyny; Misogyny and the Tawana Brawley Case," *New Republic*, September 10, 1990, 20 ff.

28. Personal communication, E. Ethelbert Miller, 1998.

29. Interview on the Larry King show, September 14, 1990.

30. Details on the case are available in Feagin and Vera, *White Racism,* chap. 4; Joe Sharkey, *Deadly Greed: The Riveting True Story of the Stuart Murder Case That Rocked Boston and Shocked the Nation* (New York: Prentice Hall, 1991).

31. Margaret Carlson, "Presumed Innocent," *Time,* January 22, 1990, 10 ff.

32. Sharkey, *Deadly Greed,* 1.

33. Ibid., 135.

34. Ibid.

35. Ibid.

36. Ibid., 137.

37. See Feagin and Vera, *White Racism,* 65.

38. Ibid., 66; Elizabeth Neuffer, "U.S. Attorney Ends Misconduct Probe in Stuart Case," *Boston Globe,* July 4, 1991 (Metro/Region), 1.

39. Feagin and Vera, *White Racism,* 67.

40. Robert Maynard, "Charles Stuart Knew America's Racist Soul," *St. Louis Post-Dispatch,* January 16, 1990, 3B.

41. Christopher Edley, "Why Everyone Believed Charles Stuart," *Legal Times,* January 22, 1990, 24 ff.

42. "Georgia Klan Leader Convicted of Murder," *Monitor of the Center for Democratic Renewal,* May 1990, 15.

43. Feagin and Vera, *White Racism,* 70–71.

44. Interestingly, Susan Smith had apparently dated a black student in high school, and both her sister-in-law and her mother-in-law had married black men. Cited in Andrea Peyser, *Mother Love, Deadly Love: The Susan Smith Murders* (New York: HarperCollins, 1995), 84.

45. Ibid., 80.

46. Ibid., 82; Maria Eftimiades, *Sins of the Mother* (New York: St. Martin's, 1995), 178, 226.

47. Susan S. Richardson, "S.C. Case Shows Racial Stereotypes Die Hard," *Austin American-Statesman,* November 5, 1994, A11.

48. "Heal Wounds of Racial Distrust," *Fort Lauderdale Sun-Sentinel,* November 12, 1994, 22A.

49. "The Kidnapping of Trust," *Boston Globe,* November 5, 1994, 12.

50. Derrick Z. Jackson, "The Black Hole," *Baltimore Sun,* November 15, 1994, 17A.

51. "South Carolina Deaths: Two Elements of Tragedy," *Durham Herald-Sun,* November 8, 1994, A8.

52. Peyser, *Mother Love, Deadly Love,* 85.

53. Ruth Sidel, *Battling Bias: The Struggle for Identity and Community on College Campuses* (New York: Viking, 1994), 81.

54. "SUNY Student Lied about Attack on Campus," *Chronicle of Higher Education*, December 14, 1994, n.p.

8. COMING CLEAN

1. Claude Steele, "Race and the Schooling of Black Americans," *Atlantic Monthly*, April 1992, 72.

2. Jan Harold Brunvand, *The Choking Doberman and Other "New" Urban Legends* (New York: Norton, 1984), 18–28.

3. Ibid., 22.

4. Ibid., 23. Another celebrity story has the wealthy star sending a new car to a passerby who stops to help when the celebrity has car trouble. Often, although not always (sometimes the story is told about Donald Trump), these celebrities are African American, such as Louis Armstrong, perhaps reminding us how difficult it may be for a black to get aid while standing on the side of the road. Jan Harold Brunvand, *Curses! Broiled Again! The Hottest Urban Legends Going* (New York: Norton, 1989), 114.

5. Brunvand, *The Choking Doberman*, 24.

6. Studs Terkel, *Race: How Blacks and Whites Think and Feel about the American Obsession* (New York: Anchor, 1993), 139.

7. Walt Harrington, "For Jesse Jackson, All the World's a Stage," *Washington Post Magazine*, January 25, 1987, 16–17.

8. Douglas C. Lyons, "Racism and Blacks Who've 'Made It,'" *Ebony*, October 1989, 112.

9. Joe Feagin and Melvin Sikes, *Living with Racism* (Boston: Beacon Press, 1994), 53.

10. Jan Harold Brunvand, *The Baby Train and Other Lusty Urban Legends* (New York: Norton, 1993), 171.

INDEX

Compositor:	Binghamton Valley Composition
Text:	10/15 Janson
Display:	Janson
Printer and binder:	Maple-Vail Book Manufacturing Group